Robin Hindson

PENGUIN BOOKS

Penguin Books Australia Ltd
487 Maroondah Highway, PO Box 257
Ringwood, Victoria 3134, Australia
Penguin Books Ltd
Harmondsworth, Middlesex, England
Viking Penguin, A Division of Penguin Books USA Inc.
375 Hudson Street, New York, New York 10014, USA
Penguin Books Canada Limited
2801 John Street, Markham, Ontario, Canada L3R 1B4
Penguin Books (N.Z.) Ltd
182–190 Wairu Road, Auckland 10, New Zealand

First published by Penguin Books Australia Ltd 1992

10 9 8 7 6 5 4 3 2 1



Produced by Viking O'Neil
56 Claremont Street, South Yarra, Victoria 3141, Australia
A Division of Penguin Books Australia Ltd

Typeset in Helvetica Medium/Light Condensed
by Typeset Gallery Sdn. Bhd., Malaysia
Printed by Longman Malaysia Sdn. Bhd., Malaysia (PA)

National Library of Australia
Cataloguing-in-Publication data

The Australian calorie counter.

ISBN 0 14 012614 7.

1. Food – Calorie content – Tables. 2. Food – Sodium content Tables. 3. Food – Cholesterol content – Tables. I. Hindson, Robin.

641.1042

# CONTENTS

**Author**
Robin Hindson DIMgt CertDiet DipEd RD
*Principal Tutor in Nutrition and Food Service, Department of Human Nutrition, Deakin University*

**Research assistants**
Frances Waterman, Catherine Cooper, Sandra Ellemor

**Chief editor**
Jane Angus

**Editorial team**
Jenny Lang, Barbara Weiss

The author and publishers would like to thank the many food manufacturers for contributing and approving the nutritional information regarding their products.

***Publisher's Note***
*Every effort has been made to give the most current and accurate information on all brand name products and their kilojoule/calorie counts at the time of going to press. However, some products may have been subsequently discontinued or their contents altered.*

# HOW TO USE THIS BOOK

There are six sections.

1 **How to use this book**.
2 **Health and eating habits** describes the components of a healthy diet; lists the foods recommended in the Dietary Guidelines for Australians; shows how to determine your healthy weight range; and tells you how to lose or gain weight.
3 The **Alcohol** section gives you information about the effects of alcohol on health, lists the alcoholic content of standard drinks, discusses safe intake levels, and includes hints for regulating your consumption.
4 The **Counter** is a detailed alphabetical list that provides you with kilojoule and calorie value for handy quantities of a huge range of foods (including brands) and drinks (including alcoholic drinks).
5 The **Introduction to the table** provides health information about fat, cholesterol, sodium (and salt), calcium and fibre, and explains how to include the right amount of each in your diet.
6 The **Table** is an alphabetical list of a wide range of foods (including brands) in selected food groups with their fat, cholesterol, sodium, calcium and fibre content.

## USING THE COUNTER AND THE TABLE

In these two sections foods and drinks are listed alphabetically (use the easy-find page headings.) Under the main items, types are listed first by description and then by brand name; for example, under *anchovies*, 'canned' and 'raw' are followed by 'Admiral' and 'John West'.

For items with a large listing (for example, *biscuits*) the same system is followed and italic type has been used to help you further. Where several foods come under the same category and have the same energy value, they appear together and are separated by a slash (/). For example, under *beetroot*, two brand names are given thus: 'Golden Circle/Edgell-Birdseye'.

## QUANTITIES AND VALUES

In most cases figures have been rounded off: this is because serving sizes often vary (for example the weight of a 'medium-sized' apple may vary greatly, depending on one's estimation of 'medium'); and because there are variations in samples according to the season, the degree of freshness, the recipe and the preparation (for example how much fat is trimmed from meat).

Within these limits, however, the figures are reliable and may be used confidently to calculate the approximate energy value of your food (in kilojoules or calories) as well as the fat, cholesterol, sodium, calcium and fibre values.

## DESCRIPTIONS OF FOODS

If no specific description is given the figures apply to the part of the food normally eaten, for example *beans, broad* will include the bean seeds but not the pods.

Where it is appropriate there is a description to help you estimate quantities in a practical way; for example the figure for *spaghetti, dried* should be used if you measure before cooking, and *spaghetti, boiled* if you estimate a serving size on your plate.

Unless specifically requested by the company concerned, all brand names in the counter are given in lower case letters.

# HEALTH AND EATING HABITS

## CHOOSING HEALTHY EATING

Not only is our food varied and excellent in quality; it is also available in great quantity – fresh, packaged, frozen or in take-away form. If, however, we combine a sedentary lifestyle with eating more than we need, we become prone to the 'Western diseases of affluence' – obesity, high blood pressure, stroke, heart disease, diabetes, gall-bladder disease and cancer.

Fortunately, good nutrition and good health can go hand in hand. Although we cannot control every aspect of our lives, we *can* exercise choice about what we eat.

If you want to eat for health you should know about the **Dietary Guidelines for Australians** issued by the Commonwealth Department of Health in 1982. There are eight broad guidelines. (For details see 'A closer look at the dietary guidelines', p. 11.)

**1** Enjoy a wide variety of nutritious foods.
**2** Control your weight.
**3** Avoid eating too much fat.
**4** Avoid eating too much sugar.
**5** Eat more breads and cereals (preferably wholegrain), and vegetables and fruit.
**6** Limit alcohol consumption.
**7** Use less salt.
**8** Promote breast-feeding.

## UNDERSTANDING YOUR WEIGHT

If you are chiefly interested in weight control you should follow guidelines 1–7 as a first step. The second step is to determine whether you *are* overweight.

Your body type, including your bone structure, is genetically determined, and will be one factor in determining your weight. For this reason, and because height influences weight, your desirable weight will fall within a range rather than being fixed.

### Height–weight chart: aged 18 onwards

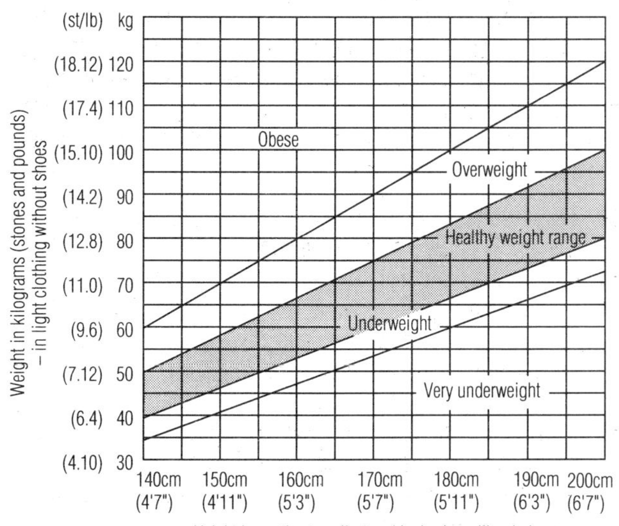


Based on the recommendations of the National Health and Medical Research Council (October 1984). Adapted from the Australian Nutrition Foundation Chart

The **height–weight chart** shown on page 5 will help you to determine your healthy weight range.

You can also understand more about your weight by working out your **Body Mass Index** (BMI), using the following formula.

$$\text{BMI} = \frac{\text{weight in kilograms}}{\text{height in metres} \times \text{height in metres}}$$

For most people a normal BMI is between 20 and 25; if your BMI is above 25 it *may* be appropriate for you to lose weight, and if it's below 20 you *may* need to gain weight.

It's important to remember, however, that these figures relate to healthy persons over 18 years of age, and that, as in the case of height–weight charts or tables, they are valuable as references but don't necessarily apply to every individual.

In addition to knowing your desirable weight range, the following information may be useful.

- The importance given to being slim, particularly in regard to women, is partly a matter of fashion.
- In Australia more men than women are overweight.
- From a health point of view it is less harmful to be a 'pear' (excess fat on the bottom and thighs) than an 'apple' (fat overhanging the waistline). Overweight women tend to be 'pears', overweight men 'apples'.
- To lose weight you must use up (through exercise) more energy than you take in (as food). To gain weight you must take in more energy than you can use, so that the body can convert it to new tissue.
- 'Going on a diet' is not recommended because, apart from

possibly missing some important nutrients, it may result in a slowing-down of your metabolic rate, so that your body uses less energy; then when you eat normally again you may put weight back on because your body is not using all the energy available. It is better to make a permanent change to nutritional eating habits and a healthy lifestyle.

- Rapid weight loss may involve losing fluid, lean-muscle tissue and important body stores of energy, leading to fatigue and headaches. It is better to reduce weight slowly and to lose fat only.

## COUNTING YOUR CALORIES

Food energy is measured in **calories** (cal) or **kilojoules** (kJ). In this book both measurements are given (1 calorie = 4.2 kilojoules).

A convenient way to calculate the food energy for a healthy weight-loss diet is to allow a set amount per day, for example 1200–1800 calories (5000–7500 kilojoules), depending on age and activity level. Nutritious foods should then be selected to meet these energy levels.

The following table sets out the energy used in various levels of activity (measured in kilojoules per minute).

## Energy expenditure for a range of activities

| Energy expenditure in kJ/min. | Occupational | Recreational |
|---|---|---|
| Less than 10 kilojoules (very light activity) | standing with light activity (e.g. sales assistant)<br>typing (electrical) | eating<br>sleeping<br>driving a car<br>strolling<br>sewing<br>knitting |
| 10–20 kilojoules (light activity) | farm work (mechanised)<br>assembly work<br>light industry<br>typing (manual)<br>housework<br>bricklaying<br>driving a truck | light gardening<br>gymnastics<br>billiards<br>fishing<br>bowling<br>slow walking (4 km/h) |

| | | |
|---|---|---|
| 20–30 kilojoules (moderate activity) | general labouring (pick and shovel)<br>painting<br>farm work (non-mechanised) | heavy gardening<br>golf (carrying clubs)<br>tennis (doubles)<br>cycling (16 km/h)<br>cricket<br>table tennis<br>moderate walking (5.5 km/h) |
| 30–40 kilojoules (heavy activity) | coalmining<br>heavy labouring | skipping<br>jogging<br>football<br>tennis (singles)<br>skiing (vigorous downhill)<br>climbing stairs<br>basketball<br>moderate swimming |
| more than 40 kilojoules (very heavy activity) | lumber work (non-mechanised) | squash<br>cross-country skiing<br>cycling (racing)<br>running<br>fast swimming |

Table, courtesy of the National Heart Foundation

## KEEPING UP THE NUTRIENTS

When you reduce your intake of calories you may also reduce your intake of other important nutrients – protein, carbohydrate, fibre, vitamins and minerals. The way to maintain your intake of these nutrients is to eat less of the most concentrated energy sources (for example fat and alcohol) and sufficient of the least concentrated (protein and carbohydrate). The following table sets out the energy values for these four sources.

### Energy value of energy-containing nutrients

| NUTRIENT | ENERGY kJ/g | cal/g |
|---|---|---|
| Protein | 17 | 4 |
| Carbohydrate | 16 | 4 |
| Fat | 37 | 9 |
| Alcohol | 29 | 7 |

From the table it can be seen that foods high in **fat** are concentrated sources of energy. These foods include butter, margarine, vegetable oils, fried foods, cream, chocolate, and many cakes, biscuits, pastries, cheeses and types of ice-cream. You need some fat in your diet to supply essential fatty acids and fat-soluble vitamins, but your total intake should be kept low (see also 'A closer look at the Dietary Guidelines', p. 11, and 'Fat', p. 155).

**Alcohol**, another concentrated energy source, is not an essential nutrient. (See also 'A closer look at the Dietary Guidelines' below, and 'Alcohol', p. 17).

**Protein** foods supply relatively smaller amounts of energy unless they are accompanied by fat; for example lean meat is low in energy but fatty meat is high, and low-fat and skim milks are lower in energy value than whole milk.

**Carbohydrate** foods such as rice, pasta, sugar-free whole-grain breakfast cereals, bread, potatoes and other fruits and vegetables are lower in energy and so can be eaten more freely. At least 50 per cent of daily energy should come from carbohydrate foods; but remember not to add fatty toppers, sauces or spreads.

## A CLOSER LOOK AT THE DIETARY GUIDELINES

The Dietary Guidelines for Australians includes the following specific information about diet.

**Enjoying a wide variety of nutritious foods** involves eating foods daily from each of the five main food groups.

1. Milk and milk products.
2. Meat, poultry, fish, and meat alternatives such as peas, beans, lentils, eggs and nuts.
3. Vegetables and fruit.
4. Bread and cereals.
5. Butter or table margarine (one tablespoon daily).

**A balanced diet** of about 1200 calories (5000 kilojoules) per day can be made up of:

- low-fat milk (300 ml), or milk products such as yoghurt (250 ml) or cheese (40 g)
- one to two serves of lean meat or meat alternative. (One serve equals 100 grams meat or poultry, 150 grams fish, two eggs, 20 grams nuts, or ¾ cup legumes)
- at least three or four different vegetables cooked or as salad, and three pieces of whole fresh fruit (cooked or canned fruit or fruit juice without sugar may be substituted for one serve)
- at least five slices of wholemeal bread, or five serves of either wholegrain cereals, brown rice or pasta
- water to drink.

**Avoid eating too much fat** because fat is the most concentrated source of energy. Look up the calorie values for 100 grams each of butter, oil, chips, chocolate and peanut butter and compare these with the calorie values for 100 grams each of bread, apples and lean chicken fillets: now you will know why foods containing fat are the most important to watch for when counting calories!

**Avoiding eating too much sugar**. In moderation sugar doesn't supply too many calories because it is a pure carbohydrate food; however, it is an extravagant way to consume energy as it provides no other nutrients. If you are counting calories, count out sugar and all foods and drinks high in sugar, especially if they are also high in fat – for example cakes, biscuits and confectionery.

**Eat more bread and cereals (preferably wholegrain), and vegetables and fruit**, because these foods supply vitamins and minerals, including Vitamin B complex and Vitamin C. The foods in this group also supply different types of fibre, each of which has a different function in the body, including reducing levels of blood cholesterol; improving bowel regularity; and giving a feeling of fullness after eating, so helping to avoid over-eating. Because high-fat, high-sugar foods supply such concentrated energy you actually eat much more of them before you feel full. The opposite is true of high-fibre foods, which are likely to make you feel full sooner, while supplying less energy: it takes over half a kilogram of apples (a high-fibre food) to provide the same energy as a small 50-gram block of chocolate (a high-fat, high-sugar food).

**Limit alcohol consumption**. Alcohol is a wasteful way of taking calories because it supplies nothing else that the body needs physiologically. If you enjoy having a drink, limit the number of drinks and try low-alcohol and non-alcohol alternatives. (See 'Alcohol', p. 17).

**Use less salt**. Two elements, sodium and chlorine, make up salt (sodium chloride). Our bodies need some sodium, but from salt added to food many people get too much. A high sodium intake is linked to high blood pressure, which can lead to other health problems. Don't eat too much processed, convenience or take-away food: these foods often have high levels of salt, and are often high in fat and calories as well.

**Enjoy water**: it contains no calories and should therefore be used freely to quench thirst instead of sweetened soft drinks, fruit juices, alcoholic drinks or high-fat, flavoured milk and milk-substitute drinks.

The **Healthy Diet Pyramid** illustrates the recommendations of the Dietary Guidelines.

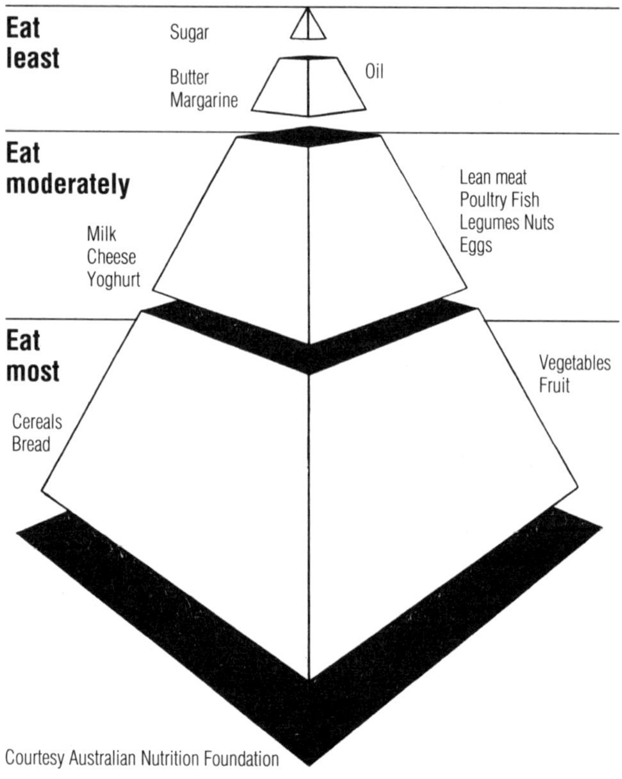


Courtesy Australian Nutrition Foundation

## GETTING IN THE EXERCISE

Remember that you will lose weight if you use more energy than you take in through eating and drinking. So you should aim to eat less and at the same time use more energy by exercising more. You may find it hard to fit in an exercise programme but every extra activity helps. Try an exercise you really enjoy – walking, swimming, gardening or ballroom dancing. Park your car further away from the shops or your place of work; use the stairs instead of the lift; and put away the remote control on your television!

## GOLDEN RULES FOR WEIGHT CONTROL

Here are some more strategies to help you lose weight.

- Set a realistic weight goal with intermediate goals, and weigh weekly, not daily.
- Alter your long-term eating patterns – don't eat 'diet' foods or 'go on a diet', especially a crash diet or one that recommends a 'magic' food.
- Use the Dietary Guidelines for the whole family.
- Eat only at the table – not on the move, when reading, or when watching television.
- Use a smaller plate to serve smaller meals.
- Eat more slowly. Chew food well, and put down your knife and fork between mouthfuls.
- Keep busy, preferably away from the kitchen and food shops.
- Avoid food-shopping when you're hungry, keep to a shopping list, and don't buy high-energy snacks and nibbles.

- Keep a food diary, so that you know when you eat or nibble most.
- Eat only when you're hungry.
- Keep a supply of low-energy instant snacks – carrot and celery sticks, fruit, orange-juice iceblocks or frozen fruit pieces (orange, watermelon or banana).
- Don't keep food hoards at work, in your handbag, or in the car.
- Avoid fried take-away foods – choose salad rolls, hamburgers with salad, or steak sandwich with salad.
- Go to the phone instead of the fridge if you're miserable.
- Look for recipe books that emphasise interesting healthy food.
- Warm up with stretching activities before strenuous exercise.

You should also be aware of the following:

- It's important to consult a doctor before reducing your energy intake to less than 4200 kilojoules (1000 calories) per day.
- Low-carbohydrate diets are not recommended – a 5000 kJ (1200 calorie) diet should supply at least 150 grams of carbohydrate.
- Many fad diets are dangerous to health, especially if followed long-term.
- Grapefruit is a low-energy fruit but otherwise has no special properties to help you lose weight.
- You can't rub or massage fat away.
- Exercise tones up muscles and improves body shape.
- Lean muscle tissue uses more energy than fat tissue.

# ALCOHOL

Alcohol provides energy at 29 kilojoules (7 calories) per gram, but alcoholic beverages provide few other nutrients. You should therefore avoid or strictly limit them if you are trying to lose weight.

## ALCOHOL AND HEALTH

In high daily doses (see 'How much is safe?', p. 19) alcohol is toxic, damaging the liver, the pancreas and the nervous system. It also alters the way the stomach and the bowel work.

Drinking too much can lead to poor nutrition, both because eating patterns may change and because the absorption of nutrients is affected by alcohol damage to the pancreas and the liver. This in turn leads to a number of other health problems.

The picture for cardiovascular health is not clear-cut. Moderate to heavy consumption of alcohol appears to lead to high blood pressure and heart-muscle damage, and heavy drinkers appear to have a greater risk of coronary heart disease. At the same time there is some evidence to suggest that *very* moderate regular drinkers (see 'How much is safe?', p. 19) may have a lower risk of coronary heart disease than either heavy drinkers or non-drinkers.

**Alcoholism** describes the condition of a person's becoming dependent on a high daily consumption of alcohol and being unable to limit drinking without the aid of therapy. As well as being responsible for the progressive effects of poor eating patterns and damage to the organs of the body, alcoholism is strongly linked to cancers of the head, neck, oesophagus, liver and colon. It also affects personal relationships and job performance.

Total abstinence from alcohol is recommended for people with alcoholism.

## ALCOHOL AND PREGNANCY

Drinking alcohol during pregnancy increases the risk of foetal abnormalities. Heavy drinking may cause the infant to be born with various developmental abnormalities, including a small head, a characteristic facial appearance, or mental retardation.

Health authorities recommend that you avoid alcohol while you are pregnant.

## ALCOHOL AND ROAD SAFETY

Safety on our roads and current drink-driving laws mean that you must be particularly aware of your alcohol consumption when you intend to drive. The table and the information below will give you the details you need to know for safety and to make sure that your alcohol consumption stays within legal limits, that is, enabling you to have a blood-alcohol reading of less than .05.

## THE STANDARD DRINK

The standard drink contains approximately 10 grams of alcohol, and is one of the following:

- 375 ml of low-alcohol beer
- 250 ml standard beer
- 100 ml wine (red or white)
- 60 ml sherry or port
- 30 ml spirits.

## HOW MUCH IS SAFE?

Recommended 'safe' limits vary – from person to person, and according to the hazard you are considering and your sex.

- Because of physiological differences and generally lower blood volumes, 'safe' levels are lower for females than for males.
- One to two standard drinks per day for women, and up to four for men, is consistent with Dietary Guidelines.
- In relation to cardiovascular health, one standard drink per day for women, and two for men, might be described as 'very moderate' (see 'Alcohol and health', p. 17).
- In relation to general health, more than 40 grams of alcohol per day for women and 60 grams per day for men is considered a high dose, and harmful, while less than 20 grams per day for women and less than 40 grams per day for men is considered safe.

- For pregnant women, and for people suffering from alcoholism, the safe level is zero.
- Road traffic authorities advise that the safest blood-alcohol count for drivers is zero. Staying within the legal limit of .05 entails having not more than one standard drink per hour for men and less than one for women.

## HOW TO REDUCE YOUR INTAKE

If you are used to drinking alcohol, try the following:

- choose low-alcohol drinks, especially light beer
- make longer drinks by adding more ice and more mixers to spirits, or by adding fruit juice, water or ice to wine.
- don't top up your glass
- drink alcohol less often, using mineral water, ice water or fruit juice as substitutes
- as a long-term measure, modify your social habits so that alcohol is not the focus.

# ALCOHOL

| | g/ 100ml | ml standard drink | av g/ standard drink |
|---|---|---|---|
| *beer* | 3.9 | glass 250 | 10 |
| | | can 375 | 15 |
| extra light | less than 1 | glass 250 | 2 |
| low-alcohol (light) | 1.6–2.6 | glass 250 | 5 |
| | | can 375 | 7.5 |
| *cider* ... dry | 3.8 | 250 | 10 |
| sweet | 3.7 | 250 | 9.5 |
| *liqueurs* ... advocaat | 12.8 | 30 | 4 |
| cherry brandy | 19 | 30 | 7 |
| curacao | 29.3 | 30 | 10 |
| *port* | 15.9 | 60 | 10 |
| *sherry* ... dry | 15.7 | 60 | 10 |
| medium | 14.8 | 60 | 9 |
| ... sweet | 15.6 | 60 | 10 |
| *spirits* ... 70% proof brandy/gin/rum/vodka/whisky | 31.7 | nip 30 | 9.5 |
| *stout* | 4.3 | glass 250 | 11 |
| | | can 375 | 16 |
| *vermouth* ... dry | 13.9 | 60 | 8.5 |
| sweet | 13 | 60 | 8 |
| *wine* ... red | 9.5 | 100 | 10 |
| rosé | 8.7 | 100 | 9 |
| white ... dry | 9.1 | 100 | 9 |
| medium | 8.8 | 100 | 9 |
| sparkling | 9.9 | 100 | 10 |
| sweet | 10.2 | 100 | 10 |

# THE COUNTER

| | MASS | KJ | CAL |
|---|---|---|---|
| *abalone* ... canned ... drained | 100g | 605 | 144 |
| raw | 100g | 410 | 98 |
| *advocaat* see *liqueurs* | | | |
| *alcohol* see individual drinks | | | |
| *ale* | 100ml | 165 | 39 |
| *alfalfa sprouts* ... 1 tbsp | 40g | 36 | 8 |
| *allbran* see *breakfast cereals* | | | |
| *almond paste* see *marzipan* | | | |
| *almonds* ... 15 | 20g | 500 | 119 |
| roasted, salted | 100g | 2625 | 625 |
| shelled, skinned | 100g | 2505 | 596 |
| sugared | 100g | 1910 | 455 |
| *anchovies* ... canned ... 1 fillet | 2g | 14 | 3 |
| raw | 100g | 925 | 220 |
| Admiral ... flat/rolled | 100g | 755 | 180 |
| John West | 100g | 940 | 224 |
| *anchovy essence* ... 1 tsp | 5ml | 15 | 4 |
| *anchovy paste* ... 1 tsp | 5g | 40 | 10 |
| *apple juice* see *fruit juices* | | | |
| *apple pie* see *pies, sweet* | | | |
| *apple strudel* see *cakes and pastries* | | | |
| *apples* ... baked/stewed ... with sugar | 100g | 345 | 82 |
| without sugar | 100g | 135 | 32 |
| canned ... sweetened | 100g | 320 | 76 |
| unsweetened | 100g | 175 | 42 |
| dried ... stewed ... with sugar | 100g | 475 | 113 |
| without sugar | 100g | 310 | 74 |
| uncooked | 100g | 1210 | 288 |
| Green's | 57g | 630 | 150 |
| raw ... average type ... 1 av | 170g | 325 | 77 |
| Delicious ... 1 av | 185g | 390 | 93 |
| Golden Delicious ... 1 av | 135g | 225 | 54 |

| | MASS | KJ | CAL |
|---|---|---|---|
| Granny Smith ... 1 av | 179g | 285 | 68 |
| Jonathan ... 1 av | 125g | 235 | 56 |
| ***apricot nectar*** ... canned | 100g | 250 | 60 |
| ***apricots*** ... canned ... in pear juice ... 3 halves + 35ml juice | 85g | 150 | 36 |
| drained ... 1 cup | 220g | 375 | 89 |
| in syrup ... 1 cup | 260g | 570 | 136 |
| drained ... 3 halves | 50g | 105 | 25 |
| artific. sweet. ... 3 halves + 40ml liquid | 90g | 90 | 21 |
| unsweetened | 100g | 140 | 33 |
| dried ... stewed ... with sugar | 100g | 510 | 121 |
| without sugar | 100g | 350 | 83 |
| uncooked ... ½ | 4g | 45 | 11 |
| raw ... 1 av | 60g | 85 | 20 |
| stewed ... with sugar | 100g | 350 | 83 |
| without sugar | 100g | 90 | 21 |
| Goulburn Valley ... in fruit juice | 100g | 190 | 45 |
| SPC ... artific. sweet | 100g | 125 | 30 |
| fruit in syrup | 100g | 300 | 71 |
| just fruit | 100g | 180 | 43 |
| SPC Little Big Fruit (snak pak) ... fruit in syrup | 140g | 420 | 100 |
| in juice | 140g | 280 | 67 |
| Weight Watchers | 100g | 125 | 30 |
| ***arrowroot*** | 100g | 1445 | 344 |
| ***artichoke hearts*** ... Admiral | 100g | 55 | 13 |

Dried apricots are a good source of fibre as well as vitamin A. For those with a sweet tooth, dried fruit are preferable to sweets.

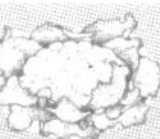

| | MASS | KJ | CAL |
|---|---|---|---|
| *artichoke, globe* ... boiled ... inner leaves + base ... 1 | 120g | 105 | 25 |
| *artichoke, Jerusalem* ... boiled ... peeled ... 1 | 320g | 330 | 79 |
| *asparagus* ... boiled ... 5 spears | 70g | 55 | 13 |
| Edgell-Birdseye | 100g | 105 | 25 |
| Farmland/John West | 100g | 100 | 25 |
| Green's/SPC | 100g | 75 | 18 |
| *asparagus rolls* ... 1 av | 45g | 185 | 44 |
| *aubergine* see *eggplant* | | | |
| *avocado* ... raw ... flesh only ... ½ | 121g | 1065 | 254 |
| *baba ghannouj* see *dips and spreads* | | | |
| *babaco* ... raw ... peeled ... flesh only ... ¼ | 277g | 225 | 54 |
| *bacon* ... fried ... medium fat ... 1 strip | 20g | 565 | 135 |
| grilled ... medium fat ... 1 strip | 20g | 555 | 132 |
| *bacon burger* ... frozen ... fried ... av all brands | 100g | 1040 | 248 |
| crumbed ... av all brands | 100g | 1535 | 365 |
| grilled ... av all brands | 100g | 1050 | 250 |
| crumbed ... av all brands | 100g | 1455 | 346 |
| Baron's Table ... 1 sv | 50g | 305 | 73 |
| *bagels* ... 1 | 85g | 950 | 226 |
| Sara Lee ... cinnamon/raisin | 100g | 945 | 225 |
| plain/poppyseed | 100g | 970 | 231 |
| *baked beans* ... Edgell-Birdseye | 100g | 345 | 82 |
| Farmland ... no added salt | 100g | 420 | 100 |
| SPC | 100g | 390 | 93 |
| *baked beans in barbecue sauce/vegetarian* ... Heinz ... 1 sv | 100g | 470 | 112 |
| *baked beans in ham sauce* ... Heinz ... 1 sv | 100g | 465 | 111 |
| *baked beans in tomato sauce* ... Heinz | 100g | 385 | 92 |

Grill bacon until crisp and most of the fat will run off and can be discarded. A 75 g rasher can reduce from 1340 kJ (320 cal) to around 715 kJ (170 cal).

| | MASS | KJ | CAL |
|---|---|---|---|
| *baklava* see *cakes and pastries* | | | |
| *balance oat bran* see *breakfast cereals* | | | |
| *bamboo shoots* ... raw | 20g | 25 | 6 |
| Admiral | 100g | 140 | 33 |
| *banana custard* see *custard, banana* | | | |
| *bananas* ... common variety ... raw ... peeled ... flesh only ... 1 | 140g | 500 | 119 |
| sugar/lady finger ... raw ... peeled ... flesh only ... 1 | 60g | 265 | 63 |
| *baps* ... 1 | 65g | 645 | 154 |
| *barbecue sauce* see *sauces, savoury* | | | |
| *barley, pearl* ... boiled ... 1 tbsp | 10g | 45 | 11 |
| dried ... uncooked ... 1 tbsp | 15g | 190 | 46 |
| *barramundi* ... baked | 100g | 410 | 98 |
| battered, fried | 100g | 835 | 199 |
| grilled | 100g | 400 | 95 |
| poached | 100g | 395 | 94 |
| poached/grilled ... no fat | 100g | 395 | 94 |
| raw | 100g | 320 | 76 |
| smoked | 100g | 335 | 80 |
| steamed | 100g | 350 | 83 |
| *bean sprouts* ... raw ... 1 cup | 90g | 75 | 18 |
| Admiral | 100g | 145 | 35 |
| *beans* ... McCain ... whole baby/golden | 100g | 115 | 27 |
| *beans, blackeye* ... dried | 100g | 1425 | 339 |
| *beans, broad* ... fresh ... boiled ... 1 cup | 170g | 295 | 70 |
| raw ... beans from 10 pods | 92g | 160 | 38 |
| Edgell-Birdseye | 100g | 440 | 105 |
| McCain | 100g | 105 | 25 |
| *beans, butter* ... boiled ... 1 cup sliced | 140g | 115 | 27 |
| cooked, cannellini style | 100g | 515 | 123 |
| frozen ... boiled | 100g | 130 | 31 |
| raw ... 10 beans | 77g | 65 | 15 |

| | | MASS | KJ | CAL |
|---|---|---|---|---|
| | Edgell-Birdseye | 100g | 115 | 27 |
| | cannellini style/ golden butter-beans | 100g | 350 | 83 |
| *beans, green* ... | canned...drained ... 1 cup | 230g | 230 | 55 |
| | dried...boiled ... 1 cup | 115g | 135 | 32 |
| | fresh...boiled ... 1 cup | 140g | 95 | 23 |
| | frozen....boiled ... 1 cup | 125g | 95 | 23 |
| | raw ... 1 cup sliced | 120g | 105 | 25 |
| | Edgell-Birdseye ... cross-cut/sliced/frozen | 100g | 110 | 26 |
| | Golden Circle ... av all brands ... sliced | 100g | 135 | 32 |
| *beans, haricot (navy)* ... | boiled | 100g | 500 | 119 |
| *beans, lima* ... | boiled | 100g | 470 | 112 |
| | dried ... boiled | 100g | 545 | 130 |
| | raw | 100g | 1420 | 338 |
| | Frionor ... baby | 100g | 480 | 114 |
| | Sanitarium ... ¼ can | 110g | 375 | 89 |
| *beans, mixed* ... | dried ... average type | 100g | 1450 | 345 |
| | cooked ... average type | 100g | 525 | 125 |
| | Masterfoods/Edgell-Birdseye | 100g | 450 | 107 |
| *beans, mung* ... | cooked (dahl) | 100g | 350 | 83 |
| | dried ... raw | 100g | 1430 | 340 |
| | raw | 100g | 980 | 233 |
| | sprouts ... canned | 100g | 40 | 10 |
| | raw | 100g | 145 | 35 |
| *beans, purple* ... | boiled ... 1 cup sliced | 140g | 170 | 40 |
| | raw ... 10 beans | 105g | 125 | 30 |
| *beans, red kidney* ... | boiled ... dried | 100g | 1060 | 255 |
| | dried ... 1 cup | 100g | 310 | 74 |
| | fresh ... 1 cup | 165g | 790 | 188 |

Bean sprouts blanched (at only 30 kJ/7 cal per 30 g) and added to rice can bulk out a lower-energy base for curries and kebabs, as well as adding a satisfying crunch.

| | MASS | KJ | CAL |
|---|---|---|---|
| Edgell-Birdseye | 100g | 410 | 98 |
| Green's | 100g | 380 | 90 |
| Masterfoods ... drained | 100g | 570 | 136 |
| *beans, snake* ... boiled ... 1 cup sliced | 140g | 135 | 32 |
| raw ... 10 beans | 120g | 115 | 27 |
| *beans, soya* ... boiled ... dried | 100g | 545 | 130 |
| dry | 100g | 1705 | 406 |
| raw ... fresh | 100g | 560 | 133 |
| Masterfoods ... drained | 100g | 465 | 111 |
| Sanitarium ... in tomato sauce ... ¼ can | 110g | 375 | 89 |
| natural ... ⅙ can | 72g | 185 | 44 |
| *beef* | | | |
| *blade steak* ... grilled ... lean ... 1 av | 112g | 830 | 198 |
| lean+fat ... 1 av | 120g | 1035 | 246 |
| *boneless average cut* ... cooked | 100g | 890 | 212 |
| lean ... 1 cup diced | 190g | 1455 | 346 |
| lean+fat ... 1 cup diced | 182g | 1805 | 430 |
| *brisket, corned* ... boiled ... lean ... 1 slice | 32g | 285 | 68 |
| lean+fat ... 1 slice | 43g | 560 | 133 |
| *chuck steak* ... simmered ... lean ... 1 cup diced | 156g | 1325 | 315 |
| lean+fat ... 1 cup diced | 179g | 1920 | 457 |
| *fillet steak* ... grilled ... lean ... 1 av | 70g | 575 | 137 |
| lean+fat ... 1 av | 77g | 750 | 179 |
| *heart* ... simmered ... 1 cup chopped | 190g | 1190 | 283 |
| *kidney* ... simmered ... 1 cup diced | 150g | 850 | 202 |
| *liver* ... simmered ... 1 cup chopped | 140g | 1290 | 307 |
| *mince* ... dry-fried | 100g | 1195 | 285 |
| regular ... simmered, drained ... 1 cup | 170g | 1300 | 310 |
| *rib steak (porterhouse)* ... grilled ... lean ... 1 av | 103g | 760 | 181 |
| lean+fat ... 1 av | 130g | 1640 | 390 |
| *rib-eye steak* ... grilled ... lean ... 1 av | 94g | 780 | 186 |
| lean+fat ... 1av | 108g | 1160 | 276 |

| | MASS | KJ | CAL |
|---|---|---|---|
| *round steak* ... grilled ... lean ... 1 av | 249g | 1840 | 438 |
| lean + fat ... 1 av | 265g | 2250 | 536 |
| *rump steak* ... fried ... 1 av | 150g | 1535 | 365 |
| grilled ... lean ... 1 av | 174g | 1400 | 333 |
| lean + fat ... 1 av | 199g | 2240 | 533 |
| *sandwich steak* ... frozen ... grilled ... av all brands | 100g | 1425 | 339 |
| *silverside* ... baked ... lean ... 1 slice | 41g | 395 | 94 |
| lean + fat ... 1 slice | 37g | 275 | 65 |
| *silverside, corned* ... boiled ... lean + fat ... 1 slice | 45g | 385 | 92 |
| lean ... 1 slice | 39g | 210 | 50 |
| *sirloin roast* ... 1 sv | 120g | 1415 | 337 |
| *sirloin steak* ... grilled ... lean ... 1 av | 104g | 840 | 200 |
| lean + fat ... 1 av | 127g | 1455 | 346 |
| *skirt steak* ... simmered ... lean ... 1 cup diced | 181g | 1430 | 340 |
| lean + fat ... 1 cup diced | 184g | 1520 | 362 |
| *tail* ... simmered ... 1 cup | 81g | 1175 | 280 |
| *tongue* ... simmered ... 1 slice | 20g | 260 | 62 |
| *topside roast* ... baked ... lean ... 1 slice | 41g | 260 | 62 |
| lean + fat ... 1 slice | 45g | 360 | 86 |

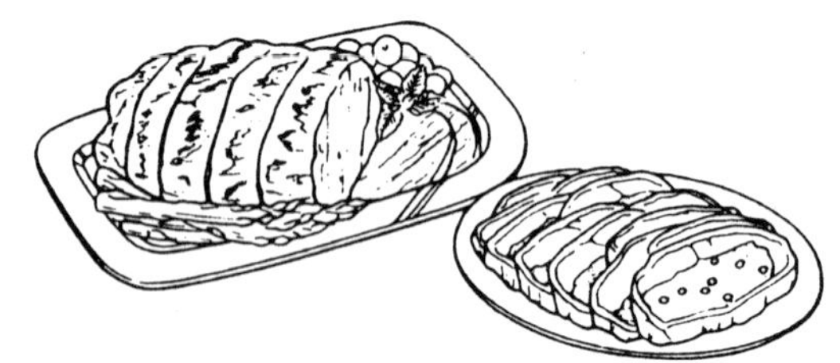

| | MASS | KJ | CAL |
|---|---|---|---|
| *tripe* ... simmered ... 1 cup chopped | 175g | 610 | 145 |
| ***beef burgers*** ... frozen ... fried ... 1 sv | 60g | 660 | 157 |
| Baron's Table ... 1 sv | 50g | 230 | 55 |
| Edgell-Birdseye ... crumbed | 100g | 1210 | 288 |
| I & J ... beefer burgers | 100g | 1105 | 263 |
| big and l'il beefers | 100g | 1125 | 268 |
| lean beefers | 100g | 485 | 116 |
| ***beef casserole*** ... 1 sv | 180g | 945 | 225 |
| with vegetables ... (chuck steak) | 100g | 710 | 169 |
| without vegetables ... (chuck steak) | 100g | 745 | 177 |
| ***beef chow mein (Chinese)*** | 100g | 580 | 138 |
| ***beef curry*** ... canned ... av commercial brands | 100g | 765 | 182 |
| Kraft ... snack pack ... 1 can | 105g | 655 | 156 |
| Vesta ... 1 pkt, made up | | 3485 | 830 |
| ***beef German*** see ***luncheon meat*** | | | |
| ***beef hot salad (Thai)*** | 100g | 390 | 93 |
| ***beef in black bean sauce*** ... Farmland ... 1 sv | 200g | 1400 | 333 |
| ***beef in oyster sauce (Chinese)*** | 100g | 625 | 149 |
| ***beef Italienne with tagliatelle*** ... Findus Lean Cuisine ... 1 sv | 250g | 985 | 235 |
| ***beef oriental*** ... Findus Lean Cuisine ... 1 sv | 245g | 1090 | 260 |
| ***beef Panang (Thai)*** | 100g | 870 | 207 |
| ***beef rissoles*** ... 1 large | 100g | 1065 | 254 |
| ***beef satay*** ... fresh/Farmland ... 1 sv | 200g | 1380 | 329 |
| ***beef satay (Chinese/Thai)*** | 100g | 805 | 191 |
| ***beef steak and vegetables*** ... Kraft | 100g | 785 | 187 |
| Farmland ... no added salt | 100g | 295 | 70 |
| ***beef teriyaki*** ... Farmland ... 1 sv | 200g | 1000 | 238 |

Grilling beefburgers on a wire rack until well done means that a substantial proportion of their fat can be cooked out and discarded. A 630 kJ (150 cal) beefburger will reduce to 480 kJ (115 cal) in this way.

| | MASS | KJ | CAL |
|---|---|---|---|
| *beef with rice curry* ... Heinz | 100g | 505 | 121 |
| *beef, corned* ... canned ... av commercial brands | 100g | 805 | 192 |
| with cereal ... av commercial brands | 100g | 825 | 196 |
| *beer* ... Boags lager/Coopers sparkling ale | 100ml | 170 | 40 |
| Cascade/Castlemaine XXX draught | 100ml | 150 | 36 |
| Castlemaine XXXX bitter | 100ml | 145 | 35 |
| Emu bitter | 100ml | 135 | 32 |
| Fosters lager | 100ml | 150 | 36 |
| Reschs pilsener/Tooheys draught/Tooth KB | 100ml | 140 | 33 |
| Swan lager | 100ml | 155 | 37 |
| Victoria bitter | 100ml | 160 | 38 |
| West End draught | 100ml | 140 | 33 |
| *beer nuts* see *snack foods* | | | |
| *beer, diet* ... Carlton diet ale | 100g | 135 | 32 |
| Coopers DB/Millers hi-lo | 100g | 115 | 27 |
| *beer, low alcohol* ... Carlton light | 100g | 125 | 30 |
| Tooheys lite | 100g | 100 | 24 |
| Tooth LA | 100g | 90 | 21 |
| XXXX lite | 100g | 105 | 25 |
| *beetroot* ... boiled ... flesh only ... 2 slices | 60g | 105 | 25 |
| Farmland ... sliced ... no added salt | 100g | 195 | 46 |
| Golden Circle/Edgell-Birdseye | 100g | 230 | 58 |
| *biscuits* | | | |
| *anzac* ... av all brands ... 1 | 19g | 360 | 86 |
| *bran* ... av all brands ... 1 | 13g | 245 | 58 |
| *brownies/chocolate chip* ... av all brands ... 1 | 12g | 245 | 58 |
| *butter* ... av all brands ... 1 | 12g | 230 | 55 |
| *carob* ... av all brands ... 1 | 18g | 375 | 89 |
| *cheese-flavoured* ... av all brands ... 1 | 3g | 60 | 14 |
| *cheese straws* ... home-made | 100g | 1905 | 454 |
| *chocolate chip and nuts* ... av all brands ... 1 | 9g | 190 | 45 |
| *chocolate-coated* ... av all brands ... 1 | 11g | 220 | 52 |

| | MASS | KJ | CAL |
|---|---|---|---|
| cream- and/or | | | |
| jam-filled ... av all brands ... 1 | 13g | 275 | 65 |
| marshmallow-filled ... av all brands ... 1 | 23g | 425 | 101 |
| *chocolate-flavoured* ... av all brands ... 1 | 9g | 160 | 38 |
| *cracker* ... high-fat ... av all brands | 100g | 2060 | 490 |
| low-fat ... av all brands | 100g | 1675 | 399 |
| medium-fat ... av all brands | 100g | 1975 | 470 |
| *cream- and jam-filled* ... av all brands ... 1 | 16g | 330 | 79 |
| *cream-filled* ... av all flavours ... av all brands ... 1 | 15g | 295 | 70 |
| *crispbread* ... rye ... av all brands | 100g | 1505 | 358 |
| wheat ... av all brands | 100g | 1735 | 413 |
| *fruit* ... av all brands ... 1 | 10g | 190 | 45 |
| *fruit and nuts* ... av all brands ... 1 | 10g | 205 | 49 |
| *fruit-filled* ... av all brands ... 1 | 15g | 250 | 60 |

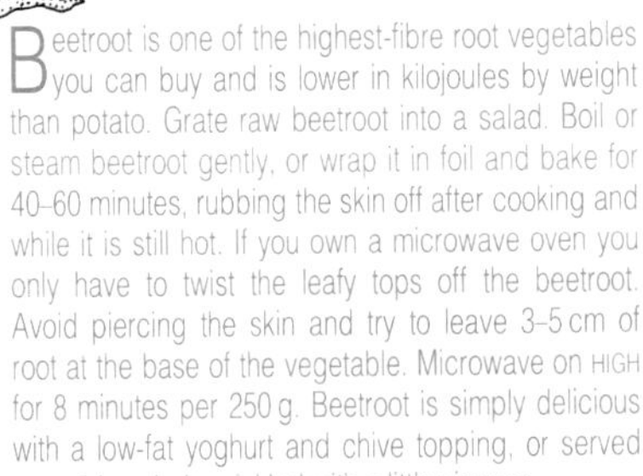

Beetroot is one of the highest-fibre root vegetables you can buy and is lower in kilojoules by weight than potato. Grate raw beetroot into a salad. Boil or steam beetroot gently, or wrap it in foil and bake for 40–60 minutes, rubbing the skin off after cooking and while it is still hot. If you own a microwave oven you only have to twist the leafy tops off the beetroot. Avoid piercing the skin and try to leave 3–5 cm of root at the base of the vegetable. Microwave on HIGH for 8 minutes per 250 g. Beetroot is simply delicious with a low-fat yoghurt and chive topping, or served as a side salad sprinkled with a little vinegar.

| | MASS | KJ | CAL |
|---|---|---|---|
| *fruit, iced* ... av all brands ... 1 | 12g | 245 | 58 |
| *ginger* ... av all brands ... 1 | 13g | 220 | 52 |
| *iced* ... av all brands ... 1 | 11g | 190 | 45 |
| *jam-filled* ... av all brands ... 1 | 13g | 225 | 54 |
| *macaroons* ... av all brands ... 1 | 10g | 200 | 48 |
| *marshmallow* ... av all brands ... 1 | 17g | 280 | 67 |
| *nuts* ... av all brands ... 1 | 11g | 225 | 54 |
| *oatmeal* ... av all brands ... 1 | 10g | 195 | 46 |
| *plain* ... av all brands ... 1 | 6g | 110 | 26 |
| salted ... av all brands ... 1 | 3g | 60 | 14 |
| sweet ... av all brands ... 1 | 8g | 155 | 37 |
| *polyunsaturated ... sweet* ... av all brands ... 1 | 14g | 250 | 60 |
| *puffed and toasted/extra-fibre* ... av all brands ... 1 | 5g | 80 | 19 |
| *rye* ... av all brands ... 1 | 8g | 105 | 25 |
| *savoury-flavoured* ... av all brands ... 1 | 2g | 40 | 10 |
| *shortbread* ... av all brands ... 1 | 12g | 240 | 57 |
| *starch-reduced* ... av all brands ... 1 | 7g | 120 | 29 |
| *wafers (filled)* ... av all brands ... 1 | 7g | 155 | 37 |
| *water crackers* ... av all brands ... 1 | 4g | 65 | 15 |
| *wheatmeal* ... av all brands ... 1 | 9g | 165 | 39 |
| *wholewheat* ... av all brands ... 1 | 5g | 90 | 21 |
| *wholewheat and sesame* ... av all brands ... 1 | 5g | 90 | 21 |
| *Arnotts* ... cheds ... 1 | | 160 | 38 |
| choc chip cream/choc fruit and nut ... 1 | | 275 | 65 |
| choc mint slice/teddy bear/choc teddy bear ... 1 | | 345 | 82 |
| chocolate ripple ... 1 | | 170 | 40 |
| chocolate royals ... 1 | | 305 | 73 |
| chocolate stiks ... 1 | | 45 | 11 |
| chocolate tee vee snacks ... 1 | | 110 | 26 |
| chocolate tim tams ... 1 | | 405 | 96 |
| clix ... 1 | | 65 | 15 |
| cruskits/thin captain, plain ... 1 | | 100 | 24 |

| | MASS | KJ | CAL |
|---|---|---|---|
| carob-coated bran/muesli ... 1 | | 365 | 87 |
| gluten-free ... 1 | | 280 | 67 |
| *Phoenix/Westons* ... choc chip cookies ... 1 | | 235 | 56 |
| crackerbread sesame ... 1 | | 140 | 33 |
| jam fancies ... 1 | | 260 | 62 |
| macaroon delights ... 1 | | 95 | 23 |
| milk chocolate wheaten ... 1 | | 485 | 115 |
| roundabouts ... 1 | | 345 | 82 |
| scotch fingers ... 1 | | 180 | 43 |
| snowballs ... 1 | | 245 | 58 |
| strawberry mallows ... 1 | | 160 | 38 |
| vitawheat ... 1 | | 95 | 23 |
| wagon wheels ... 1 | | 860 | 205 |
| *Premier Japan* ... rice crackers ... 1 | | 60 | 14 |
| *Sunshine* ... choc galore ... 1 | | 275 | 65 |
| cream treats/lemon cream/orange cream ... 1 | | 355 | 85 |
| custard cream ... 1 | | 365 | 87 |
| ginger crunch ... 1 | | 110 | 26 |
| marie/milk coffee ... 1 | | 155 | 37 |
| nice/shortbread treats ... 1 | | 175 | 42 |
| orange crunch ... 1 | | 210 | 50 |
| *Willow Valley* ... oat bran with choc chips ... 1 | | 565 | 135 |
| with fruit and nuts ... 1 | | 600 | 143 |
| ***black pudding (sausage)*** ... av commercial brands | 100g | 1080 | 257 |
| ***blackberries*** ... canned ... sweetened | 100g | 300 | 71 |
| unsweetened | 100g | 165 | 39 |
| raw | 100g | 245 | 58 |
| stewed ... with sugar | 100g | 255 | 61 |
| without sugar | 100g | 125 | 30 |
| ***blackcurrants*** ... raw | 100g | 245 | 58 |
| ***bogong moth*** ... abdomen | 100g | 1910 | 455 |
| ***bonox*** ... Kraft ... 1 tsp | 8g | 30 | 7 |

| | MASS | KJ | CAL |
|---|---|---|---|
| ***Boston bun*** see ***buns*** | | | |
| ***bourghul*** ... dried ... Lowans | 100g | 1480 | 354 |
| see also ***bulgar*** | | | |
| ***brains*** see ***lamb***; ***veal*** | | | |
| ***braised beef steak*** ... canned | 100g | 885 | 211 |
| ***braised beef steak and onions*** ... canned ... av all brands | 100g | 715 | 170 |
| ***bran*** see ***breakfast cereals*** | | | |
| ***brandy*** see ***spirits*** | | | |
| ***brazil nuts*** ... shelled ... snack-size | 50g | 1335 | 318 |
| ***bread*** | | | |
| *flat breads* ... chapati ... + fat | 100g | 1385 | 330 |
| no fat | 100g | 860 | 205 |
| Lebanese ... white ... 24 cm diam | 110g | 1234 | 294 |
| wholemeal ... 24 cm diam | 110g | 1086 | 259 |
| matzo | 30g | 490 | 117 |
| pita ... Oasis ... 1 | 80g | 860 | 205 |
| with oat fibre ... 1 | 75g | 780 | 186 |
| pocket ... white/wholemeal ... 1 | 45g | 510 | 121 |
| sorj ... 1 | 100g | 1205 | 287 |

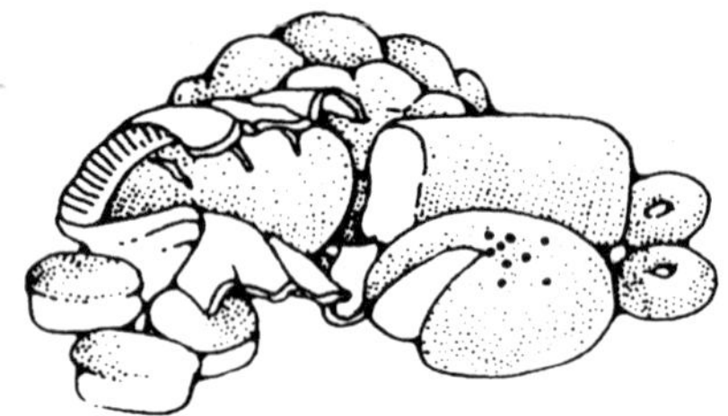

| | MASS | KJ | CAL |
|---|---|---|---|
| *loaves* ... brown sandwich ... 1 slice | 28g | 270 | 64 |
| toasted ... 1 slice | 23g | 265 | 63 |
| fruit bread ... brown ... heavy ... 1 slice | 45g | 535 | 127 |
| continental fruit ... 1 slice | 20g | 205 | 49 |
| white ... light ... 1 slice | 30g | 305 | 73 |
| pumpernickel ... 1 slice | 60g | 460 | 110 |
| raisin ... 1 slice | 60g | 655 | 156 |
| rye ... dark ... 1 slice | 50g | 425 | 101 |
| light ... 1 slice | 37g | 375 | 89 |
| starch-reduced ... 1 slice | 20g | 205 | 49 |
| Vienna ... 1 slice | 30g | 310 | 74 |
| white ... high-fibre ... toasted ... 1 slice | 23g | 265 | 63 |
| sandwich ... 1 slice | 28g | 290 | 69 |
| toasted ... 1 slice | 23g | 285 | 68 |
| wholemeal sandwich ... 1 slice | 28g | 290 | 69 |
| 1 toast-size-slice | 33g | 310 | 74 |
| Buttercup ... country split white (450-g loaf) ... 1 slice | | 245 | 68 |
| gold medal 'oat bran' ... 1 slice | | 265 | 63 |
| golden bake multi-grain ... 1 slice | | 255 | 61 |
| golden bake white/white 'oat bran' ... 1 slice | | 245 | 58 |
| low-salt wholemeal/super-soft ... white ... 1 slice | | 285 | 68 |

### Eating Too Little Can Hinder Weight Loss

A diet of 3350 kJ (800 cal) a day reduces the possibility that the body will obtain the wide range of nutrients it requires, and actually constitutes a kind of 'famine' intake because the quantity of kilojoules is inadequate. Over a long period, inadequate energy intake has the effect of making the body feel that famine is imminent, so that it strenuously resists further weight loss.

| | MASS | KJ | CAL |
|---|---|---|---|
| natural-grain toast ... 1 slice | | 335 | 80 |
| natural-grain toast reduced-salt ... 1 slice | | 350 | 83 |
| Oz varieties ... 1 slice | | 255 | 60 |
| toasty ... 1 slice | | 340 | 81 |
| toasty reduced-salt ... 1 slice | | 345 | 82 |
| wholemeal ... 1 slice | | 285 | 68 |
| wholemeal toast ... 1 slice | | 340 | 81 |
| Sunicrust ... Raisin Bread | 100g | 1180 | 281 |
| Suni-Sandwich ... white | 100g | 995 | 237 |
| wholemeal | 100g | 1025 | 244 |
| Suni-7-Grains | 100g | 995 | 237 |
| Suni-Toast ... white | 100g | 995 | 237 |
| wholemeal | 100g | 1025 | 244 |
| Wholemeal Grain | 100g | 895 | 213 |
| Taylors ... wholemeal ... 1 slice | 40g | 490 | 117 |
| Tip Top ... Bornhoffen ... av per slice | | 310 | 74 |
| harvest wholemeal wholegrain ... av av per slice | | 390 | 93 |
| spicy fruit ... av per slice | | 300 | 71 |
| Weight Watchers ... av per slice | | 185 | 44 |
| wholemeal ... av per slice | | 265 | 63 |
| Vogel ... family-size ... 1 slice | 37g | 375 | 89 |
| *rolls* ... cheese ... 1 | 65g | 710 | 169 |
| dinner ... 1 | 30g | 300 | 71 |
| hamburger ... 1 | 65g | 645 | 154 |
| horseshoe/knot/mixed-grain/torpedo ... 1 | 60g | 595 | 142 |
| *sticks* ... French bread stick ... 1 slice | 20g | 200 | 48 |
| garlic bread ... 2 slices | 67g | 1140 | 271 |
| grissini ... 2 sticks | 20g | 300 | 71 |
| white | 90g | 975 | 232 |
| wholemeal | 105g | 1050 | 250 |

| | MASS | KJ | CAL |
|---|---|---|---|
| see also *bagels; baps; buns; croissants; crumpets; muffins* | | | |
| *breadcrumbs* ... 1 cup | 100g | 1330 | 317 |
| *bread mix* ... gluten-free ... Country Harvest ... made up | 100g | 955 | 227 |
| high-fibre made up | 100g | 885 | 211 |
| multi-mix made up | 100g | 945 | 225 |
| *breadfruit* ... canned ... drained | 100g | 275 | 65 |
| raw | 100g | 445 | 106 |
| *breakfast cereals* ... | | | |
| *baby cereal* ... 1 bowl | 30g | 225 | 54 |
| *bran flakes* ... 1 bowl | 30g | 465 | 111 |
| *bran, rice* ... 1 tbsp | 8g | 144 | 34 |
| *bran, wheat* ... 1 tbsp | 5g | 33 | 9 |
| *muesli* ... swiss-style ... 1 cup | 125g | 1786 | 421 |
| toasted ... 1 cup | 110g | 1860 | 443 |
| *oatmeal* ... boiled ... ⅓ cup | 85g | 250 | 60 |
| dry ... raw ... 2 tbsp | 30g | 490 | 117 |
| *oats* ... rolled ... boiled ... 1 cup | 260g | 550 | 131 |
| *puffed corn/puffed rice* ... 1 bowl | 30g | 135 | 32 |
| *puffed wheat* ... 1 cup | 12g | 180 | 43 |

## Don't Skip Breakfast

Missing breakfast can mean burning almost 6 per cent fewer kilojoules during the day. Most of the kilojoules we use each day are to maintain the body's metabolic rate, which is increased by eating breakfast after we've slept. A good breakfast should supply at least 10 per cent of the day's energy intake to stimulate the metabolism for the whole day. Without breakfast our metabolism slows down and we burn fewer kilojoules.

Another danger allied to skipping breakfast is the temptation to snack during the morning on foods that will not provide the same nutrients that can be gained from a good breakfast. It may also be more difficult to control your kilojoule intake.

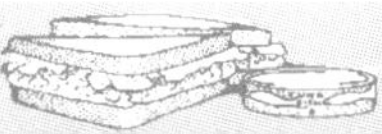

| | MASS | KJ | CAL |
|---|---|---|---|
| *rice bubbles* ... 1 cup | 30g | 445 | 106 |
| *semolina* ... cooked ... 1 cup | 200g | 260 | 62 |
| Fountain ... raw | 30g | 455 | 108 |
| *wheatgerm* ... 1 tbsp | 6g | 67 | 16 |
| *Alevita* ... muesli with fruit ... no added sugar | 30g | 420 | 100 |
| *Anchor* ... oatbran | 30g | 480 | 114 |
| *Arrowhead Mills* ... oatbran flakes | 30g | 460 | 110 |
| *Cerola* ... crunchy toasted muesli/apricot toasted muesli | 30g | 540 | 129 |
| light 'n' crunchy | 30g | 530 | 126 |
| natural muesli | 30g | 475 | 113 |
| *Country Harvest* ... rice pops | 30g | 460 | 110 |
| *Farmland* ... minute oats | 30g | 460 | 110 |
| toasted muesli | 30g | 580 | 138 |
| *Green's* ... natural bran | 30g | 135 | 32 |
| oatbran cereal | 30g | 270 | 64 |
| wheatgerm ... 1 tbsp | | 75 | 18 |
| *Home Brand* ... fruit rings/rice puffs | 30g | 490 | 117 |
| *John Bull* ... rolled oats | 30g | 460 | 110 |
| *Kellogg's* ... all-bran | 30g | 320 | 76 |
| balance oat bran | 45g | 790 | 188 |
| bran flakes/sultana bran | 30g | 365 | 87 |
| corn flakes/frosties/just right/ready wheats/ rice bubbles | 30g | 460 | 110 |
| froot loops | 30g | 490 | 117 |
| honey smacks | 30g | 485 | 115 |
| komplete natural muesli/coco pops | 30g | 465 | 111 |
| nutri-grain/puffed wheat/special K | 30g | 480 | 114 |
| sustain | 30g | 440 | 105 |
| toasted muesli | 30g | 545 | 130 |
| *Morning Sun* ... natural muesli | 30g | 440 | 105 |
| toasted tropical muesli | 30g | 495 | 118 |
| *Norco* ... whey cereal delite | 30g | 85 | 20 |

| | MASS | KJ | CAL |
|---|---|---|---|
| *Purina* ... natural bran | 30g | 270 | 64 |
| processed bran | 30g | 330 | 79 |
| Swiss formula muesli | 30g | 415 | 99 |
| toasted muesli | 30g | 500 | 119 |
| toasted muesli flakes | 30g | 430 | 102 |
| *Quaker* ... instant porridge ... 1 sachet | 34g | 520 | 124 |
| *Sanitarium* ... bix biscuits ... 3 biscuits | 22g | 345 | 82 |
| cornflakes | 30g | 440 | 105 |
| crunchy granola | 30g | 540 | 129 |
| fruit bran | 30g | 340 | 81 |
| goodstart ... 2 biscuits | 40g | 590 | 140 |
| honey weets/weeta puffs | 30g | 450 | 107 |
| puffed wheat | 30g | 430 | 102 |
| toasted muesli | 30g | 560 | 133 |
| tropical muesli/unsweetened muesli | 30g | 420 | 100 |
| weet-bix ... 2 biscuits | 30g | 395 | 94 |
| weet-bix hi-bran ... 2 biscuits | 40g | 410 | 98 |
| weeta-flakes | 30g | 400 | 95 |
| weeta-germ (betta B) ... 2 tbsp | 15g | 410 | 98 |
| *Sunfarm*... rice bran ... 2 tbsp | 15g | 265 | 63 |
| *The Old Grain Mill* ... minute oats/wholegrain rolled oats | 30g | 485 | 115 |

| | MASS | KJ | CAL |
|---|---|---|---|
| natural bran | 30g | 280 | 67 |
| natural muesli | 30g | 445 | 106 |
| natural oatbran/natural wheatgerm | 30g | 475 | 113 |
| tropical fruit toasted muesli | 30g | 430 | 102 |
| wholegrain barley flakes/triticale flakes | 30g | 445 | 106 |
| wholegrain wheat flakes | 30g | 425 | 101 |
| *Uncle Toby's* ... 1-minute oats/instant porridge ... ⅓ cup ... dry | 30g | 460 | 110 |
| apricot and almond natural muesli | 30g | 440 | 105 |
| fibre plus | 30g | 395 | 94 |
| fruit and bran flakes | 30g | 395 | 94 |
| fruit and nut weeties | 30g | 415 | 99 |
| muesli clusters | 30g | 505 | 120 |
| oat bran/Swiss muesli | 30g | 445 | 106 |
| pro vita weat harts ... 1 tbsp | 12g | 160 | 38 |
| vita brits weeties | 30g | 415 | 99 |
| X-tra-G/shredded wheat/muesli flakes | 30g | 425 | 101 |
| ***bream*** ... battered, deep-fried | 100g | 970 | 231 |
| floured, pan-fried in oil | 100g | 830 | 198 |
| steamed | 100g | 580 | 138 |
| ***broccoli*** ... boiled/raw | 50g | 50 | 12 |
| McCain/Edgell-Birdseye | 100g | 120 | 29 |
| ***brussels sprouts*** ... boiled ... 5 | 100g | 105 | 29 |
| Edgell-Birdseye | 100g | 150 | 36 |
| McCain | 100g | 160 | 38 |
| ***bubble 'n' squeak*** ... Edgell-Birdseye | 100g | 400 | 95 |
| ***buckwheat*** ... raw ... ½ cup | 100g | 1520 | 362 |
| The Old Grain Mill ... kernels | 100g | 1400 | 333 |
| ***bulgur*** ... boiled ... 1 cup | 265g | 955 | 227 |
| dry ... 1 cup | 180g | 2250 | 536 |
| soaked ... 1 cup | 205g | 1305 | 311 |
| ***buns*** ... 1 | 60g | 610 | 145 |
| brioche | 100g | 1720 | 410 |

| | MASS | KJ | CAL |
|---|---|---|---|
| cinnamon ... 1 medium | 55g | 680 | 162 |
| finger | 100g | 1240 | 295 |
| fruit (Boston/coffee scroll/currant) ... 1 | 76g | 940 | 224 |
| hot cross ... 1 | 90g | 915 | 218 |
| *butter* ... salted/unsalted ... av all commercial brands ... 1 tbsp | 20g | 610 | 146 |
| Dairy Farmers | 100g | 3030 | 721 |
| reduced-fat dairy spread | 100g | 1550 | 369 |
| Devondale ... dairy extra soft ... 1 tbsp | 15g | 285 | 68 |
| Western Star ... Less reduced-fat spread | 10g | 160 | 38 |
| see also *margarine* | | | |
| *buttermilk* see *milk* | | | |
| *butterscotch* see *confectionery* | | | |
| *cabbage rolls (Lebanese)* | 100g | 495 | 118 |
| *cabbage* ... Chinese ... raw ... 1 cup shredded | 80g | 35 | 8 |
| common/savoy/white ... boiled ... 1 cup shredded | 135g | 90 | 21 |
| raw ... 1 cup shredded | 85g | 60 | 14 |
| mustard ... raw ... 1 cup shredded | 60g | 40 | 10 |
| red ... boiled ... 1 cup shredded | 130g | 90 | 21 |
| raw ... 1 cup shredded | 95g | 90 | 21 |
| Edgell-Birdseye | 100g | 160 | 38 |
| *caffex* see *coffee substitutes* | | | |
| *cake and pudding mixes* | | | |
| *Country Harvest* ... gluten-free ... cakes ... made up | 100g | 1810 | 431 |
| puddings ... vanilla/ choc ... made up | 100g | 665 | 758 |
| *Green's* ... light and moist ... chocolate cake/vanilla/golden butter ... made up | 50g | 670 | 160 |
| carrot cake/madeira with sultanas ... made up | 50g | 670 | 160 |
| sponge cake ... made up | 25g | 295 | 70 |
| date loaf ... made up | 50g | 1120 | 267 |

| | MASS | KJ | CAL |
|---|---|---|---|
| microbake puddings ... chocolate ... made up | 50g | 1165 | 277 |
| sultana ... made up | 50g | 1055 | 251 |
| self-saucing sponge puddings ... chocolate ... made up | 100g | 1070 | 255 |
| lemon/forestberry/ butterscotch ... made up | 100g | 1000 | 238 |
| *White Wings* | | | |
| apple and oatmeal cake ... av all varieties ... made up | 50g | 685 | 163 |
| bake o scone mix ... made up | 100g | 1360 | 324 |
| banana cake ... made up | 50g | 710 | 169 |
| chocolate cheese cake ... made up | 80g | 1180 | 281 |
| chocolate sponge/lemon cake ... made up | 50g | 650 | 155 |
| date loaf ... made up | 50g | 590 | 140 |
| French tea cake/apple spice tea/carrot ... made up | 50g | 670 | 160 |
| madeira cake ... made up | 50g | 690 | 164 |
| microwave moist ... chocolate chip pudding ... made up | 55g | 915 | 218 |
| chocolate cake ... made up | 50g | 790 | 188 |
| microwave moist self-icing cake ... banana ... made up | 50g | 765 | 182 |
| chocolate ... made up | 50g | 830 | 198 |

For a lower-kilojoule treat choose light and airy cakes such as fat-free whisked sponge filled with a moist fruit puree. Manufacturers tend to whisk more air into their products than their non-commercial counterparts so you may often find that bought cakes have fewer kilojoules than those you can make at home.

If you have prepared or bought a special cake for a particular occasion and there are likely to be leftovers to tempt you, try cutting only as much of the cake as you think you will need and freeze the rest.

| | MASS | KJ | CAL |
|---|---|---|---|
| moist orange cake/moist lemon ... made up | 50g | 645 | 154 |
| puffin self-saucing sponge cake ... made up | 100g | 750 | 179 |
| real fruit dessert ... av all varieties ... made up | 125g | 415 | 99 |
| rich chocolate sponge/choc cake ... made up | 50g | 680 | 162 |
| self-saucing sponge puddings ... | | | |
| av all varieties except choc ... | | | |
| made up | 125g | 1020 | 243 |
| chocolate ... made up | 125g | 1090 | 260 |
| sultana buttercake ... made up | 50g | 770 | 183 |
| *cakes and pastries* | | | |
| *angel-food cake* | 100g | 1135 | 270 |
| *apple strudel* ... 1 slice | 128g | 1120 | 267 |
| *baklava* ... Greek | 100g | 1580 | 376 |
| Lebanese | 100g | 2080 | 495 |
| *black forest cake* ...1 slice | 80g | 1140 | 271 |
| *carrot cake* ... 1 slice | 103g | 1425 | 339 |
| *cheesecake* ... 1 slice | 165g | 2350 | 560 |
| *chocolate cake, iced* ... 1 slice | 55g | 825 | 204 |
| *chocolate eclair* ... 1 | 70g | 1115 | 265 |
| *Christmas cake* ... light | 100g | 1490 | 355 |
| rich | 100g | 1595 | 380 |
| *cream puffs* ... with custard filling | 100g | 965 | 230 |
| *cupcake* ... 1 | 40g | 620 | 148 |
| *custard tart* ... 1 | 134g | 1465 | 349 |
| *Danish pastry* ... 1 | 100g | 1290 | 307 |
| *date and nut loaf* ... 1 | 100g | 1500 | 357 |
| *fruit cake* ... boiled ... 1 slice | 60g | 1015 | 242 |
| dark ... commercial ... 1 slice | 50g | 695 | 165 |
| light ... commercial ... 1 slice | 50g | 720 | 171 |
| rich ... 1 slice | 85g | 1145 | 273 |
| wedding | 100g | 1485 | 354 |
| *fruit mince slice* ... 1 | 170g | 1495 | 356 |

| | MASS | KJ | CAL |
|---|---|---|---|
| *galactobureko (Greek)* | 100g | 896 | 213 |
| *gingerbread* | 100g | 1330 | 317 |
| *jam tart* ... 1 | 45g | 670 | 160 |
| *kataifi (Greek)* | 100g | 1245 | 296 |
| *lamington* ... 1 | 73g | 950 | 226 |
| *madeira cake* | 100g | 1480 | 352 |
| *meringue* ... 1 | 26g | 400 | 95 |
| *muesli slice* ... 1 | 78g | 1335 | 318 |
| *plain cake* ... 1 slice | 40g | 590 | 140 |
| *rock cakes* | 100g | 1670 | 398 |
| *sponge cake* ... iced ... 1 thin slice | 60g | 755 | 180 |
| jam + cream, not iced ... ⅛ cake | 53g | 715 | 170 |
| *sweet mince tarts* | 100g | 1825 | 435 |
| *Swiss roll* ... 1 slice | 30g | 410 | 98 |
| *vanilla slice* ... 1 | 135g | 1155 | 275 |
| *Edgell-Birdseye* ... apple rolls | 100g | 1080 | 257 |
| apple strudel | 100g | 1015 | 242 |
| *Farmland* ... pastries ... av all flavours ... 1 | | 1060 | 252 |

| | MASS | KJ | CAL |
|---|---|---|---|
| *Herbert Adams* ... Danish pastries ...apple/apricot | 100g | 1270 | 302 |
| fruit cake | 100g | 1320 | 314 |
| *Sara Lee* ... banana cake ... ⅛ cake | 45g | 600 | 143 |
| black forest ... ¼ cake | 50g | 615 | 146 |
| celebration cake ... ¼ cake | 50g | 705 | 168 |
| cheesecake ... blueberry ... ⅛ cake | 60g | 650 | 155 |
| snack ... 1 | 50g | 525 | 125 |
| chocolate Bavarian ... ⅛ cake | 75g | 1095 | 261 |
| chocolate cake ... ⅛ cake | 45g | 650 | 155 |
| Danish pastry ... apple pull-apart/ raspberry ... 1 | 58g | 755 | 180 |
| blueberry | 100g | 1080 | 257 |
| cherry | 100g | 1040 | 248 |
| pecan ... 1 piece | 85g | 1300 | 310 |
| hazelnut/mocca gâteau ... 1 sv | 72g | 1075 | 256 |
| light desserts ... berry topped cheese/ strawberry French cheese | 100g | 770 | 183 |
| double choc mousse | 100g | 810 | 193 |
| pound cake ... all-purpose ... ⅛ cake | 40g | 635 | 151 |
| chocolate ... ⅛ cake | 40g | 620 | 148 |
| coconut/sultana ... ⅛ cake | 40g | 570 | 136 |
| sponge ... av all flavours ... ¼ cake | 50g | 600 | 143 |
| *calamari* ... fried (Lebanese) | 100g | 1170 | 279 |
| raw ... 1 tube | 180g | 590 | 140 |
| sliced, floured, fried ... 1 cup | 95g | 725 | 173 |
| *camp pie* ... canned | 100g | 710 | 169 |
| *cannelloni* ... dried ... Leggo's ... 1 sv | 33g | 495 | 118 |
| shells ... uncooked | 100g | 1540 | 367 |
| Findus Lean Cuisine ... 1 sv | 260g | 1135 | 270 |
| La Deliziosa ... ½ pkt | 250g | 1700 | 405 |
| McCain | 400g | 2270 | 540 |
| *canola oil* | 100ml | 3700 | 881 |

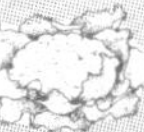

| | MASS | KJ | CAL |
|---|---|---|---|
| *cantaloupe/rockmelon* see *melon* | | | |
| *cape gooseberry* | 100g | 200 | 48 |
| *capers* ... 5 | 5g | 5 | 1 |
| *cappuccino* ... 1 cup | 250ml | 510 | 121 |
| *capsicum* ... green ... boiled ... 1 cup chopped | 110g | 110 | 26 |
| raw ... 1 cup chopped | 120g | 80 | 19 |
| red ... boiled ... 1 cup chopped | 145g | 170 | 40 |
| raw ... 1 cup chopped | 120g | 125 | 30 |
| Edgell-Birdseye ... diced | 100g | 135 | 32 |
| *carambola* ... flesh + skin + seeds ... 1 av | 125g | 290 | 69 |
| *caramels* see *confectionery* | | | |
| *caro* see *coffee substitutes* | | | |
| *carob bars* see *health-food bars* | | | |
| *carob drink powder* ... Healtheries | 100g | 1465 | 349 |
| *carob flour* ... 1 cup | 100g | 755 | 180 |
| *carob powder* | 100g | 1555 | 370 |
| *carrot cake* see *cakes and pastries* | | | |
| *carrots* ... baby ... boiled/raw ... peeled ... 1 av | 16g | 20 | 5 |
| Edgell-Birdseye ... canned | 100g | 115 | 27 |
| frozen | 100g | 165 | 39 |
| Farmland/Golden Circle/McCain | 100g | 120 | 29 |
| mature ... boiled ... peeled ... 1 cup | 140g | 155 | 37 |
| canned | 100g | 135 | 32 |
| raw ... peeled ... 1 med | 81g | 80 | 19 |
| Edgell-Birdseye ... julienne ... canned | 100g | 150 | 3[illegible] |
| Edgell-Birdseye ... rings ... frozen | 100g | 165 | [illegible] |
| *cashew nuts* ... roasted ... 15 | 30g | 715 | 1[illegible] |
| see also *snack foods* | | | |
| *cassaba* see *melon, honeydew* | | | |
| *cassava* ... boiled ... peeled ... ¼ | 145g | 800 | 190 |
| see also *tapioca* | | | |
| *cassava bread* | 100g | 1575 | 375 |

| | MASS | KJ | CAL |
|---|---|---|---|
| *cassava flour* | 100g | 1435 | 342 |
| *cauliflower* ... boiled ... 1 stem+floweret | 90g | 70 | 17 |
| canned | 100g | 100 | 24 |
| frozen ... av all brands | 100g | 95 | 23 |
| raw ... 1 stem+floweret | 70g | 55 | 13 |
| *cauliflower and vegetables in sauce* ... McCain ... av all varieties | 100g | 245 | 58 |
| *cauliflower cheese* | 100g | 470 | 112 |
| *caviar* ... lumpfish roe ... black ... 1 tbsp | 19g | 73 | 17 |
| red ... 1 tbsp | 19g | 120 | 29 |
| *celeriac* ... boiled ... peeled ... ½ | 115g | 150 | 36 |
| raw ... peeled ... ½ | 127g | 150 | 36 |
| *celery* ... boiled ... 1 cup chopped | 125g | 70 | 17 |
| raw ... 1 stick | 20g | 10 | 2 |
| *cereals* see *breakfast cereals* | | | |
| *champagne* | 100ml | 345 | 82 |
| *champignons* ... Admiral | 100g | 80 | 19 |
| Edgell-Birdseye | 100g | 75 | 18 |
| Farmland ... whole ... no added salt | 100g | 100 | 24 |
| *chapati* see *bread* | | | |
| *chapati flour* | 100g | 1410 | 336 |

## Cauliflower and Vegetable Soup

*4 cups chicken stock*
*¼ large cauliflower*
*1 medium-sized potato*
*1 medium-sized carrot*
*1 stick celery*
*1 medium-sized onion*
*2 tablespoons dry sherry*

Place stock in a large saucepan. Roughly chop the vegetables and add them to the chicken stock. Bring to the boil and then simmer for 30 minutes, or until vegetables are tender. Remove from heat and blend in a food processor until smooth. Return soup to saucepan, add the dry sherry and reheat. Serves 4 at 388 kJ (92cal) per portion.

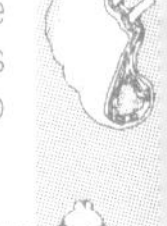

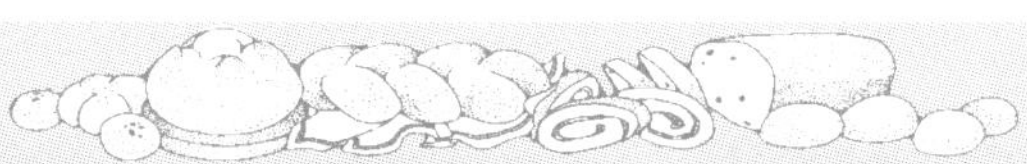

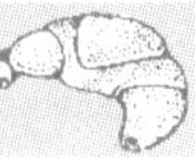

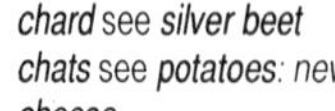

| | MASS | KJ | CAL |
|---|---|---|---|
| *chard* see *silver beet* | | | |
| *chats* see *potatoes: new* | | | |
| *cheese* | | | |
| *bel paese* | 100g | 2560 | 610 |
| *blue vein* | 30g | 480 | 114 |
| *brie, Australian* | 30g | 425 | 101 |
| *camembert* ... av Australian/imported | 30g | 390 | 93 |
| *cheddar* ... matured | 30g | 505 | 120 |
| reduced-fat | 30g | 410 | 98 |
| reduced-salt | 30g | 515 | 123 |
| *cheshire/colby* | 30g | 485 | 115 |
| ***cottage*** creamed ... 2 tbsp | 25g | 130 | 31 |
| low-fat ... 2 tbsp | 25g | 105 | 25 |
| uncreamed ... 2 tbsp | 25g | 95 | 23 |
| *cotto* | 30g | 265 | 63 |
| *cream cheese* | 30g | 430 | 102 |
| *Danish blue* | 30g | 410 | 98 |
| *edam* | 30g | 450 | 107 |
| *fetta* | 30g | 380 | 90 |
| low-salt | 30g | 470 | 112 |
| reduced-fat | 30g | 290 | 69 |

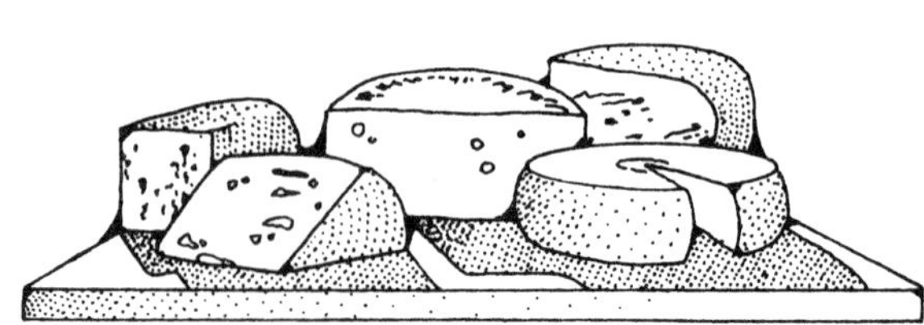

| | MASS | KJ | CAL |
|---|---|---|---|
| *fruited* | 30g | 405 | 96 |
| *gloucester* | 30g | 510 | 121 |
| *goat* | 30g | 320 | 76 |
| *gorgonzola* | 30g | 470 | 112 |
| *gouda* | 30g | 465 | 111 |
| *gruyère* | 30g | 520 | 124 |
| *havarti* | 30g | 505 | 120 |
| *Jarlsberg* | 30g | 435 | 104 |
| *mascarpone* | 30g | 550 | 131 |
| *mozzarella/pizza* | 30g | 400 | 95 |
| reduced-fat | 30g | 360 | 86 |
| *neufchatel* | 30g | 380 | 90 |
| *parmesan* | 30g | 535 | 127 |
| *pecorino* | 30g | 445 | 106 |
| *processed* ... cheddar ... canned | 30g | 420 | 100 |
| sliced and packaged | 30g | 400 | 95 |
| *quark* | 30g | 170 | 40 |
| low-fat | 30g | 95 | 23 |
| *raclette/provolone* | 30g | 460 | 110 |
| *ricotta* | 30g | 185 | 44 |
| reduced-fat | 30g | 165 | 39 |
| *romano* | 30g | 470 | 112 |
| *roqueforte* | 30g | 465 | 111 |
| *stilton* | 30g | 575 | 137 |
| *Swiss* | 30g | 475 | 113 |
| *Avalanche* ... almond and curacao | 30g | 370 | 88 |
| pepper log | 30g | 430 | 102 |
| pineapple rum | 30g | 385 | 92 |
| poppyseed fruit/smoky bacon | 30g | 410 | 98 |

Although high in kilojoules, the flavour of parmesan cheese goes a long way, so substitute it for ordinary cheese as a topping for cooked meals.

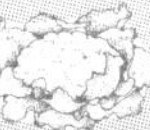

| | MASS | KJ | CAL |
|---|---|---|---|
| *Bega* ... natural cheddar ... mild/tasty/vintage | 30g | 510 | 121 |
| processed ... cheddar/super slices | 30g | 415 | 99 |
| cheddar super-slims (slices) | 30g | 265 | 63 |
| *Bodalla* ... edam ... blocks/slices | 30g | 450 | 107 |
| gouda ... blocks/slices | 30g | 465 | 111 |
| natural cheddar ... slices | 30g | 505 | 120 |
| reduced-fat and -salt cheddar | 30g | 435 | 104 |
| *Chateau* ... neufchatel | 30g | 380 | 90 |
| *Dairy Farmers* ... low-fat, reduced-salt cottage | 30g | 115 | 27 |
| natural creamed cottage... av all flavours | 30g | 130 | 31 |
| *Devondale* ... trim n' tasty cheddar | 30g | 435 | 104 |
| *Jalna* ... dessert/farm/Polish/slicing | 30g | 150 | 36 |
| fetta | 30g | 225 | 54 |
| keren quark | 30g | 135 | 32 |
| quark ski | 30g | 80 | 19 |
| slimming | 30g | 130 | 31 |
| *Kraft* ... cheesestiks | 20g | 285 | 68 |
| cracker barrel/mil-lel | 25g | 420 | 100 |
| Danish blue | 25g | 345 | 82 |
| Danish camembert | 25g | 335 | 80 |
| edam ... reduced-fat | 25g | 320 | 76 |
| traditional | 25g | 345 | 82 |
| gouda ... reduced-fat | 25g | 340 | 80 |
| traditional | 25g | 400 | 95 |
| havarti ... danish | 25g | 445 | 106 |
| Philadelphia ... cream/soft cream | 25g | 355 | 85 |
| light cream | 25g | 205 | 49 |
| processed ... cheddar packets/loaf cans | 20g | 265 | 63 |
| deluxe cheddar slices ... 1 slice | 21g | 280 | 69 |
| light singles ... 1 slice | 21g | 215 | 51 |
| singles ... 1 slice | 21g | 250 | 58 |
| romano ... traditional | 25g | 375 | 89 |

| | MASS | KJ | CAL |
|---|---|---|---|
| Swiss reduced-fat | 25g | 335 | 80 |
| *Lactos* ... Cradle Valley edam | 30g | 420 | 100 |
| Cradle Valley spring onion ... processed | 30g | 395 | 94 |
| Mersey Valley club | 30g | 490 | 117 |
| neufchatel ... chocolate | 30g | 480 | 114 |
| plain | 30g | 325 | 77 |
| strawberry | 30g | 425 | 101 |
| Tasmanian reduced-fat swiss | 30g | 375 | 89 |
| Tasmanian camembert | 30g | 440 | 105 |
| with peppercorns | 30g | 385 | 92 |
| *Mainland* ... av all flavours processed | 30g | 425 | 101 |
| blue vein | 30g | 445 | 106 |
| edam | 30g | 425 | 101 |
| gouda | 30g | 460 | 110 |
| mild cheddar | 30g | 520 | 124 |
| mozzarella | 30g | 345 | 82 |
| parmesan | 30g | 580 | 138 |
| processed cheddar | 30g | 420 | 100 |
| tasty cheddar/vintage tasty | 30g | 520 | 124 |
| tasty colby | 30g | 495 | 118 |
| *Meadow Gold* ... creamed cottage ... av all flavours | 30g | 125 | 30 |
| *Norco* ... jack/Nimbin natural | 30g | 480 | 114 |
| pizza | 30g | 360 | 86 |
| ricotta | 30g | 140 | 33 |
| *Oak* ... cheddar varieties | 30g | 535 | 127 |
| cottage | 30g | 175 | 42 |
| cream | 30g | 430 | 102 |
| *Pauls* ... continental-style low-fat | 30g | 110 | 26 |
| cottage ... low-fat reduced-salt | 30g | 110 | 26 |
| plain/gherkin/garden salad | 30g | 125 | 30 |
| *Perfect Cheese* ... grated/parmesan | 30g | 575 | 137 |
| mozzarella | 30g | 420 | 100 |

| | MASS | KJ | CAL |
|---|---|---|---|
| pecorino | 30g | 520 | 124 |
| romano | 30g | 520 | 124 |
| *Peters Farm* ... cottage | 30g | 125 | 30 |
| low-fat cottage | 30g | 110 | 26 |
| *Renaissance* ... edam ... reduced-fat | 25g | 320 | 76 |
| gouda ... reduced-fat | 25g | 340 | 80 |
| Swiss ... reduced-fat | 25g | 335 | 80 |
| tasty | 25g | 420 | 100 |
| *Riviana* ... blue vein | 30g | 460 | 110 |
| brandied orange roll/rum roll | 30g | 470 | 112 |
| brie | 30g | 420 | 100 |
| camembert | 30g | 385 | 92 |
| fruit ... av all flavours | 30g | 415 | 99 |
| pepper roll | 30g | 425 | 101 |
| *Weight Watchers* ... cottage | 30g | 115 | 27 |
| *cheese souffle* | 100g | 950 | 226 |
| *cheese spreads* see *dips and spreads* | | | |
| *cheesecake* see *cakes and pastries* | | | |
| *cherries* ... glacé | 100g | 1420 | 338 |
| raw ... 10 cherries | 45g | 85 | 20 |
| stewed without sugar ... inc stone ... 20 cherries | 100g | 140 | 33 |
| John West ... black in syrup | 100g | 265 | 63 |
| SPC ... in syrup | 100g | 345 | 82 |
| *chestnuts* ... 4 | 20g | 145 | 35 |
| *chewing gum* see *confectionery* | | | |
| *chick pea spread* see *dips and spreads: homous* | | | |
| *chick peas* ... boiled | 100g | 685 | 163 |
| canned | 100g | 495 | 118 |
| cooked (dahl) | 100g | 610 | 145 |
| dry seed | 100g | 1315 | 313 |
| *chicken* | | | |
| *average cut* ... roast ... meat+skin ... 1 sv | 100g | 1005 | 239 |

| | MASS | KJ | CAL |
|---|---|---|---|
| rotisseried ... lean+skin ... from ½ chicken | 195g | 1975 | 470 |
| *boneless, average* ... baked ... lean+skin ... from ½ chicken | 268g | 2765 | 658 |
| lean only ... from ½ chicken | 213g | 1665 | 396 |
| skin only ... skin from ½ chicken | 55g | 1105 | 263 |
| *breast* ... baked ... lean ... ½ breast | 79g | 520 | 124 |
| lean+skin ... from ½ breast | 97g | 885 | 211 |
| from whole baked chicken | 100g | 900 | 214 |
| lean+skin+stuffing ... from whole rotisseried chicken | 100g | 900 | 214 |
| *crisp-skin (Chinese)* | 100g | 860 | 205 |
| *drumstick* ... baked ... lean+skin ... from whole baked chicken | 48g | 480 | 114 |
| lean only ... from whole baked chicken | 43g | 375 | 89 |
| *leg qtr* ... rotisseried ... lean+skin ... 1 av | 99g | 1120 | 267 |
| *liver* ... floured, fried ... 1 sv | 130g | 1460 | 348 |
| *Findus Lean Cuisine* ... glazed chicken with vegetable rice ... 1 sv | 240g | 1135 | 270 |
| *Inghams* | | | |
| big dippers ... 1 sv | 50g | 720 | 171 |
| breast patties ... 1 sv | 85g | 1010 | 240 |
| crumbed chicken fillets/breast tenders | 100g | 1045 | 249 |
| drumsticks ... edible portion | 100g | 1065 | 254 |
| honey-roasted drumsticks ... edible portion | 100g | 715 | 170 |
| honey-roasted mid wings ... edible portion | 100g | 1035 | 246 |
| mini-drums ... edible portion | 100g | 1270 | 302 |
| *Plumrose* ... deli chicken | 100g | 580 | 138 |
| ***chicken a la king*** | 100g | 800 | 190 |

Avoid fatty meats when choosing cold meats for salads. Lean meats such as chicken, turkey and lean boiled ham should appear on your shopping list in place of salami and patés.

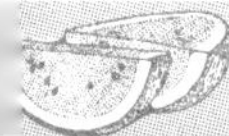

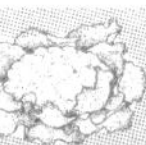

| | MASS | KJ | CAL |
|---|---|---|---|
| *chicken and almonds (Chinese)* | 100g | 575 | 137 |
| *chicken and coconut* ... Findus Lean Cuisine ... 1 sv | 260g | 1090 | 260 |
| *chicken and vegetable casserole* ... 1 sv | 200g | 700 | 167 |
| *chicken basil (Thai)* | 100g | 780 | 186 |
| *chicken cacciatore* | 100g | 525 | 125 |
| *chicken chop suey (Chinese)* | 100g | 410 | 98 |
| *chicken chow mein (Chinese)* | 100g | 705 | 168 |
| *chicken cordon bleu* ... Baron's Table ... 1 sv | 138g | 1530 | 364 |
| *chicken croquettes* ... deep-fried ... one | 55g | 615 | 146 |
| *chicken curry* ... Vesta ... 1 pkt made up | | 3480 | 829 |
| *chicken curry (Thai)* | 100g | 570 | 136 |
| *chicken duets* ... Inghams ... creamy cheese and asparagus ... ½ pkt | 150g | 1570 | 374 |
| tasty cheese and ham ... ½ pkt | 150g | 1350 | 321 |
| *chicken fricassee* | 100g | 675 | 161 |
| *chicken ginger (Thai)* | 100g | 770 | 183 |
| *chicken in peach sauce* ... 1 sv | 200g | 1400 | 333 |
| *chicken kiev* ... Baron's Table ... 1 sv | 175g | 1915 | 456 |
| Inghams ... 1 sv | 100g | 1170 | 279 |
| *chicken lemon (Chinese)* | 100g | 820 | 195 |
| *chicken-liver pâté* | 100g | 1285 | 306 |
| *chicken marsala, breast of* ... Findus Lean Cuisine ... 1 sv | 230g | 800 | 190 |
| *chicken nuggets* ... Inghams ... ⅕ pkt | 100g | 1340 | 319 |
| *chicken salad (Thai)* | 100g | 495 | 118 |
| *chicken schnitzel* ... Baron's Table ... 1 sv | 150g | 1615 | 385 |
| *chicken supreme* ... Vesta ... 1 pkt made up | | 3950 | 940 |
| *chicken, take-away* see *Hungry Jacks; Kentucky Fried Chicken; McDonalds* | | | |
| *chicory* ... boiled ... 1 cup chopped | 145g | 95 | 23 |
| raw ... 1 | 48g | 25 | 6 |
| *chiko roll* ... deep-fried ... 1 | 165g | 1560 | 371 |
| *chilli con carne* ... McCain | 400g | 2120 | 505 |
| *chilli pickle* | 100g | 1120 | 267 |

| | MASS | KJ | CAL |
|---|---|---|---|
| *chilli sauce* see *sauces, savoury* | | | |
| *chillies* ... banana ... boiled ... 1 av | 55g | 35 | 8 |
| green ... boiled ... 1 av | 20g | 15 | 4 |
| long, thin ... boiled ... 1 av | 19g | 20 | 5 |
| red ... boiled ... 1 av | 18g | 25 | 6 |
| raw ... 1 av | 20g | 25 | 6 |
| *Chinese broccoli* ... raw | 80g | 120 | 29 |
| *Chinese cabbage* see *cabbage* | | | |
| *Chinese chard* ... raw | 75g | 35 | 8 |
| *Chinese chives* ... 1 tbsp chopped | 4g | 5 | 1 |
| *Chinese gooseberry* see *kiwifruit* | | | |
| *Chinese parsley* ... raw | 10g | 13 | 3 |
| *Chinese salted fish* ... steamed | 100g | 660 | 157 |
| *Chinese spinach* see *spinach* | | | |
| *Chinese stirfry (vegetables)* ... McCain | 100g | 380 | 90 |
| *Chinese zucchini* ... raw | 69g | 60 | 14 |
| *chips* see *potato chips* | | | |
| *chives* ... raw ... 1 tbsp chopped | 4g | 5 | 1 |
| see also *spices, dried* | | | |
| *chocolate biscuits* see *biscuits* | | | |
| *chocolate cake* see *cakes and pastries* | | | |
| *chocolate eclair* see *cakes and pastries; confectionery* | | | |
| *chocolate* see *confectionery* | | | |
| *chokoes* ... boiled ... peeled ... 1 cup chopped | 140g | 115 | 27 |
| *chop suey* see *chicken chop suey; pork chop suey* | | | |
| *chops* see *lamb; pork; veal* | | | |
| *chow mien* ... Vesta ... 1 pkt made up | | 2740 | 652 |
| *chow mien* see *chicken chow mein (Chinese)* | | | |
| *Christmas cake* see *cakes and pastries* | | | |
| *Christmas pudding* see *desserts and puddings* | | | |
| *chutney* ... av all flavours ... 1 tsp | 5g | 45 | 11 |
| *cider* ... alcoholic | 100ml | 165 | 39 |

| | MASS | KJ | CAL |
|---|---|---|---|
| Strongbow ... draught | 100ml | 185 | 44 |
| dry | 100ml | 155 | 37 |
| sweet | 100ml | 215 | 51 |
| Woodpecker | 100ml | 180 | 43 |
| non-alcoholic ... sweet | 100ml | 190 | 45 |
| *clams* ... canned | 100g | 470 | 112 |
| fresh ... without shells | 100g | 410 | 98 |
| *clobaci* see *luncheon meat* | | | |
| *coating mix* see *seasoning mix* | | | |
| *Coca Cola* see *drinks, carbonated* | | | |
| *cockles* ... boiled | 100g | 205 | 49 |
| *cocktail frankfurts* see *frankfurters* | | | |
| *cocktails* ... bloody mary | 100ml | 325 | 77 |
| bourbon and soda | 100ml | 380 | 90 |
| daiquiri | 100ml | 775 | 185 |
| gin and tonic | 100ml | 320 | 76 |
| manhattan | 100ml | 940 | 224 |
| martini | 100ml | 555 | 132 |
| pina colada | 100ml | 780 | 186 |
| screwdriver | 100ml | 345 | 82 |
| tequila sunrise | 100ml | 460 | 110 |
| tom collins | 100ml | 230 | 55 |
| whisky sour | 100ml | 570 | 136 |
| see also *spirits* | | | |
| *cocoa powder* ... 1 tsp | 5g | 95 | 23 |
| *coconut* ... dessicated ... ½ cup | 45g | 1120 | 267 |
| fresh meat | 100g | 1525 | 363 |

Energy from alcohol has a strong tendency to be converted to fat because it is treated by the body as a poison, rather than as fuel for the metabolism. Alcohol can't be made directly into glucose and it is likely to be stored as fat in your liver.

| | MASS | KJ | CAL |
|---|---|---|---|
| shredded ... dry ... 1 cup | 100g | 2815 | 670 |
| *coconut cream* ... from grated coconut meat | 100g | 1480 | 352 |
| *coconut milk* ... canned ... 1 tbsp | 20g | 165 | 39 |
| drained from fresh nut | 100g | 90 | 21 |
| *cod* ... baked | 100g | 710 | 169 |
| dried, salted ... cooked | 100g | 585 | 139 |
| raw | 100g | 545 | 130 |
| fried in batter | 100g | 835 | 199 |
| grilled | 100g | 400 | 95 |
| poached | 100g | 395 | 94 |
| inc bones + skin | 100g | 345 | 82 |
| raw | 100g | 320 | 76 |
| smoked ... simmered | 100g | 395 | 94 |
| steamed | 100g | 350 | 83 |
| inc bones + skin | 100g | 285 | 68 |
| Baron's Table ... uncooked | 100g | 325 | 77 |
| Edgell-Birdseye ... fillets | 100g | 320 | 76 |
| Frionor ... filllets | 100g | 325 | 77 |
| *cod liver oil* | 100g | 3700 | 881 |
| *coffee* ... black | 250ml | 25 | 6 |
| black + 1 sugar | 250ml | 140 | 33 |
| black + 1 sugar + cream | 250ml | 445 | 106 |
| black, decaffeinated, instant | 250ml | 25 | 5 |
| dry ...instant ... 1 tsp | 2.5g | 10 | 2 |
| iced + cream | 250ml | 445 | 106 |
| iced + cream + ice-cream | 250ml | 645 | 153 |
| white ... ¼ cup milk | 250ml | 195 | 46 |
| 2 tsp milk | 250ml | 55 | 13 |
| 30ml milk+ 1 sugar | 250ml | 220 | 53 |
| all milk ... reduced-fat | 250ml | 535 | 127 |
| all milk ... whole | 250ml | 700 | 167 |

| | MASS | KJ | CAL |
|---|---|---|---|
| *coffee substitutes* ... caffex ... 1 tsp | 1g | 15 | 4 |
| caro ... 1 tsp | 2.5g | 40 | 10 |
| ***combination chow mein (Chinese)*** | 100g | 625 | 149 |
| ***confectionery*** | | | |
| *butterscotch* | 100g | 1760 | 419 |
| *caramels* ... plain | 100g | 1710 | 407 |
| plain + nuts | 100g | 1790 | 426 |
| *carob bars* see ***health-food bars*** | | | |
| *chewing gum* | 100g | 1325 | 315 |
| *chocolate* ... average ... 5–6 squares | | 610 | 145 |
| coated almond fudge | 100g | 1800 | 429 |
| diabetic | 100g | 2305 | 549 |
| nut milk | 100g | 2275 | 542 |
| plain ... dark | 100g | 2235 | 532 |
| milk | 100g | 2250 | 536 |
| *fondant* ... chocolate | 100g | 1715 | 408 |
| plain | 100g | 1525 | 363 |
| *fudge* ... chocolate/vanilla | 100g | 1670 | 398 |

| | MASS | KJ | CAL |
|---|---|---|---|
| *gumdrops/jelly beans/liquorice allsorts* | 100g | 1465 | 349 |
| *lollypops* | 100g | 1585 | 377 |
| *marshmallow* ... chocolate | 100g | 1695 | 404 |
| plain | 100g | 1350 | 321 |
| *muesli bars* see ***health-food bars*** | | | |
| *pastilles* | 100g | 1065 | 254 |
| *peanut brittle* | 100g | 1800 | 429 |
| *peppermint* | 100g | 1635 | 389 |
| *sweets, boiled* | 100g | 1370 | 326 |
| *toffee* ... mixed | 100g | 1870 | 445 |
| *turkish delight* ... no nuts | 100g | 1255 | 299 |
| *Allens* ... anticol/butter menthol/soothers | 100g | 1600 | 382 |
| bananas | 100g | 1625 | 387 |
| fruit tingles /steam rollers | 100g | 1600 | 382 |
| gums, e.g. raspberries/pythons/snakes/strawberries and cream | 100g | 1395 | 333 |
| jelly beans | 100g | 1535 | 365 |
| kool fruits/kool mints | 100g | 1620 | 386 |
| *Cadbury* | | | |
| bars ... cherry ripe | 100g | 1840 | 438 |
| chomp ... av all flavours | 100g | 1995 | 475 |
| crunchie | 100g | 2010 | 479 |
| flake | 100g | 2210 | 526 |
| moro | 100g | 1910 | 455 |
| picnic | 100g | 2125 | 506 |
| turkish delight | 100g | 1610 | 383 |
| caramello koala | 100g | 2060 | 490 |
| caramello rolls/peppermint rolls | 100g | 2010 | 479 |
| chocolate blocks ... coconut delight (classic) | 100g | 2210 | 526 |
| dairy milk | 100g | 2195 | 523 |
| energy | 100g | 2120 | 505 |
| fruit and nut | 100g | 2025 | 482 |

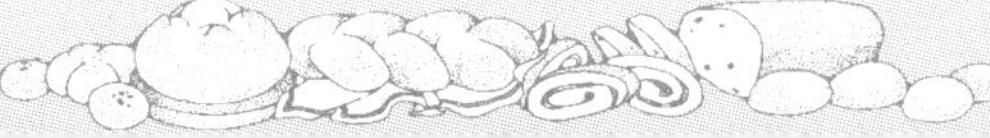

| | MASS | KJ | CAL |
|---|---|---|---|
| nut | 100g | 2155 | 513 |
| premium dark | 100g | 2100 | 500 |
| snack | 100g | 1955 | 465 |
| soft centres | 100g | 1931 | 460 |
| swiss chalet | 100g | 2140 | 510 |
| top deck | 100g | 2270 | 540 |
| white | 100g | 2300 | 547 |
| freddo ... av all flavours | 100g | 2035 | 485 |
| white/milk | 100g | 2190 | 521 |
| Fry's bars ... Fry's cream/five fruits | 100g | 1805 | 430 |
| garfield ... caramel | 100g | 1980 | 471 |
| chocolate | 100g | 2200 | 524 |
| honeycomb | 100g | 2050 | 488 |
| *Lifesavers* ... all flavours ... 1 pack | | 330 | 79 |
| *Mars* ... Bounty bar | 50g | 1000 | 238 |
| M & Ms ... peanut | 50g | 1055 | 251 |
| plain | 50g | 1020 | 243 |

| | MASS | KJ | CAL |
|---|---|---|---|
| Maltesers | 50g | 800 | 190 |
| Mars bar | 60g | 1110 | 264 |
| Mars Almond bar | 50g | 980 | 233 |
| Milky Way ... choc whip | 25g | 430 | 102 |
| milk whip | 25g | 450 | 107 |
| Snickers bar | 60g | 1175 | 280 |
| Twix bar | 50g | 1145 | 273 |
| *Nestlé block chocolate* ... Alpine Fruits | 100g | 1880 | 449 |
| Club | 100g | 2190 | 523 |
| Club Roasted Almond | 100g | 2330 | 556 |
| Cooking | 100g | 2240 | 535 |
| Crunch | 100g | 2210 | 527 |
| Fruit and Nut | 100g | 2270 | 542 |
| Full Cream Milk | 100g | 2240 | 535 |
| Milky Bar | 100g | 2240 | 535 |
| *Pascal* ... barley sugar/fruit bonbons/fruit drops | 100g | 1555 | 370 |
| big strap/laces/rails | 100g | 1510 | 360 |
| butterscotch | 100g | 1760 | 419 |
| chews/choc/columbines/licorice | 100g | 1420 | 338 |
| chocolate eclairs | 100g | 1885 | 449 |
| clinkers/country mints | 100g | 1910 | 455 |
| jars ... barley sugar/bonbons/bulls eyes/humbugs | 100g | 1550 | 369 |
| butterscotch/chocmint crunchies | 100g | 1660 | 395 |
| jellies/jelly babies | 100g | 1315 | 313 |
| jelly beans | 100g | 1535 | 365 |
| jubes | 100g | 1405 | 335 |
| licorice allsorts | 100g | 1585 | 377 |
| marshmallows ... av all varieties | 100g | 1480 | 352 |
| spearmint chews | 100g | 1395 | 332 |

If you brush your teeth straight after eating, the fresh taste in your mouth may help you to resist snacking.

| | MASS | KJ | CAL |
|---|---|---|---|
| twists ... chocolate | 100g | 1740 | 414 |
| other varieties | 100g | 1510 | 360 |
| *Red Tulip* ... after-dinner mints/thins | 100g | 1860 | 443 |
| choc-coated nuts | 100g | 2245 | 548 |
| fruit jellies | 100g | 1350 | 321 |
| liqueur cherries | 100g | 1830 | 436 |
| liqueur cremes | 100g | 1905 | 454 |
| *Rowntree Hoadley* ... aero | 100g | 2230 | 531 |
| bertie beetle | 100g | 2090 | 498 |
| fantales/jaffas | 100g | 1825 | 434 |
| fruit gums/fruit pastilles | 100g | 1460 | 348 |
| kit kat | 100g | 2090 | 496 |
| minties | 100g | 1405 | 335 |
| smarties | 100g | 1875 | 447 |
| violet crumble | 100g | 1905 | 454 |
| *Scanlens* ... Big Charlie ... fruit ... av all flavours ... 1 | | 25 | 6 |
| *Stimorol* ... bubble gum ... av all flavours ... 1 | | 90 | 21 |
| original /sportlife... sugarfree ... 1 | | 14 | 4 |
| *Wander* ... ovalteenie tablets | 100g | 1600 | 381 |
| see also ***health-food bars*** | | | |
| ***cooking chocolate ...*** Cadbury | 100g | 2100 | 500 |
| ***cooking compound ...*** Unicorp ... dark | 100g | 2260 | 538 |
| ***copha*** ... 1 tbsp | 20g | 740 | 176 |
| ***cordials ...*** average diluted (1:4) ... 1 glass | 250ml | 290 | 69 |
| average undiluted ... 2 tbsp | 40ml | 225 | 54 |
| Diet Cottees ... low-joule ... lemon ... 1 glass | 250ml | 20 | 5 |
| lime/coola ... 1 glass | 250ml | 50 | 12 |
| orange ... 1 glass | 250ml | 40 | 10 |
| raspberry ... 1 glass | 250ml | 25 | 6 |
| So Slim ... all flavours ... 1 glass | 250ml | 25 | 6 |
| Weight Watchers ... low-joule orange/lemon/orange and lemon/raspberry cordial ... 1 glass | 250ml | 25 | 6 |

| | MASS | KJ | CAL |
|---|---|---|---|
| *corn* see *sweetcorn* | | | |
| *corn bread* | 100g | 1575 | 375 |
| *corn chips* see *snack foods* | | | |
| *corn meal* | 100g | 1465 | 349 |
| *corn pasta* Country Harvest ... gluten-free ... all types | 100g | 1520 | 362 |
| *corn syrup ...* ⅓ cup | | 240 | 57 |
| *corned beef* see *beef* | | | |
| *cornflakes* see *breakfast cereals* | | | |
| *cornflour* ... av all brands ... 1 tbsp | 10g | 145 | 35 |
| *cottage pie* see *shepherds pie* | | | |
| *courgettes* see *zucchini* | | | |
| *couscous* ... cooked | 100g | 950 | 226 |
| *cow peas* see *beans, blackeye* | | | |
| *crab* ... boiled | 100g | 535 | 127 |
| canned ... in brine ... meat only ... 1 cup | 190g | 985 | 235 |
| steamed ... meat only | 100g | 390 | 93 |
| Admiral ... crabmeat | 100g | 405 | 97 |
| Green's ... shredded crabmeat | 100g | 420 | 100 |
| *crab in black-bean sauce (Chinese)* | 100g | 645 | 154 |
| *crackers* see *biscuits* | | | |
| *cranberries* ... raw | 100g | 195 | 46 |
| *cranberry sauce* see *sauces, sweet* | | | |
| *crayfish* see *lobster* | | | |
| *cream* ... aerosol | 20g | 245 | 58 |
| fresh ... 1 tbsp | 20ml | 305 | 73 |
| pure (35% fat) ... 1 tbsp | 20g | 280 | 67 |
| reduced-fat ... canned/fresh ... 1 tbsp | 20g | 220 | 52 |
| single ... 1 tbsp | 20ml | 180 | 43 |
| thickened ... av all brands ... 1 tbsp | 20g | 285 | 68 |
| whipped ... 1 tbsp | 12g | 174 | 41 |
| Meadow Gold/Pauls ... 1 tbsp | 20ml | 350 | 52 |
| *cream powder* ... Oak ... full-cream powder | 100g | 2100 | 500 |

| | MASS | KJ | CAL |
|---|---|---|---|
| *cream, sour* ... 35% fat ... 1 tbsp | 20g | 295 | 70 |
| reduced-fat (18% fat) ... 1 tbsp | 21g | 190 | 45 |
| Dairy Farmers ... 1 tbsp | 20ml | 280 | 67 |
| Jalna ... 1 tbsp | 20ml | 200 | 48 |
| light ... Bulla/Meadow Gold ... 1 tbsp | 20ml | 175 | 42 |
| Calorie Counters ... 1 tbsp | 20ml | 190 | 45 |
| Dairy Farmers/Oak/Pauls ... 1 tbsp | 20ml | 165 | 39 |
| *crème fraîche* | 100g | 1840 | 438 |
| *crispbread* see *biscuits* | | | |
| *crisps* see *snack foods* | | | |
| *croissants* .... 1 | 60g | 890 | 212 |
| Sara Lee ... all-butter ... 1 | 50g | 670 | 160 |
| ham and cheese ... 1 | 125g | 1410 | 336 |
| *crumpets* .... 1 | 55g | 390 | 93 |
| *cucumber* ... apple ... raw ... unpeeled ... 1 | 320g | 95 | 23 |
| common ... raw ... peeled ... 5 slices | 40g | 20 | 5 |
| unpeeled ... 5 slices | 45g | 15 | 4 |
| Lebanese ... raw ... unpeeled ... 1 | 97g | 45 | 11 |
| pickled ... 1 large | 100g | 40 | 10 |
| Always Fresh ... dill | 100g | 50 | 12 |
| garlic dill/polskie ogorki | 100g | 70 | 17 |
| sweet-and-sour | 100g | 175 | 42 |
| sweet baby | 100g | 210 | 50 |
| telegraph ... raw ... unpeeled ... 5 slices | 45g | 20 | 5 |
| *cucumber and yoghurt dip* see *dips and spreads* | | | |
| *cumquat* see *kumquat* | | | |
| *currants* .... dried | 100g | 1145 | 273 |
| *curried prawns* ... Griffs | 100g | 1095 | 261 |
| *curried prawns and rice (Chinese)* | 100g | 560 | 133 |
| *curried rice* ... Griffs | 100g | 310 | 74 |
| *curry* .... Tandaco ... one-pan dinner ... 1/4 pkt | 50g | 655 | 156 |
| *custard* .... baked with cereal | 100g | 720 | 171 |

| | MASS | KJ | CAL |
|---|---|---|---|
| banana | 100g | 450 | 107 |
| with egg, baked/boiled | 100g | 455 | 108 |
| Dairy Farmers | 100g | 430 | 102 |
| Norco ... Nimbin low-fat | 100g | 300 | 71 |
| Yomix ... vanilla/banana | 100g | 450 | 107 |
| ***custard apple ...*** raw ... peeled ... flesh only ... 1/4 | 120g | 365 | 87 |
| ***custard mix ...*** Bingo ... egg-custard mix | 100g | 1700 | 405 |
| Foster Clark's ... egg | 100g | 1700 | 405 |
| quick | 100g | 1685 | 401 |
| Green's ... instant ... 1 sachet | 60g | 1365 | 325 |
| ***custard powder ... av all brands ...*** 1 tbsp | 14g | 200 | 48 |
| ***cyclamate*** see ***sugar subtitutes*** | | | |
| ***dahl*** see ***chick peas; beans, mung; lentils*** | | | |
| ***dairy dessert*** see ***desserts and puddings*** | | | |
| ***damson plums*** see ***plums*** | | | |
| ***dates ...*** dried ... pitted ... 1 av | 7g | 80 | 19 |
| fresh ... raw ... inc stone | 100g | 600 | 143 |
| raw ... diced | 100g | 1055 | 251 |
| ***desserts and puddings*** | | | |
| *apple crumble* | 100g | 1145 | 273 |
| *blancmange* | 100g | 460 | 110 |
| *bread-and-butter pudding* | 100g | 670 | 160 |

### Slimmer's Tuna, Cucumber and Chives Dip

*75 g peeled and chopped cucumber*
*100 g tuna in brine, drained and mashed*
*3 tablespoons buttermilk*
*2 level tablespoons low-fat natural yoghurt*
*1 teaspoon Worcestershire sauce*
*salt and pepper to taste*
*chopped chives*

Blend cucumber and tuna until smooth. Add remaining ingredients and season to taste. Chill and sprinkle with chives before serving. Serves 1 at 288 kJ (69 cal).

| | MASS | KJ | CAL |
|---|---|---|---|
| *chocolate mousse* | 100g | 2165 | 515 |
| *Christmas pudding* | 100g | 1325 | 315 |
| *golden syrup dumplings* | 100g | 885 | 211 |
| *lemon delicious* | 100g | 935 | 223 |
| *milk pudding* | 160g | 880 | 210 |
| *pavlova* ... + cream + strawberries | 100g | 1600 | 381 |
| *plum pudding* ... canned | 90g | 875 | 208 |
| *rice pudding* ... canned | 100g | 385 | 92 |
| *sponge pudding* ... jam-filled | 100g | 1280 | 305 |
| steamed | 100g | 1395 | 332 |
| *steamed pudding* ... chocolate | 100g | 1495 | 356 |
| plain | 100g | 1395 | 332 |
| *trifle* | 100g | 620 | 148 |
| *ETA* ... blueberry meringue single-serve | 100g | 1515 | 361 |
| lemon meringue single-serve | 100g | 1900 | 452 |
| pine and coconut meringue single-serve | 100g | 1400 | 333 |
| *Farmland* ... cheesecake ... original/strawberry | 100g | 1225 | 292 |
| chocolate bavarian | 100g | 1360 | 324 |
| *Foster Clark's* ... snak pak ... av all flavours | 150g | 795 | 190 |
| *Fruche* ... av all flavours ... 1 | | 465 | 111 |
| *Oak* ... dairy dessert | 100g | 590 | 140 |
| low-cholesterol frozen dessert | 100g | 840 | 200 |

| | MASS | KJ | CAL |
|---|---|---|---|
| *Pampas* ... filo apple strudel | 100g | 1140 | 271 |
| lovebites ... apple | 100g | 1350 | 321 |
| berry | 100g | 1195 | 285 |
| *Peters Farm* ... dairy dessert | | | |
| creme caramel/choc | 100g | 535 | 127 |
| *Yogo* see *yoghurt* | | | |
| *Yomix* ... dairy dessert ... varieties | 100g | 415 | 99 |
| see also *custard; pies, sweet* | | | |
| ***dim sim*** deep-fried ... 1 | 50g | 465 | 111 |
| ***dips and spreads*** | | | |
| *baba ghannouj (eggplant dip)* | 20g | 200 | 48 |
| *cheddar spread* | 20g | 245 | 58 |
| *cheese wiz* | 20g | 220 | 52 |
| *cream cheese dip* ... flavoured ... 1 tbsp | 22g | 230 | 58 |
| *cream cheese spread* | 20g | 285 | 68 |
| *Danish blue* | 20g | 300 | 71 |
| *fish paste* ... canned ... 1 tsp | 5g | 30 | 7 |
| *gorgonzola* | 20g | 290 | 69 |
| *homous (chick pea spread)* | 20g | 190 | 45 |
| *marmite* ... 1 tsp | 5g | 40 | 10 |
| *meat paste* | 5g | 40 | 10 |
| *nutella (hazelnut spread)* | 20g | 450 | 107 |
| *peanut butter* | 20g | 530 | 126 |
| *skordalia (Greek)* | 20g | 110 | 26 |
| *taramasalata* | 20g | 200 | 48 |
| *tzatziki (cucumber and yoghurt dip)* | 20g | 110 | 26 |
| *vegemite* | 5g | 35 | 8 |
| *Dairy Farmers* ... dips ... av all flavours ... 1 tbsp | 20g | 170 | 40 |
| *ETA* ... peanut butter ... crunchy/smooth | 20g | 470 | 112 |
| *Farmland* ... *peanut butter* ... crunchy/smooth ... no added salt | 20g | 535 | 127 |
| *Kraft* ... barbeque dip | 20g | 205 | 49 |
| cheese spread | 20g | 260 | 62 |

| | MASS | KJ | CAL |
|---|---|---|---|
| cream cheese spread | 20g | 305 | 73 |
| curried beef spread/devilled beef and ham ... 1 tsp | 5g | 40 | 10 |
| curried salmon and prawn spread ... 1 tsp | 5g | 30 | 7 |
| French onion dip/gherkin | 20g | 205 | 49 |
| onion and bacon style dip | 20g | 215 | 51 |
| salmon, lobster and tomato spread ... 1 tsp | 5g | 25 | 6 |
| salmon pastes ... av ... 1 tsp | 5g | 30 | 7 |
| sandwich relish | 20ml | 130 | 31 |
| smoked oyster dip | 20g | 205 | 49 |
| spicy Mexican-flavour dip | 20g | 205 | 49 |
| *Masterfoods* ... lemon butter ... 1 tsp | 10g | 125 | 30 |
| meat/fish ... av all varieties | 5g | 45 | 11 |
| promite ... 1 tsp | 5g | 35 | 8 |
| *Paul's* ... cracka dips ... av all flavours | 20g | 155 | 37 |
| *Perfect Cheese* ... smooth ricotta spread ... 1 tsp | 10g | 40 | 10 |
| *Peters Farm* ... dips ... av all flavours | 20g | 250 | 60 |
| *Riviana Swirle* ... av all flavours | 125g | 1550 | 369 |
| *Sanitarium* ... honey and glucose ... 1 tbsp | 27g | 355 | 85 |
| ***dolmades*** see ***vine leaves, stuffed*** | | | |
| ***doughnuts ...*** cinnamon and sugar ... 1 | 50g | 770 | 183 |
| iced ... 1 | 80g | 1425 | 339 |
| Herbert Adams ... iced ring donuts | 100g | 1500 | 357 |
| jam ball donuts | 100g | 1470 | 350 |
| ***dressing*** see ***salad dressing*** | | | |
| ***drinking chocolate powder ...*** Cadbury ... 1 sv | 10g | 160 | 38 |
| ***drinks, carbonated ...*** *creamy soda* | 100ml | 195 | 46 |
| *dry ginger ale* | 100ml | 125 | 30 |
| *lemonade/lime* | 100ml | 185 | 44 |
| *mineral water* ... lemon | 100ml | 120 | 29 |
| natural | 100ml | 0 | 0 |
| *sarsaparilla* | 100ml | 195 | 46 |
| *soda water* | 100ml | 0 | 0 |

| | MASS | KJ | CAL |
|---|---|---|---|
| *tonic water* | 100ml | 150 | 36 |
| *Bisleri* ... chinotto | 100ml | 184 | 44 |
| lemon, lime and bitters | 100ml | 100 | 24 |
| orange/lemon | 100ml | 115 | 27 |
| *Bulmer* ... sparkling apple fruit-juice drink | 100ml | 155 | 37 |
| *Coca-Cola* | 100ml | 170 | 40 |
| *Cottees* ... lemonade/passiona | 100ml | 180 | 43 |
| *Deep Spring Mineral Water ... lemon and lime* | 100ml | 140 | 33 |
| *lemon, lime and orange* | 100ml | 160 | 38 |
| orange/orange and mango/sparkling apple | 100ml | 170 | 40 |
| orange and passionfruit | 100ml | 150 | 36 |
| *Devondale* ... sparkling apple juice | 100ml | 155 | 37 |
| *Diet Coke* | 100ml | 1 | 0 |
| *Diet Deep Spring* ...lemon/lemon, lime and orange/ orange | 100ml | 15 | 4 |
| *Diet Fanta* | 100ml | 3 | 1 |
| *Diet Lift* | 100ml | 7 | 2 |
| *Diet Sprite* | 100ml | 5 | 1 |
| *Fanta ... orange* | 100ml | 220 | 52 |
| *Kirks* ... bitter lemon/club lemon/sarsaparilla | 100ml | 205 | 49 |
| creamy soda/drinking dry ginger ale | 100ml | 190 | 45 |
| lemonade/orange soda squash | 100ml | 200 | 48 |
| mixer dry ginger ale | 100ml | 120 | 29 |
| tonic water | 100ml | 145 | 35 |

## Low-Joule Cheese, Garlic and Onion Dip

*75 g onion, finely chopped*
*2 cloves garlic, crushed*
*3 tablespoons low-fat natural yoghurt*
*120 ml buttermilk*
*1 tablespoon grated parmesan cheese*
*chopped parsley*

Mix together the onion and garlic and fold into yoghurt, buttermilk and cheese. Chill and sprinkle with parsley before serving. Serves 1 at 260 kJ (62 cal).

| | MASS | KJ | CAL |
|---|---|---|---|
| *Lift* | 100ml | 7 | 2 |
| *Marchants* ... club lemon soda squash/raspberry/lemonade | 100ml | 190 | 45 |
| lime | 100ml | 220 | 52 |
| pasito | 100ml | 195 | 46 |
| pineapple/portello | 100ml | 170 | 40 |
| *Sprite* ... lemonade | 100ml | 165 | 39 |
| *Tarax* ... bitter lemon/wild raspberry | 100ml | 170 | 40 |
| creamy soda/lemonade/tropical lime | 100ml | 180 | 43 |
| low-joule lemonade | 100ml | 4 | 1 |
| orange drink/sunshine pine | 100ml | 190 | 45 |
| *Weight Watchers* ... low-joule lemon mineral water | 100ml | 5 | 1 |
| low-joule lemonade | 100ml | 5 | 1 |
| low-joule orange mineral water | 100ml | 10 | 2 |
| low-joule orange and mango mineral water | 100ml | 10 | 2 |
| ***dripping*** see ***lard*** | | | |
| ***drop scones ...*** 2 | 50g | 640 | 152 |
| ***duck ...*** raw ... meat only | 100g | 515 | 123 |
| roasted | 100g | 1310 | 312 |
| ***dumplings ...*** plain | 100g | 885 | 211 |
| ***dumplings, golden syrup*** see ***desserts and puddings*** | | | |
| ***eel ...*** fresh ... grilled/stewed | 100g | 840 | 200 |
| raw | 100g | 700 | 167 |
| smoked | 100g | 1380 | 329 |
| ***egg ...*** boiled ... from 1 egg (55g) | 48g | 305 | 73 |
| dried | 100g | 2455 | 585 |
| fried ... from 1 egg (55g) | 35g | 375 | 89 |
| poached ... from 1 egg (55g) | 47g | 295 | 70 |
| raw ... from 1 egg (55g) | 48g | 285 | 68 |
| scrambled ... 1 sv | 110g | 750 | 179 |
| ***egg substitute*** | 100g | 680 | 162 |
| ***egg white ...*** raw ... from 1 egg (55g) | 31g | 60 | 14 |

| | MASS | KJ | CAL |
|---|---|---|---|
| *egg yolk ...* raw ... from 1 egg (55g) | 17g | 225 | 54 |
| *eggnog* see *milk, flavoured* | | | |
| *eggplant ...* baked | 100g | 260 | 62 |
| boiled ... 1 cup sliced | 195g | 160 | 38 |
| *eggplant dip see dips and spreads* | | | |
| *eggs, duck ...* boiled | 100g | 820 | 195 |
| *eggs, turtle* | 100g | 895 | 213 |
| *enchirito ...* with cheese, beef and beans | 100g | 745 | 178 |
| *endive ...* raw ... 1 cup chopped | 55g | 20 | 5 |
| *equal* see *sugar substitutes* | | | |
| *farfalle ...* dry, uncooked | 100g | 1540 | 367 |
| *felafel* | 100g | 990 | 236 |
| *fennel* | | | |
| boiled/raw ... 1/2 bulb | 165g | 130 | 31 |
| *fenugreek leaves ...* raw | 100g | 145 | 35 |
| *fettuccine ...* dry ... uncooked | 100g | 1540 | 367 |
| *figs* ... dried | 100g | 1130 | 269 |
| glacé | 100g | 1250 | 298 |
| raw ... 1 av | 40g | 70 | 17 |
| *fish* ... baked | 100g | 300 | 71 |
| battered, deep-fried ... 1 sv | 145g | 1535 | 365 |
| commercial ... battered, deep-fried ... 1 sv | 145g | 1535 | 365 |
| crumbed, fried | 100g | 1060 | 252 |
| fried ... 1 av fillet | | 900 | 214 |
| steamed/grilled ... 1 fillet | 65g | 260 | 62 |

Scrambled eggs can be one of the most fattening ways to prepare eggs. Two with toast can amount to 1675 kJ (400 cal). If you scramble 2 eggs with 2 tablespoons of skim milk in a non-stick pan and forgo butter on your toast the kilojoule content drops to 1090 kJ (260 cal).

| | MASS | KJ | CAL |
|---|---|---|---|
| Edgell-Birdseye ... oven-fried battered fillets | 100g | 1090 | 260 |
| oven-fried crumbed fillets | 100g | 1045 | 249 |
| portions in batter | 100g | 1040 | 248 |
| portions in golden crumbs | 100g | 510 | 121 |
| I & J ... light and crispy ... crispy crumbs | 100g | 865 | 206 |
| extra-light | 100g | 700 | 167 |
| golden batter | 100g | 1040 | 248 |
| lemon | 100g | 1010 | 240 |
| seasoned | 100g | 985 | 235 |
| see also names of individual fish | | | |
| *fish balls (Chinese)* ... steamed | 100g | 220 | 52 |
| *fish burgers* ... Frionor | 100g | 670 | 160 |
| *fish cakes* ... deep-fried | 80g | 920 | 219 |
| frozen ... fried ... 1 | 70g | 680 | 162 |
| Thai | 100g | 695 | 165 |
| *fish cocktail* ... battered, fried ... fish pieces ... 1 | 30g | 350 | 83 |
| *fish curry* | 100g | 1050 | 250 |
| *fish fingers* ... frozen ... grilled ... 1 | 23g | 215 | 51 |
| Edgell-Birdseye ... frozen ... pan-fried ... 1 | 23g | 255 | 61 |
| I & J ... chunky | 100g | 755 | 180 |
| standard | 100g | 785 | 187 |
| tasty | 100g | 785 | 187 |
| *fish in cheese sauce* ... I & J | 100g | 415 | 99 |
| Findus Lean Cuisine | 200g | 610 | 145 |

  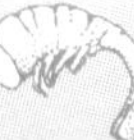   

| | MASS | KJ | CAL |
|---|---|---|---|
| *fish in lemon sauce* ... I & J | 100g | 440 | 105 |
| Findus Lean Cuisine | 200g | 830 | 198 |
| *fish in parsley sauce* ... I & J | 100g | 320 | 76 |
| Findus Lean Cuisine | 200g | 640 | 152 |
| *fish in seafood sauce* ... I & J | 100g | 265 | 63 |
| *fish in white sauce* | 100g | 605 | 144 |
| *fish spreads* see *dips and spreads* | | | |
| *fish stew* | 100g | 520 | 124 |
| *fish sticks* ... frozen ... pan-fried ... 1 | 22g | 160 | 38 |
| Edgell-Birdseye | 100g | 1055 | 251 |
| *five-corner fruit* see *carambola* | | | |
| *flake* ... battered, deep-fried ... 1 fillet | 145g | 1235 | 294 |
| crumbed, pan-fried ... 1 fillet | 165g | 1225 | 292 |
| steamed | 100g | 525 | 125 |
| *flapjacks* see *pancakes* | | | |
| *flathead* ... battered, deep-fried | 100g | 954 | 227 |
| floured, pan-fried | 100g | 740 | 176 |
| steamed | 100g | 485 | 115 |
| *flounder* ... baked | 100g | 845 | 201 |
| battered, fried | 100g | 1165 | 277 |
| crumbed, fried | 100g | 950 | 226 |
| grilled | 100g | 400 | 95 |
| poached | 100g | 395 | 94 |
| raw | 100g | 330 | 79 |
| smoked | 100g | 505 | 120 |
| inc bones + skin | 100g | 335 | 80 |
| steamed | 100g | 350 | 83 |
| inc bones + skin | 100g | 210 | 50 |
| Edgell-Birdseye | 100g | 330 | 79 |
| Frionor ... fillets | 100g | 350 | 83 |
| *flour, arrowroot* | 100g | 1560 | 371 |
| *flour, corn* see *cornflour* | | | |

| | MASS | KJ | CAL |
|---|---|---|---|
| *flour, gluten* | 30g | 475 | 113 |
| *flour, maize* see *cornflour* | | | |
| *flour, millet* | 100g | 1480 | 352 |
| *flour, potato* | 100g | 2070 | 493 |
| *flour, rice* | 100g | 1525 | 363 |
| *flour, rye* ... wholemeal | 100g | 1235 | 294 |
| *flour, soya* ... full-fat | 100g | 1755 | 418 |
| low-fat | 100g | 1485 | 354 |
| The Old Grain Mill | 100g | 1760 | 419 |
| *flour, wheat* ... fortified | 100g | 1525 | 363 |
| plain ... white | 100g | 1475 | 351 |
| wholemeal | 100g | 1410 | 336 |
| self-raising ... white | 100g | 1525 | 363 |
| wholemeal | 100g | 1175 | 280 |
| White Wings ... av all types | 100g | 1485 | 354 |
| *foule moudamass (Lebanese)* | 100g | 305 | 73 |
| *frankfurters* ... battered, deep-fried ... 1 | 100g | 1280 | 305 |
| boiled ... 2 | 100g | 1160 | 276 |
| canned ... av commercial brands | 100g | 865 | 206 |
| *French beans* see *beans, green* | | | |
| *fried rice* ... Griffs | 100g | 675 | 161 |
| *fried rice (Chinese)* | 100g | 930 | 221 |
| *frijoles* ... with cheese | 100g | 566 | 135 |
| *fruit* see individual fruits | | | |
| *fruit bread* see *bread* | | | |
| *fruit cake* see *cakes and pastries* | | | |
| *fruit cocktail ...* Golden Circle | 100g | 345 | 82 |
| SPC ... artific. sweet | 100g | 120 | 29 |
| in syrup | 100g | 260 | 62 |
| *fruit conserve* see *jams and marmalades* | | | |
| *fruit drinks* ... Break ... apple and blackcurrant/ apple and strawberry | 100ml | 185 | 44 |

| | MASS | KJ | CAL |
|---|---|---|---|
| apple and raspberry | 100ml | 170 | 40 |
| tropical | 100ml | 185 | 44 |
| Golden Circle ... av all flavours | 100ml | 180 | 43 |
| Oak | 100ml | 170 | 40 |
| Prima ... av all flavours | 100ml | 180 | 43 |
| Sunburst ... av all flavours | 100ml | 185 | 44 |
| Sunrise ... 25% fruit juice/50% fruit juice ... all flavours | 100ml | 170 | 40 |
| *fruit juices* | | | |
| *grapefruit* ... fresh | 100ml | 150 | 36 |
| *lemon/lime* ... fresh | 100ml | 115 | 27 |
| *orange* ... fresh | 100ml | 185 | 44 |
| frozen concentrate ... undiluted ... unsweetened | 100g | 655 | 156 |
| *pineapple* ... canned | 100g | 225 | 54 |
| *prune* ... canned | 100g | 320 | 76 |
| *tomato* ... canned | 100ml | 85 | 20 |
| *Berri* ... tomato ... unsweetened | 100g | 70 | 17 |
| *Berrivale* ... grapefruit ... unsweetened | 100ml | 140 | 33 |
| orange ... unsweetened | 100ml | 155 | 37 |
| apple | 100ml | 170 | 40 |
| *Big O* ... apple 100%/six fruits 100%, NAS | 100ml | 200 | 48 |
| apple, NAS | 100ml | 180 | 43 |
| orange,NAS | 100ml | 155 | 37 |
| orange, apple and mango 100%/orange 100%, NAS | 100ml | 160 | 38 |
| *Devondale* ... apple | 100ml | 155 | 37 |
| *Glen Park* ... apple 100% | 100ml | 170 | 40 |
| *Golden Circle* ... apple/pineapple | 100ml | 210 | 50 |
| Estrel tetra pak ... av all flavours | 100ml | 195 | 46 |
| unsweetened pineapple | 100ml | 185 | 44 |
| *Heinz* ... tomato | 100ml | 75 | 18 |
| *Mildura* ... chilled 100% ... orange ... unsweetened | 100ml | 155 | 37 |
| *Mr Juicy* ... chilled 100% ... no added sugar ... apple | 100ml | 170 | 40 |

| | MASS | KJ | CAL |
|---|---|---|---|
| grapefruit | 100ml | 140 | 33 |
| orange | 100ml | 155 | 37 |
| *Oak* | 100ml | 170 | 40 |
| *Popper* ... apple | 100g | 190 | 45 |
| pineapple and orange/orange and mango/orange | 100g | 165 | 39 |
| UHT ... av all flavours | 100g | 180 | 43 |
| *Prima* ... orange 100% | 100ml | 155 | 37 |
| av all others | 100ml | 190 | 45 |
| *Sanitarium* ... apple ... reconstituted | 100ml | 180 | 43 |
| grape ... dark shiraz/golden muscatel | 100ml | 330 | 79 |
| med. dry red/white | 100ml | 280 | 67 |
| sparkling red/white | 100ml | 300 | 71 |
| orange/apple ... fresh | 100ml | 155 | 37 |
| *Schweppes* ... orange | 100ml | 165 | 39 |
| tomato | 100ml | 105 | 25 |
| av all others | 100ml | 200 | 48 |
| *Spring Valley* ... apple blends/pineapple/tropical ... av | 100ml | 185 | 44 |
| nectars ... av | 100ml | 200 | 47 |
| sparkling ... av | 100ml | 190 | 45 |
| *Sunburst* ... orange 100%/grapefruit | 100ml | 155 | 37 |
| tomato | 100ml | 100 | 24 |
| av all others | 100ml | 200 | 48 |
| *Sunpak* ... orange, apple and mango/orange | 100ml | 150 | 36 |
| sultana grape/dark grape | 100ml | 255 | 61 |
| *Sunraysia* ... prune juice | 100ml | 265 | 63 |
| *Sunup* ... 100% ... no added sugar ... apple and blackcurrant | 100ml | 170 | 40 |
| grapefruit | 100ml | 140 | 33 |

Many fruit juices are relatively high in sugar and kilojoules. Diluting juices with mineral water or soda water cuts down on energy intake while making for a flavoursome, refreshing drink.

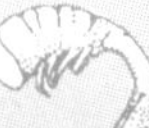

| | MASS | KJ | CAL |
|---|---|---|---|
| orange mango/ orange/orange and passionfruit | 100ml | 155 | 37 |
| tropical | 100ml | 170 | 40 |
| *Valencio* ... four-fruits | 100ml | 160 | 38 |
| ***fruit mince*** ... Robertsons | 100g | 1150 | 274 |
| with rum ... Robertsons | 100g | 1170 | 279 |
| ***fruit salad*** ... canned ... in heavy syrup ... 1 cup | 270g | 895 | 213 |
| in pear juice ... 1 cup | 255g | 450 | 107 |
| in syrup ... 1 cup | 260g | 530 | 126 |
| fresh | 100g | 265 | 63 |
| Golden Circle | 100g | 345 | 82 |
| unsweetened | 100g | 185 | 44 |
| Goulburn Valley ... in fruit juice | 100g | 175 | 42 |
| Letona ... trim fruit | 100ml | 205 | 49 |
| ***fruit salad, tropical*** ... canned ... in heavy syrup ... 1 cup | 270g | 905 | 215 |
| in pineapple juice ... 1 cup | 260g | 525 | 125 |

***fudge*** see ***confectionery***

### Tutti Frutti Dessert

*1 level teaspoon powdered gelatine*
*1 tablespoon water*
*15 g slivered almonds*
*1 small carton low-fat natural yoghurt*
*25 g dried apricots, chopped*
*15 g glacé cherries, chopped*
*1 level tablespoon raisins*
*few angelica leaves*

Sprinkle gelatine over the water in a small basin and leave to stand for 15 minutes. Stand basin in a pan of simmering water until the gelatine has dissolved. Heat almonds in a small non-stick saucepan, tossing until golden. Mix yoghurt with cooled gelatine and stir in fruit and almonds. Spoon mixture into a mould. Chill until set. Turn dessert out onto a plate and decorate with angelica. Serves 1 at 1255 kJ (299 cal).

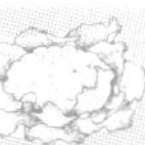

| | MASS | KJ | CAL |
|---|---|---|---|
| *galactobureko (Greek)* see *cakes and pastries* | | | |
| *gammon* see *ham* | | | |
| *garfish* ... baked | 100g | 410 | 98 |
| grilled | 100g | 400 | 95 |
| poached | 100g | 395 | 94 |
| raw | 100g | 320 | 76 |
| smoked | 100g | 335 | 80 |
| steamed | 100g | 350 | 83 |
| *garlic* ... boiled ... peeled ... 2 cloves | 5g | 20 | 5 |
| raw ... peeled ... 2 cloves | 6g | 25 | 6 |
| White Wings ... granules | 100g | 920 | 219 |
| *garlic bread* see *bread: sticks* | | | |
| *garlic prawns (Chinese)* | 100g | 510 | 121 |
| *garlic prawns (Thai)* | 100g | 820 | 195 |
| *gelatine powder* | 100g | 1540 | 367 |
| *gemfish* ... battered, deep-fried | 100g | 1195 | 285 |
| crumbed, pan-fried | 100g | 1155 | 275 |
| steamed | 100g | 940 | 224 |
| *ghee* | 100g | 3695 | 880 |
| Allowrie/Q.B.B | 100g | 3700 | 881 |
| *gherkins* | 100g | 75 | 18 |
| *gin* see *spirits* | | | |
| *ginger* ... boiled ... peeled ... 5 slices | 10g | 10 | 2 |

| | MASS | KJ | CAL |
|---|---|---|---|
| crystallised | 100g | 1425 | 339 |
| ground | 5g | 55 | 13 |
| raw ... peeled ... 1 tbsp grated | 12g | 15 | 4 |
| *gingerbread see cakes and pastries* | | | |
| *glucose* ... liquid | 100g | 1330 | 317 |
| powder | 100g | 1600 | 381 |
| *goat* ... meat + skin | 100g | 610 | 145 |
| *goat cheese* see *cheese* | | | |
| *goat milk* see *milk, goat's* | | | |
| *golden syrup* see *syrup, golden* | | | |
| *golden syrup dumplings* see *desserts and puddings* | | | |
| *goose* ... meat + skin | 100g | 1850 | 440 |
| roasted, meat only | 100g | 1330 | 317 |
| *gooseberries* ... canned ... sweetened | 100g | 375 | 89 |
| unsweetened | 100g | 110 | 26 |
| fresh | 100g | 180 | 43 |
| stewed ... with sugar | 100g | 215 | 51 |
| *gooseberries, chinese* see *kiwifruit* | | | |
| *gourd, wax* ... raw ... peeled ... 1 cup diced | 140g | 30 | 7 |
| *granadilla* see *passionfruit* | | | |
| *grape juice* see *fruit juices* | | | |
| *grapefruit* ... grilled ... 1/2 | 103g | 430 | 102 |
| raw ... peeled ... 1/2 | 103g | 115 | 27 |
| John West ... canned ... in syrup | 100g | 250 | 60 |
| *grapefruit cocktail* | 100g | 340 | 81 |
| *grapefruit juice* see *fruit juices* | | | |
| *grapes* ... black ... raw ... 1 cup | 175g | 470 | 112 |
| black muscatel ... raw ... 10 grapes | 39g | 130 | 31 |
| Cornichon ... raw ... 10 grapes | 60g | 140 | 33 |
| green ... raw ... 1 cup | 170g | 435 | 104 |
| green sultana/ruby sultana ... raw ... 10 grapes | 30g | 75 | 18 |
| Waltham Cross ... raw ... 10 grapes | 50g | 125 | 30 |

| | MASS | KJ | CAL |
|---|---|---|---|
| *gravy* ... Continental ... instant gravy ... brown onion ... made up | 100ml | 170 | 40 |
| chicken ... made up | 100ml | 205 | 49 |
| roast meat ... made up | 100ml | 185 | 44 |
| Gravox ... gravy maker/supreme ... made up | 100ml | 75 | 18 |
| light brown (salt-reduced)/chicken ... made up | 100ml | 80 | 19 |
| low-joule ... made up | 100ml | 70 | 17 |
| Gravox Carvery ... all flavours ... made up | 60ml | 85 | 20 |
| Gravy Quik ... 1/4 cup as prepared | 6g | 80 | 19 |
| Gravyboat ... instant gravy mix ... av all flavours ... made up | 20g | 280 | 65 |
| Maggi ... rich gravy ... made up | 100ml | 120 | 29 |
| Sanitarium ... gravy quick ... 1/4 cups as prepared | 6g | 80 | 19 |
| White Wings ... brown gravy mix ... made up | 100ml | 160 | 38 |
| gravy mix ... made up | 100ml | 75 | 18 |
| light and golden gravy mix ... made up | 100ml | 145 | 35 |
| *Greek foods* see names of individual foods | | | |
| *green pepper* see *capsicum* | | | |
| *greengage plums* see *plums* | | | |
| *grissini sticks* see *bread: sticks* | | | |
| *grouse* ... roasted ... boneless | 100g | 730 | 174 |
| *guavas* ... canned in syrup | 100g | 255 | 61 |
| raw ... flesh + skin seeds ... 1 av | 113g | 115 | 27 |
| *guinea fowl* ... raw | 100g | 665 | 158 |
| *gurnard, long finned* ... baked | 100g | 410 | 98 |
| grilled | 100g | 400 | 95 |
| poached | 100g | 395 | 94 |
| raw | 100g | 320 | 76 |
| smoked | 100g | 335 | 80 |
| steamed | 100g | 350 | 83 |
| *haddock* ... fried | 100g | 690 | 164 |

| | MASS | KJ | CAL |
|---|---|---|---|
| raw | 100g | 320 | 76 |
| smoked | 100g | 430 | 102 |
| steamed | 100g | 415 | 99 |
| steamed ... inc bones + skin | 100g | 315 | 75 |
| Frionor ... fillets | 100g | 350 | 83 |
| *haggis* ... boiled | 100g | 1290 | 307 |
| *hake* ... raw | 100g | 350 | 83 |
| *halibut, tropical* ... baked | 100g | 410 | 98 |
| grilled | 100g | 400 | 95 |
| poached | 100g | 395 | 94 |
| raw | 100g | 320 | 76 |
| smoked | 100g | 335 | 80 |
| steamed | 100g | 350 | 83 |
| *halva* | 100g | 2570 | 612 |
| *ham* ... leg ... canned ... av all brands | 100g | 470 | 112 |
| lean ... 1 slice | 25g | 105 | 25 |
| lean and fat ... canned ... 2 slices | 35g | 165 | 39 |
| non-canned ... 1 slice | 25g | 145 | 35 |
| with fat ... cured ... boned ... pressed slices | 100g | 455 | 108 |
| on the bone ... cooked ... slices without bone | 100g | 950 | 226 |
| prosciutto | 100g | 1445 | 344 |
| shoulder ... canned ... av commercial brands | 100g | 495 | 118 |
| cured ... boned, pressed slices | 100g | 465 | 111 |
| lean ... non-canned ... 1 slice | 25g | 115 | 27 |
| lean + fat ... canned ... 2 slices | 35g | 175 | 42 |
| unspecified cut ... lean + fat ... 1 slice | 25g | 130 | 31 |
| non-canned ... 2 slices | 35g | 170 | 40 |
| Plumrose ... deli | 100g | 580 | 138 |
| leg | 100g | 545 | 130 |
| shoulder | 100g | 605 | 144 |
| *ham and cheese submarine* ... with potato crisps ... 1 sv | 215g | 2625 | 625 |
| Pizza Hut | 100g | 1240 | 295 |

| | MASS | KJ | CAL |
|---|---|---|---|
| *ham sandwich* see *sandwiches* | | | |
| *ham steak* ... grilled | 100g | 680 | 162 |
| raw | 100g | 520 | 124 |
| *hamburger mince* ... simmered, drained ... 1 cup | 170g | 1535 | 365 |
| *hamburger patties* ... crumbed ... frozen ... fried ... av all brands | 100g | 1420 | 338 |
| frozen ... fried ... av all brands | 100g | 1205 | 287 |
| grilled ... av all brands | 100g | 1100 | 262 |
| Edgell-Birdseye | 100g | 1090 | 260 |
| Farmland | 50g | 630 | 150 |
| *hamburgers* ... plain ... 1 | 170g | 1590 | 379 |
| with bacon ... 1 | 185g | 1955 | 465 |
| with cheese ... 1 | 195g | 2110 | 502 |
| with onions | 100g | 1095 | 261 |
| *hazelnut spread* see *dips and spreads* | | | |
| *hazelnuts* ... shelled | 100g | 2680 | 638 |
| *health-food bars* | | | |
| *Cadbury* ... chewy muesli ... apricot/blackcurrant | 100g | 1675 | 399 |
| fruit and nut | 100g | 1795 | 427 |
| tour-fruits muesli/muesli | 100g | 2115 | 504 |
| *Europe* ... apricot | 100g | 1245 | 296 |
| apricot and coconut | 100g | 1310 | 312 |
| carob ... coconut crisp | 100g | 2280 | 543 |
| fruit and nut bar/block | 100g | 1960 | 467 |
| nutty crisp | 100g | 2220 | 529 |
| muesli crisp | 100g | 1890 | 450 |
| fruit nougat | 100g | 1350 | 321 |
| ginger | 100g | 1585 | 377 |
| honey log | 100g | 2075 | 494 |
| sesame | 100g | 1880 | 448 |
| summer roll | 100g | 2025 | 482 |
| *Gold Crest* ... muesli ... apricot choc chip ... 1 | 35g | 625 | 149 |
| apricot/orchard fruit muesli lites ... 1 | 25g | 350 | 83 |

| | MASS | KJ | CAL |
|---|---|---|---|
| cherry coconut choc chip ... 1 | 35g | 620 | 148 |
| choc chip ... 1 | 35g | 635 | 151 |
| peanut choc chip ... 1 | 35g | 685 | 163 |
| muesli bites ... cherry and coconut choc-coated ... 1 | 20g | 375 | 89 |
| cherry coconut and choc chip ... 1 | 20g | 370 | 88 |
| *Uncle Toby's* ... chewy muesli ... apricot and coconut ... 1 | | 480 | 114 |
| choc chip/banana choc chip ... 1 | | 545 | 130 |
| peanut butter ... 1 | | 525 | 125 |
| peppermint/orange choc chip ... 1 | | 555 | 132 |
| three fruits/tropical fruit ... 1 | | 485 | 115 |
| yoghurt top ... av all flavours ... 1 | | 575 | 137 |
| crunchy muesli ... apricot ... 1 | | 500 | 119 |
| fruit roll-ups ... 1 | | 235 | 56 |
| muesli wraps ... apricot and coconut ... 1 | | 585 | 140 |
| cherry and coconut ... 1 | | 580 | 139 |
| nut combo ... 1 | | 645 | 154 |
| peppermint ... 1 | | 630 | 150 |

*heart* see *beef*; *lamb*

*herbs* see *spices, dried*

| | MASS | KJ | CAL |
|---|---|---|---|
| *herrings* ... canned | 100g | 840 | 200 |
| in tomato sauce | 100g | 740 | 176 |
| fried | 100g | 975 | 232 |
| inc bones | 100g | 860 | 205 |
| grilled | 100g | 830 | 198 |
| inc bones | 100g | 560 | 133 |

Aim to get between 50 per cent to 60 per cent of your daily kilojoules in the form of cereals and complex carbohydrates (pasta, rice, bread and potatoes).

| | MASS | KJ | CAL |
|---|---|---|---|
| kippered | 100g | 905 | 215 |
| pickled | 100g | 930 | 221 |
| raw | 100g | 970 | 231 |
| Admiral ... herring fillets ... assorted | 100g | 715 | 170 |
| John West ... in tomato sauce | 100g | 820 | 195 |
| King Oscar ... fillets in tomato sauce | 100g | 860 | 205 |
| *herrings, Atlantic* ... raw | 100g | 735 | 175 |
| *herrings, Pacific* ... raw | 100g | 410 | 98 |
| *homous* see *dips and spreads* | | | |
| *honey* ... av all brands ... 1 tbsp | 27g | 365 | 87 |
| *honeydew melon* see *melon* | | | |
| *horseradish* | 100g | 250 | 60 |
| *horseradish cream* ... Masterfoods | 5g | 30 | 7 |
| *hot cross buns* see *buns* | | | |
| *hot dog* ... roll + frankfurt + sauce ... 1 av | | 1290 | 307 |
| *hundreds and thousands* ... 1 tbsp | 5ml | 65 | 15 |
| *Hungry Jacks* ... Apple Pie ... 1 | | 1005 | 239 |
| Bacon Double Cheeseburger ... 1 | | 2105 | 501 |
| Bacon Double Cheeseburger Deluxe ... 1 | | 2415 | 575 |
| Chicken Nuggets ... with plum sauce ... 4 pieces | | 100 | 24 |
| with sweet-and sour-sauce ... 4 pieces | | 105 | 25 |
| French Fries ... small | | 950 | 226 |
| Great Aussie Burger ... 1 | | 2475 | 589 |
| Grilled Chicken Burger ... 1 | | 1725 | 411 |
| Onion Rings ... 7–9 rings | | 915 | 218 |
| Sundae ... caramel ... 1 | | 1030 | 246 |
| chocolate ... 1 | | 1010 | 240 |

Plan before you start your diet. Understand the strengths and weaknesses in your eating habits and take them into account. Try to build into your shopping list low-fat, low-sugar and high-fibre alternatives to your staple foods.

| | MASS | KJ | CAL |
|---|---|---|---|
| strawberry ... 1 | | 915 | 218 |
| Thickshake ... av all flavours ... 1 | | 1170 | 279 |
| Whaler Fish Sandwich ... 1 | | 1610 | 383 |
| Whopper ... 1 | | 2515 | 599 |
| Whopper Junior ... 1 | | 1445 | 344 |
| Whopper Junior with Cheese ... 1 | | 1630 | 388 |
| Whopper Sandwich ... 1 | | 2515 | 599 |
| Whopper with Bacon/Cheese | | 2890 | 688 |
| Whopper with Egg ... 1 | | 2640 | 629 |
| Yumbo ... 1 | | 1415 | 337 |
| *ice-block mix powder* | 100g | 1240 | 295 |
| *ice-cream /ice confections* | | | |
| *vanilla ice-cream* ... commercial ... av all brands ... 1 scoop | 45g | 375 | 89 |
| *vanilla ice confection* ... commercial ... av all brands ... 1 scoop | 45g | 330 | 79 |
| *Buskin Robins* ... plain ... 1 sv | 90g | 1110 | 264 |
| *Buttercup* ... vanilla ... 1 sv | 50g | 400 | 95 |
| *Cadbury* ... crunchie | 70ml | 860 | 205 |
| *Dairy Bell* ... standard ... 3 scoops | 150ml | 570 | 136 |
| *Jalna* ... soft-serve | 100g | 535 | 127 |
| *Nice-n-Lite* ... 1 sv | 50g | 250 | 60 |
| *Norco* ... natural | 100g | 850 | 202 |
| *Norgen Vaaz* ... plain ... 1 sv | 90g | 1110 | 264 |
| *Oak* | 100g | 840 | 200 |
| *Pauls* ... dessert whip | 50g | 705 | 168 |
| extra cream ... double choc chip/ butterscotch brickle/peppermint choc mint chip/mocha almond fudge | 50g | 465 | 110 |
| hava-heart ... 1 | 77g | 935 | 223 |
| *Peters* ... billabong ... barney banana/choc/strawb | 50g | 410 | 98 |
| bubbleberry | 50g | 550 | 130 |

| | MASS | KJ | CAL |
|---|---|---|---|
| choc twist | 50g | 590 | 140 |
| triple swirl | 50g | 440 | 105 |
| carbohydrate-modified | 50g | 270 | 64 |
| chill stik | 77g | 195 | 46 |
| choc wedge ... av all flavours ... 1 | 68g | 760 | 180 |
| classic ... cafe macadamia/choc mousse supreme ... av | 50g | 535 | 127 |
| vanilla francaise | 50g | 480 | 114 |
| crazy critters ... 1 | 84g | 325 | 77 |
| Donald Duck | 51g | 620 | 148 |
| drumstick ... mintchip vanilla/vanilla ... 1 | 73g | 850 | 202 |
| mocha choc chip ... 1 | 91g | 1030 | 245 |
| toffee sundae ... 1 | 77g | 940 | 224 |
| triple choc ... 1 | 77g | 910 | 217 |
| Eskimo pie ... vanilla | 72g | 880 | 210 |
| chocolate | 72g | 910 | 216 |
| Frisco | 70g | 840 | 200 |
| Frisco treats | 39g | 485 | 115 |
| frozen yoghurt ... av all flavours ... 1 | 86g | 535 | 127 |
| fruit de light | 63g | 220 | 52 |
| icy poles ... raspberry lemonade ... 1 | 77g | 200 | 48 |
| light ... choc swirl/strawb swirl ... av | 50g | 305 | 73 |
| vanilla | 50g | 290 | 69 |
| Michel Mouse | 65g | 655 | 155 |
| monaco bar ... 1 | 73g | 835 | 199 |
| natural ... dixie cup ... 1 | 53g | 430 | 102 |
| vanilla/vanilla with apricots/ fruit salad ... av | 50g | 410 | 97 |
| vanilla with raspberry | 50g | 430 | 102 |
| party cake | 50g | 410 | 98 |
| royal ... vanilla/chocolate ... av | 50g | 440 | 105 |
| skona ... apricot ... 1 | 72g | 525 | 125 |

| | MASS | KJ | CAL |
|---|---|---|---|
| split ... pine-lime | 64g | 350 | 83 |
| pine-orange | 63g | 315 | 75 |
| raspberry | 63g | 265 | 63 |
| twister ... av all flavours | 89g | 715 | 170 |
| white wedge ... 1 | 78g | 820 | 195 |
| *Plumes* ... 1 sv | 90g | 1110 | 264 |
| *Sara Lee Premium* ... French vanilla | 100g | 1110 | 264 |
| peach mango | 100g | 940 | 224 |
| strawberry | 100g | 925 | 220 |
| ultra chocolate | 100g | 1200 | 287 |
| *Snow Boy* ... polyunsat. van. ice/no-milk van. honey ... 3 scoops | 150ml | 570 | 136 |
| *Streets* ... blue ribbon hearts ... 1 | | 795 | 189 |
| bubble-o-bill ... 1 | | 695 | 165 |
| cal control slices ... 1 | | 195 | 46 |
| calippo ... lemon ... 1 | | 505 | 120 |
| orange ... 1 | | 505 | 120 |
| choc block ... chocolate ... 1 | | 860 | 205 |
| vanilla ... 1 | | 900 | 214 |
| cornetto ... choc mint ... 1 | | 850 | 202 |
| chocolate ripple | | 720 | 171 |
| vanilla ... 1 | | 725 | 172 |

| | MASS | KJ | CAL |
|---|---|---|---|
| dude food ... 1 | | 385 | 92 |
| feast ... 1 | | 1230 | 293 |
| fresh ... 1 | | 715 | 170 |
| golden gaytime ... 1 | | 860 | 205 |
| ice-cream slices ... 1 | | 400 | 95 |
| logs ... coffee walnut | 100ml | 385 | 92 |
| vienetta ... chocolate | 100ml | 550 | 131 |
| magnifico ... chocolate ... 1 | | 970 | 231 |
| Oz block ... cola/lemonade/raspberry ... 1 | | 230 | 55 |
| paddle pops ... banana ... 1 | | 510 | 121 |
| caramel choc ... 1 | | 560 | 133 |
| chocolate ... 1 | | 650 | 155 |
| splice ... pine lime ... 1 | | 395 | 94 |
| strawberry triple treat ... 1 | | 935 | 223 |
| tubs ... blue ribbon ... chocolate/vanilla | 100ml | 385 | 92 |
| coffee cream | 100ml | 465 | 111 |
| wild strawberry | 100ml | 420 | 100 |
| quality favourites ... vanilla/neapolitan/ chocolate | 100ml | 375 | 89 |
| super saver ... vanilla/neapolitan | 100ml | 400 | 95 |
| Vienna chocolate ... 1 | | 620 | 148 |
| winner ... 1 | | 905 | 215 |
| *Taranto's* ... gelato classico ... milk-based | 100ml | 300 | 71 |
| water-based | 100ml | 200 | 48 |
| premium natural ice-cream | 100ml | 380 | 90 |
| tofu glace | 100ml | 295 | 70 |
| *Weight Watchers* ... 1 sv | 50g | 280 | 67 |
| ***ice-cream cones*** ... unfilled ... 1 small | 5g | 80 | 19 |
| ***ice-cream mix*** ... Pauls ... UHT soft-serve mix | 100g | 540 | 129 |
| ***icing*** ... almond see ***marzipan*** | | | |
| chocolate | 100g | 1460 | 348 |
| fondant | 100g | 1605 | 382 |

| | MASS | KJ | CAL |
|---|---|---|---|
| marshmallow | 100g | 1264 | 301 |
| warm | 100g | 1405 | 335 |
| *icing sugar* ... pure/soft | 100g | 1635 | 389 |
| Green's ... chocolate-icing mix | 100g | 1580 | 376 |
| plain icing mix | 100g | 1755 | 418 |
| *Irish stew* ... canned ... av commercial brands | 100g | 360 | 86 |
| home-made | 100g | 520 | 124 |
| Farmland | 100g | 515 | 123 |
| Harvest ... hot packs | 100g | 270 | 64 |
| *jackfruit* ... raw ... peeled ... flesh only ... 1/4 | 201g | 650 | 155 |
| *jams and marmalades* ... jam ... all flavours ... av ... 1 tsp | 10g | 110 | 26 |
| marmalade ... all flavours ... av ... 1 tsp | 10g | 110 | 26 |
| Country Harvest ... av all flavours ... 1 tsp | 10g | 50 | 12 |
| IXL ... apricot jam ... 1 tsp | 10g | 105 | 25 |
| av all other flavours ... 1 tsp | 10g | 110 | 26 |
| Kraft ... conserve/marmalade ... av all flavours ... 1 tsp | 10g | 110 | 26 |
| Monbulk ... av all flavours ... 1 tsp | 10g | 115 | 27 |
| Quality Foods ... av all flavours ... 1 tsp | 10g | 65 | 15 |
| Robertsons ... marmalade ... av all flavours ... 1 tsp | 10g | 110 | 26 |
| SPC ... av all flavours ... 1 tsp | 10g | 115 | 27 |

| | MASS | KJ | CAL |
|---|---|---|---|
| *jelly* ... low-joule ... made up | 100g | 15 | 4 |
| made with milk ... made up | 100g | 365 | 87 |
| made with water ... made up | 100g | 250 | 60 |
| Aero Premium/Aeroplane ... made up | 100g | 265 | 63 |
| Aeroplane low-joule/Diet Cottees ... made up | 100g | 30 | 7 |
| Country Harvest ... all flavours ... made up | 100g | 385 | 92 |
| Gold Crest ... so slim ... made up | 100g | 35 | 8 |
| Pioneer ... low-joule ... strawberry ... made up | 100g | 30 | 7 |
| *jelly beans* see *confectionery* | | | |
| *jelly crystals* | 100g | 1235 | 294 |
| Country Harvest ... low-protein ... all flavours | 100g | 1570 | 374 |
| *John Dory* ... fried | 100g | 905 | 215 |
| steamed | 100g | 385 | 92 |
| *junket* | 100g | 330 | 79 |
| *kafta (Lebanese)* | 100g | 910 | 217 |
| *kale* ... boiled | 100g | 160 | 38 |
| raw | 100g | 180 | 43 |
| *kangaroo meat* | 100g | 625 | 149 |
| *kedgeree* | 100g | 635 | 151 |
| *Kentucky Fried Chicken* ... bacon and cheese chicken fillet burger | 193g | 2065 | 491 |
| bean salad ... 1 sv | 100g | 565 | 134 |
| chicken fillet burger | 170g | 1785 | 425 |
| coleslaw ... 1 sv | 100g | 400 | 95 |
| Colonel Burger | 114g | 1195 | 285 |
| Kentucky Nuggets | 18g | 165 | 39 |
| mashed potato and gravy | 100g | 560 | 133 |
| original recipe ... chicken, av pieces | 93g | 895 | 213 |
| potato salad ... 1 sv | 100g | 415 | 99 |
| thigh drumstick ... 1 piece | 68g | 900 | 214 |
| wing ... inc bone ... 1 piece | 55g | 550 | 131 |

| | MASS | KJ | CAL |
|---|---|---|---|
| *kibbi (Lebanese)* ... fried | 100g | 910 | 217 |
| vegetarian ... baked | 100g | 1075 | 256 |
| *kibbi nayeh (Lebanese)* | 100g | 710 | 169 |
| *kidney* see *beef*; *lamb* | | | |
| *kippers* ... baked | 100g | 855 | 204 |
| John West ... fillets | 100g | 950 | 226 |
| *kiwifruit* ... flesh + seeds ... 1 fruit | 78g | 160 | 38 |
| *kohlrabi* ... boiled ... peeled ... 1 cup sliced | 175g | 265 | 63 |
| raw ... peeled ... 1 cup sliced | 150g | 205 | 49 |
| *kumara* see *sweet potato* | | | |
| *kumiss* | 100g | 1615 | 385 |
| *kumquat* ... canned | 100g | 575 | 137 |
| raw ... 1 small | 7g | 10 | 2 |
| | | | |
| *lady fingers (Lebanese)* | 100g | 1195 | 285 |
| *lady fingers vegetarian (Lebanese)* | 100g | 1365 | 325 |
| *lamb* | | | |
| *boneless* ... average cut | | | |
| cooked ... lean ... 1 cup diced | 190g | 1455 | 346 |
| lean + fat ... 1 cup diced | 182g | 1805 | 430 |
| *brains* ... crumbed, fried | 100g | 1220 | 290 |
| simmered ... 1 set | 80g | 450 | 107 |
| *breast* ... boneless ... rolled ... baked | 100g | 1210 | 288 |
| rolled, stuffed, baked ... 1 boneless slice | 60g | 725 | 173 |
| *chump chop* ... grilled ... lean ... 1 av | 56g | 770 | 183 |
| lean + fat ... 1 av | 65g | 475 | 113 |
| *cutlets* ... crumbed, fried ... lean | 100g | 1435 | 342 |
| lean + fat | 100g | 1945 | 463 |
| *heart* ... baked ... 1 av | 70g | 540 | 129 |

Check nutritional information accompanying food you buy. Avoid any food containing more than 3 grams of fat per 420 kJ (100 cal).

| | MASS | KJ | CAL |
|---|---|---|---|
| *kidney* ... fried | 100g | 890 | 212 |
| simmered ... 1 cup sliced | 150g | 915 | 218 |
| *leg* ... baked ... lean ... 1 boneless slice | 41g | 305 | 73 |
| lean+fat ... 1 boneless slice | 45g | 420 | 100 |
| *liver* ... fried ... 1 slice | 40g | 405 | 96 |
| *mid-loin chop* ... grilled ... lean ... 1 av | 34g | 250 | 60 |
| lean+fat ... 1 av | 48g | 735 | 175 |
| *mince* ... cooked | 100g | 1265 | 301 |
| *neck chop* ... simmered ... lean ... 1 av | 40g | 425 | 101 |
| lean+fat ... 1 av | 50g | 740 | 176 |
| *rib-loin cutlet* ... grilled ... lean ... 1 av | 29g | 235 | 56 |
| lean+fat ... 1 av | 39g | 555 | 132 |
| *shank* ... simmered ... lean ... 1 av | 87g | 655 | 156 |
| lean+fat ... 1 av | 99g | 925 | 220 |
| *shoulder* ... baked ... lean ... 1 boneless slice | 22g | 170 | 40 |
| lean+fat ... 1 boneless slice | 30g | 360 | 86 |
| *tongue* ... canned ... av all brands ... 5 slices | 100g | 810 | 193 |
| simmered ... 1 av | 55g | 635 | 151 |
| *lamb and spring vegetables* ... McCain | 400g | 1525 | 363 |
| *lamb casserole* ... with vegetables | 100g | 585 | 139 |
| without vegetables | 100g | 615 | 146 |
| *lamb's fry and bacon* ... fried | 100g | 1840 | 438 |
| *Lancashire hotpot* | 100g | 480 | 114 |
| *lard/dripping* | 20g | 755 | 180 |
| *lasagne* ... dried ... uncooked | 100g | 1540 | 367 |
| Leggo's ... 1 sv | 50g | 760 | 181 |
| Tandaco ... one-pan dinner ... 1/4 pkt | 50g | 565 | 134 |
| fresh-baked | 100g | 575 | 137 |
| frozen ... av all brands | 100g | 530 | 126 |
| *lasagna, tuna* see *tuna lasagna* | | | |
| *lasagna, zucchini* see *zucchini lasagna* | | | |
| *lassi* | 100g | 1575 | 375 |

| | MASS | KJ | CAL |
|---|---|---|---|
| *Lean Cuisine* see names of individual meals | | | |
| *leatherjacket* ... fried | 100g | 730 | 174 |
| raw | 100g | 310 | 74 |
| steamed | 100g | 415 | 99 |
| *Lebanese bread* see *bread: flat breads* | | | |
| *Lebanese foods* see names of individual foods | | | |
| *lecithin* ... The Old Grain Mill ... 98% unbleached granules ... | 1 tbsp | 210 | 50 |
| *leeks* ... boiled ... 1 cup sliced | 165g | 165 | 39 |
| raw ... 1 av | 83g | 90 | 21 |
| *lemon butter/curd* | 100g | 1215 | 289 |
| *llemon ginger sauce with vegetables* ... Kan Tong | 100g | 295 | 70 |
| *lemon juice* ... fresh | 100ml | 110 | 26 |
| *lemon meringue* see *pies, sweet* | | | |
| *lemonade* see *drinks, carbonated* | | | |
| *lemons* ... raw ... peeled ... flesh only ... 1 lemon | 99g | 95 | 23 |
| *lentils* ... boiled (dahl) | 100g | 460 | 110 |
| dried ... 1/2 cup | 100g | 1405 | 335 |
| Sanitarium ... savoury brown ... 1/4 can | 110g | 265 | 63 |
| *lettuce* ... butter .... raw ... 3 leaves | 100g | 60 | 14 |
| common ... raw ... 1 leaf | 50g | 15 | 4 |
| cos ... raw ... 1 cup shredded | 65g | 45 | 11 |
| iceberg ... raw | 100g | 55 | 13 |
| mignonette ... raw ... 1 cup pieces | 45g | 25 | 6 |
| radicchio ... raw | 50g | 15 | 4 |
| *lime juice* ... fresh | 100ml | 115 | 27 |

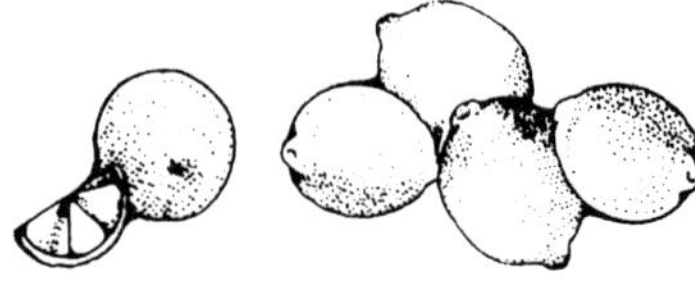

| | MASS | KJ | CAL |
|---|---|---|---|
| *limes* ... raw .. peeled ... flesh only ... 1 | 49g | 45 | 11 |
| *ling* ... raw | 100g | 370 | 88 |
| *linguine* ... dried ... uncooked | 100g | 1540 | 367 |
| *linseed* ... ground ... Healtheries | 100g | 2295 | 546 |
| *liqueurs* ... apricot/peach brandy/kirsch | 20ml | 135 | 32 |
| benedictine/chartreuse/galliano/ouzo/sambuca | 20ml | 335 | 80 |
| cherry brandy | 20ml | 215 | 51 |
| cointreau/van der hum/grand marnier/advocaat | 20ml | 235 | 56 |
| creme de menthe/malibu/tia maria/baileys/ drambuie/kahlya | 20ml | 250 | 60 |
| curacao | 20ml | 260 | 62 |
| *liver* see *beef*; *chicken*; *veal* | | | |
| *liver paste* see *liverwurst* | | | |
| *liver pâté* see *pâté* | | | |
| *liverwurst* | 100g | 1420 | 338 |
| calf | 100g | 1285 | 306 |
| chicken | 100g | 1300 | 310 |
| *lobster* ... boiled ... meat only ... 1 cup | 165g | 670 | 160 |
| canned | 100g | 400 | 95 |
| raw | 100g | 370 | 88 |
| *lobster mayonnaise* | 100g | 1100 | 262 |
| *lobster paste* | 100g | 755 | 180 |
| *lobster thermidor* ... 1 in shell | 400g | 1700 | 405 |
| *lobster with ginger and shallots (Chinese)* | 100g | 560 | 133 |
| *locusts* | 100g | 565 | 135 |
| *loganberries* ... canned ... sweetened | 100g | 295 | 70 |
| raw ... 1 av | 13g | 15 | 4 |
| *loquats* ... canned | 100g | 350 | 83 |
| *lotus tubers* ... canned | 100g | 65 | 15 |
| *lucozade* | 100ml | 300 | 71 |
| *luffa, angled* ... raw ... peeled ... 1 cup diced | 135g | 70 | 17 |
| *luncheon meat* ... beef German/ham and chicken roll | 100g | 970 | 231 |

| | MASS | KJ | CAL |
|---|---|---|---|
| Berliner fleischwurst | 100g | 945 | 225 |
| cabanossi | 100g | 1525 | 363 |
| chicken roll | 100g | 630 | 150 |
| Devon/chicken Devon/ham and chicken | 100g | 980 | 233 |
| fritz | 100g | 1015 | 242 |
| garlic roll | 100g | 1030 | 245 |
| ham sausage | 100g | 1140 | 271 |
| liverwurst | 100g | 1155 | 275 |
| luncheon roll | 100g | 1225 | 292 |
| mortadella/clobaci | 100g | 1355 | 323 |
| Polish | 100g | 1005 | 239 |
| polony | 100g | 1170 | 279 |
| salami ... av all varieties | 100g | 1785 | 425 |
| Strasbourg | 100g | 1025 | 244 |
| *lychees* ... canned | 100g | 290 | 69 |
| flesh only ... 1 av | 14g | 40 | 10 |
| *macadamia nuts* ... shelled | 100g | 2960 | 705 |
| *macaroni* ... boiled | 100g | 475 | 113 |
| dried ... uncooked | 100g | 1540 | 367 |
| *macaroni cheese* ... Kraft ... cheese dinner | 100g | 680 | 162 |
| deluxe cheese dinner | 100g | 525 | 125 |
| spiral cheese and bacon | 100g | 720 | 171 |
| *mackerel* ... canned | 100g | 760 | 181 |
| raw | 100g | 785 | 187 |
| Admiral ... in brine | 100g | 710 | 169 |
| sgombri in oil | 100g | 765 | 182 |
| John West ... in brine | 100g | 635 | 151 |
| in oil | 100g | 1040 | 249 |
| *maize meal* ... refined ... 60% | 100g | 1485 | 354 |
| whole ... 90% | 100g | 1520 | 362 |
| *maize oil* | 100ml | 3700 | 881 |

| | MASS | KJ | CAL |
|---|---|---|---|
| *malt extract* ... Saunders | 100g | 1250 | 298 |
| *malt powder* | 100g | 1510 | 360 |
| Horlicks ... 1 tsp | 5g | 85 | 20 |
| *mandarins* ... canned | 100g | 270 | 64 |
| raw ... 1 av | 80g | 100 | 24 |
| Ellendale ... raw ... 1 av | 115g | 145 | 35 |
| John West ... in juice | 100g | 140 | 33 |
| in syrup | 100g | 215 | 51 |
| *mangoes* ... canned | 100g | 330 | 79 |
| raw ... flesh only ... 1 av | 148g | 350 | 83 |
| Admiral ... sliced | 100g | 300 | 72 |
| *maple syrup* see *sauces, sweet* | | | |
| *margarine, cooking* | 100g | 3015 | 718 |
| Tulip | 100g | 3000 | 714 |
| *margarine, table* ... av all brands ... 1 tbsp | 15g | 455 | 108 |
| Devondale ... dairy extra soft ... 1 tbsp | 15g | 285 | 68 |
| ERA ... polyunsaturated reduced-fat spread ... 1 tbsp | 15g | 240 | 57 |
| Flora Light ... polyunsaturated ... 1 tbsp | 15g | 285 | 68 |
| Meadow Lea ... polyunsaturated lite spread ... 1 tbsp | 15g | 225 | 54 |
| Mrs McGregors ... lite spread ... 1 tbsp | 15g | 230 | 55 |
| *marmalade* see *jams and marmalades* | | | |
| *marmite* see *dips and spreads* | | | |
| *marrow, vegetable* ... boiled ... peeled ... 1 cup diced | 220g | 175 | 42 |
| raw ... peeled ... 1 cup diced | 135g | 95 | 23 |
| *martini* see *cocktails* | | | |

*The season of mango madness is one of many dangers. Who knows what crazy idea a Commisar might come up with while under the influence of the dreaded mango fruit.*

**Northern Territory News**, 22 September 1984

| | | MASS | KJ | CAL |
|---|---|---|---|---|
| *marzipan* | | 30g | 555 | 132 |
| *mayonnaise* | Country Harvest ... soya ... 1 tbsp | 20g | 615 | 146 |
| | Eta ... 1 tbsp | 20g | 180 | 43 |
| | Hain/Hain eggless imitation ... 1 tbsp | 20g | 615 | 146 |
| | Heinz ... 1 tbsp | 20g | 300 | 71 |
| | Kraft ... cholesterol free ... 1 tbsp | 20g | 165 | 39 |
| | light ... 1 tbsp | 20g | 205 | 49 |
| | natural ... 1 tbsp | 20g | 280 | 67 |
| | Nature's Garden ... 1 tbsp | 20g | 640 | 152 |
| | Praise/McCormick ... 1 tbsp | 20g | 570 | 136 |
| | Praise ... light ... 1 tbsp | 20g | 275 | 65 |
| *McDonald's* ... | apple pie ... 1 | 85g | 1105 | 263 |
| | big mac ... 1 | 215g | 2100 | 500 |
| | cheese burger ... 1 | 115g | 1315 | 313 |
| | chicken mcnuggets ... 1 | 19g | 225 | 54 |
| | chocolate thick shake ... 1 | 304ml | 1410 | 336 |
| | cookies ... 1 box ... 19 | 60g | 1190 | 283 |
| | egg mcmuffin ... 1 | 142g | 1490 | 355 |
| | English muffin ... 1 | 68g | 805 | 192 |
| | filet-o-fish ... 1 | 152g | 1605 | 384 |
| | French fries ... large carton | | 1380 | 329 |
| | small carton | | 835 | 199 |
| | hash browns ... 1 | 56g | 730 | 174 |
| | hot fudge sundae ... 1 | 163g | 1115 | 265 |
| | junior burger ... 1 | 100g | 1120 | 267 |
| | mcfeast ... 1 | 225g | 2100 | 500 |
| | quarterpounder with cheese ... 1 | 200g | 2425 | 577 |
| | sauces (for mcnuggets) ... per portion | 31g | 185 | 44 |

Weigh yourself regularly, say once a week in the morning. Don't hop on and off the scales every day as weight fluctuation, which can be the product of many different factors, could be discouraging.

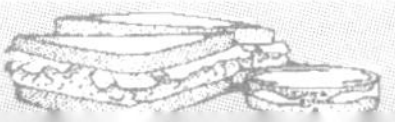

| | MASS | KJ | CAL |
|---|---|---|---|
| sausage mcmuffin ... 1 | 116g | 1415 | 338 |
| sausage mcmuffin with egg ... 1 | 165g | 1770 | 423 |
| scrarmbled eggs and muffin ... 1 | 160g | 1520 | 362 |
| *meat loaf* ... baked | 100g | 835 | 199 |
| *meat* see individual types | | | |
| *meat spreads* see *dips and spreads* | | | |
| *meat substitutes* ... Sanitarium ... BBQ links ... 1 | 43g | 325 | 77 |
| Bologna ... 2 slices | 54g | 455 | 108 |
| casserole mince ... 1/8 can | 55g | 175 | 42 |
| nut meat ... 2 slices | 54g | 400 | 95 |
| nutolene ... 2 slices | 54g | 495 | 118 |
| salad loaf ... 2 slices | 72g | 345 | 82 |
| savoury brown lentils ... 1/4 can | 110g | 265 | 63 |
| savoury pie ... 1/3 can | 110g | 770 | 183 |
| soya loaf ... 2 slices | 72g | 545 | 130 |
| Swiss rounds ... 1 | 110g | 705 | 168 |
| tender bits ... 1/6 can | 72g | 245 | 58 |
| TVP ... roast flavour ... 1/2 cup rehydr | 22g | 295 | 70 |
| veg country stew ... 1/4 can | 110g | 350 | 83 |
| veg rediburger ... 2 slices | 60g | 410 | 98 |
| vegecuts ... 2 slices | 72g | 300 | 71 |
| vegelinks ... 2 | 75g | 525 | 125 |
| vegetarian sausages ... 2 | 85g | 580 | 138 |
| Soy Feast ... burger mix | 50g | 705 | 168 |
| *mee grob (Thai)* | 100g | 1525 | 363 |
| *melon* ... bitter melon ... raw ... 1 av | 126g | 25 | 6 |
| canteloupe/rockmelon ... raw flesh only ... 1 cup diced | 165g | 150 | 36 |
| hairy melon ... raw ... 1 cup diced | 130g | 60 | 14 |
| honeydew ... raw ... flesh only ... 1 cup diced | 165g | 215 | 51 |
| watermelon ... raw ... flesh only ... 1 cup diced | 195g | 185 | 44 |

| | MASS | KJ | CAL |
|---|---|---|---|
| *meringues* see *cakes and pastries* | | | |
| *milk* | | | |
| *buttermilk* | 100ml | 165 | 39 |
| Jalna | 100g | 135 | 32 |
| *condensed, sweetened* ... skim ... canned | 100g | 1135 | 270 |
| 1 cup | 335g | 3800 | 905 |
| whole | 100g | 1370 | 326 |
| 1 cup | 325g | 4445 | 1058 |
| *evaporated* ... reduced-fat ... canned | 100g | 385 | 92 |
| 1 cup | 265g | 1015 | 242 |
| skim ... canned | 100g | 315 | 75 |
| 1 cup | 268g | 840 | 200 |
| whole ... canned | 100g | 600 | 143 |
| 1 cup | 262g | 1575 | 375 |
| Bear Brand ... reduced-fat | 100ml | 410 | 98 |
| *powdered/dried* | 100g | 145 | 35 |
| skim ... 3 tbsp | 24g | 355 | 85 |
| whole ... 3 tbsp | 24g | 485 | 115 |

| | MASS | KJ | CAL |
|---|---|---|---|
| *reduced-fat, protein-increased* | 100g | 225 | 54 |
| 1 cup | 260g | 585 | 139 |
| *skim* | 100g | 145 | 35 |
| 1 cup | 260g | 585 | 139 |
| *Skinny* | 100ml | 160 | 38 |
| *whole* | 100ml | 270 | 66 |
| fresh/UHT ... 1 cup | 258g | 700 | 167 |
| *Balance* ... UHT high calcium | 100ml | 195 | 46 |
| *Dairy Farmers* ... cultured buttermilk | 100ml | 205 | 49 |
| Hi-Lo/UHT | 100ml | 235 | 56 |
| Lite-White | 100ml | 215 | 51 |
| Shape | 100ml | 195 | 46 |
| *Diploma* ... UHT | 100ml | 270 | 64 |
| *Diploma Challenge* ... UHT reduced-fat | 100ml | 245 | 58 |
| *Farmhouse* | 100ml | 310 | 74 |
| *Ideal Dairy* ... Rev | 100ml | 205 | 49 |
| *Joyhill* ... UHT ... light (reduced-fat) | 100ml | 220 | 52 |
| *New Rev* | 100ml | 205 | 49 |
| *Norco* ... shape | 100ml | 195 | 46 |
| *Oak* ... Lite | 100ml | 240 | 57 |
| Lite White | 100ml | 215 | 51 |
| *Pauls* ... buttermilk | 100ml | 200 | 48 |
| *Pauls/ Suncoast* ... Shape/Trim | 100ml | 185 | 44 |
| *Sandhurst* ... PhysiCAL | 100ml | 220 | 52 |
| Trim and Terrific | 100ml | 180 | 43 |
| ***milk, buffalo*** | 100g | 430 | 102 |
| ***milk, flavoured*** | 100ml | 375 | 89 |
| milk shake ... 1 | 340ml | 1735 | 413 |
| Akta-vite ... made up ... | 20g + 300ml milk | 1160 | 276 |
| Berri Iced ... av all flavours | 100ml | 245 | 58 |
| Big M ... av all flavours | 100ml | 320 | 76 |
| Dairy Farmers ... Good One ... av all flavours | 100ml | 385 | 92 |

| | MASS | KJ | CAL |
|---|---|---|---|
| Moove ... av all flavours | 100ml | 315 | 75 |
| UHT Moove ... av all flavours | 100ml | 325 | 77 |
| Healtheries ... carob drink | 2 tsp + 200ml milk | 540 | 129 |
| Lift ... av all flavours | 100ml | 290 | 69 |
| McDonalds ... thick shake ... 1 | 340ml | 1150 | 274 |
| Milo ... made up | 20g + 200ml milk | 930 | 222 |
| Norco ... av all flavours | 100ml | 330 | 79 |
| Oak ... av all flavours | 100ml | 380 | 90 |
| Ovaltine ... made up | 10g + 240 ml milk | 320 | 76 |
| UHT ... ready to go | 100ml | 320 | 76 |
| Pauls ... chocolate shayk | 100ml | 320 | 76 |
| eggnog | 100g | 290 | 69 |
| Pauls/Suncoast ... reduced-fat flavoured modified dairy drink ... breaka/choc/strawb/ french van./honeycomb | 100ml | 260 | 62 |
| iced coffee breaka | 100ml | 240 | 57 |
| UHT breaka ... av all flavours | 100ml | 285 | 68 |
| QUF Industries ... Good One ... malt and honey | 100ml | 305 | 73 |
| Spring Valley ... UHT ... Baco Luxury ... av all flavours | 100ml | 255 | 61 |
| Sustagen Gold | 100ml | 470 | 112 |
| *milk, goat's* | 100ml | 280 | 67 |
| Nanny Goat Lane/Simply Better | 100ml | 280 | 67 |
| *milk, human* | 100ml | 295 | 70 |
| *milk, sheep's* | 100ml | 450 | 107 |
| *milk, soya bean* see *soya drink* | | | |

Thirst quenching should not cost you kilojoules. Milk-based drinks and even fruit juices should be regarded as food rather than liquid replacement. Herbal teas are a welcome refresher, being perfect to drink without milk and with the added benefit of being caffeine-free.

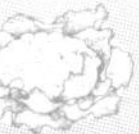

| | MASS | KJ | CAL |
|---|---|---|---|
| *millet* | 100g | 1350 | 321 |
| *Milo ...* powder ... 1 tsp | 5g | 85 | 20 |
| *mince pies, fruit* see *pies, sweet* | | | |
| *mince* see *beef*; *lamb*; *pork* | | | |
| *mincemeat (fruit filling)* | 20g | 235 | 56 |
| *mineral water* see *drinks, carbonated* | | | |
| *mint jelly* ... Masterfoods | 5g | 55 | 13 |
| *miso ...* 1 tbsp | 20ml | 170 | 40 |
| *mixed peel ... candied* | 100g | 1325 | 315 |
| *molasses ...* black | 100g | 900 | 214 |
| light | 100g | 1075 | 256 |
| *Mongolian lamb* ... Farmland ... uncooked ... 1 sv | 200g | 1140 | 271 |
| *mornay chicken ...* Harvest ... hot packs | 100g | 270 | 64 |
| *mortadella* see *luncheon meat* | | | |
| *morwong ...* battered, deep-fried | 100g | 870 | 207 |
| crumbed, pan-fried | 100g | 835 | 199 |
| steamed | 100g | 530 | 126 |
| *moussaka (Greek) ...* fresh-cooked | 100g | 640 | 152 |
| *muesli bars* see *health-food bars* | | | |
| *muesli* see *breakfast cereals* | | | |
| *muffins* ... 1 | 65g | 600 | 143 |
| Sara Lee ... apple/blueberry ... 1 | 75g | 970 | 231 |
| oatbran ... 1 | 75g | 865 | 206 |
| Tip Top ... 1 | 67g | 600 | 143 |
| apple cinnamon/spicy fruit ... 1 | 65g | 640 | 152 |
| Bornhoffen/multigrain ... 1 | 67g | 615 | 146 |
| Weight Watchers ... 1 | 55g | 490 | 117 |
| *mulberries ...* flesh + seeds ... raw ... 1 cup | 130g | 160 | 38 |
| *mullet ...* battered, deep-fried | 100g | 1225 | 292 |
| floured, pan-fried | 100g | 860 | 205 |
| steamed | 100g | 560 | 133 |
| *mulloway ...* battered, deep-fried | 100g | 1000 | 238 |

| | MASS | KJ | CAL |
|---|---|---|---|
| crumbed, pan-fried | 100g | 800 | 190 |
| steamed | 100g | 540 | 129 |
| *mung bean sprouts* see *beans, mung* | | | |
| *mushrooms* ... Chinese | 100g | 1180 | 281 |
| dried | 100g | 1150 | 274 |
| raw ... 1 cup sliced | 70g | 70 | 17 |
| sauteed in butter | 100g | 460 | 110 |
| straw ... canned ... drained | 100g | 125 | 30 |
| Edgell-Birdseye ... sliced ... in brine | 100g | 120 | 29 |
| in butter sauce | 100g | 190 | 45 |
| Farmland ... no added salt | 100g | 130 | 31 |
| SPC ... sliced | 100g | 75 | 18 |
| in butter sauce | 100g | 210 | 50 |
| *mushrooms, button* see *champignons* | | | |
| *mushrooms, oyster* | 100g | 85 | 20 |
| *mussels* ... boiled | 100g | 365 | 87 |
| canned | 100g | 480 | 114 |
| smoked ... canned in oil ... drained ... 1 cup | 160g | 1300 | 310 |
| Admiral | 100g | 1030 | 246 |
| John West | 100g | 860 | 205 |
| *mustard* ... Masterfoods ... av all types | 5g | 25 | 6 |
| *mustard pickles* see *pickles* | | | |
| *mustard powder* | 5g | 97 | 23 |
| *mutton curry with vegetables* | 100g | 585 | 139 |
| *mutton stew with potatoes and onions* see *Irish stew* | | | |

With almost no fat, cholesterol, salt or sugar, and as a significant supplier of valuable dietary fibre, the mushroom is one of the dieter's allies in the fight against weight gain. Mushrooms are a rich source of vitamins, especially in the B-complex group including riboflavin, niacin, thiamin and pantothenic acid. They are also one of the very few vegetable sources of vitamin B12.

| | MASS | KJ | CAL |
|---|---|---|---|
| *nachos* ... with cheese | 100g | 1280 | 306 |
| *nectarines* ... raw ... 1 av | 80g | 115 | 27 |
| *noodles* ... egg ... boiled | 100g | 500 | 119 |
| dried ... uncooked ... all types | 100g | 1540 | 367 |
| *nut meat* see *meat substitutes* | | | |
| *nuts* see individual types of nuts; *snack foods* | | | |
| *oat bran* see *breakfast cereals* | | | |
| *oatmeal/oats* see *breakfast cereals* | | | |
| *octopus* see *calamari* | | | |
| *offal* see *beef*; *lamb*; *veal* | | | |
| *oils* ... av all types | 100g | 3700 | 881 |
| 1 tbsp | 12g | 445 | 106 |
| *okra* ... boiled ... 10 pods | 100g | 95 | 23 |
| raw ... 10 pods | 111g | 95 | 23 |
| *olive oil* | 100g | 3700 | 881 |
| *olives* ... black | 100g | 830 | 198 |
| green ... pickled | 100g | 535 | 127 |
| Always Fresh ... black | 100g | 850 | 203 |
| green | 100g | 535 | 128 |
| kalamata | 100g | 580 | 138 |
| stuffed | 100g | 535 | 128 |
| *omelette* ... chicken (Chinese) | 100g | 895 | 213 |
| Lebanese | 100g | 710 | 169 |
| plain | 100g | 1040 | 248 |
| prawn (Chinese) | 100g | 765 | 182 |
| *onions* ... dried/flakes ... Dewcrisp ... easy-serve dried chopped | 100g | 205 | 49 |
| fried ... average type | 100g | 1425 | 339 |
| pickled ... 5 small | 50g | 65 | 15 |
| Always Fresh ... sweet-and-sour/home-style | 100g | 280 | 67 |
| Edgell-Birdseye ... chopped | 100g | 145 | 35 |
| McCain | 100g | 295 | 70 |

| | MASS | KJ | CAL |
|---|---|---|---|
| *onions, brown* ... boiled ... 1 cup chopped | 220g | 250 | 60 |
| raw ... 1 | 98g | 100 | 24 |
| *onions, spring* ... raw ... 1 | 14g | 15 | 4 |
| *onions, white* ... boiled ... 1 | 70g | 85 | 20 |
| raw ... 1 cup chopped | 125g | 140 | 33 |
| *orange juice* see *fruit juices* | | | |
| *orange peel, candied* | 100g | 1325 | 310 |
| *orange ruff* see *ruff, tommy/orange* | | | |
| *oranges* ... fresh ... raw ... 1 av | 165g | 190 | 45 |
| navel ... 1 av | 205g | 255 | 61 |
| valencia ... 1 av | 225g | 245 | 58 |
| *oriental beef with vegetable and rice* ... Findus Lean Cuisine ... 1 sv | 245g | 1090 | 260 |
| *osso bucco (Italian)* | 100g | 805 | 192 |
| *ouzo* see *spirits* | | | |
| *Ovaltine* ... powder ... 2 tsp | 10g | 160 | 38 |
| see also *milk, flavoured* | | | |
| *oysters* ... fresh ... 1 dozen | 59g | 180 | 43 |
| fried in butter | 100g | 1000 | 238 |
| smoked ... canned in oil ... drained ... 5 | 30g | 260 | 62 |
| Admiral | 100g | 850 | 203 |
| John West | 100g | 950 | 226 |
| *pad thai (Thai)* | 100g | 860 | 205 |
| *paella* ... Vesta ... 1 pkt made up ... 2 svs | | 2665 | 634 |
| *pancake mix* ... White Wings | 100g | 810 | 193 |
| *pancakes* ... plain ... fresh-cooked ... 16 cm diam ... 1 | 80g | 990 | 236 |
| *pandanus* | 100g | 330 | 79 |
| *papaya* see *pawpaw* | | | |
| *pappadums* ... raw | 100g | 1155 | 275 |
| *parsley, common* ... raw ... 10 sprigs | 10g | 5 | 1 |
| *parsely, continental* ... raw ... 1 tbsp chopped | 5g | 5 | 1 |

| | MASS | KJ | CAL |
|---|---|---|---|
| *parsnip* ... boiled ... 1 cup chopped | 150g | 310 | 74 |
| *partridge* ... roasted ... meat only | 100g | 890 | 212 |
| *passionfruit* ... raw ... flesh only ... 1 av | 21g | 40 | 10 |
| *pasta* ... dried ... uncooked | 100g | 1540 | 367 |
| egg ... boiled | 100g | 547 | 130 |
| spinach ... boiled | 100g | 542 | 129 |
| white ... boiled | 100g | 497 | 118 |
| wholemeal ... boiled | 100g | 435 | 104 |
| see also specific types, e.g. *macaroni* | | | |
| *pasta and sauce* ... Continental ... 1 pkt made up ... | | | |
| chicken curry ... 4 svs | | 2530 | 604 |
| fettucini verdi ... 4 svs | | 1295 | 309 |
| pumpkin with wholemeal pasta ... 4 svs | | 1905 | 455 |
| sour cream and mushroom ... 4 svs | | 2515 | 599 |
| tomato and onion ... 4 svs | | 2400 | 573 |
| *pasticcio (Greek)* | 100g | 645 | 154 |

## Curried Parsnip Soup

*1 teaspoon oil*
*450 g peeled and sliced parsnips*
*1 onion, chopped*
*1 level teaspoon curry powder*
*850 ml water*
*1 vegetable stock cube*
*1 level teaspoon mango chutney*
*salt and pepper to taste*
*25 g skim milk powder*
*1 level teaspoon chopped fresh coriander (optional)*

Heat oil in a large non-stick pan. Add parsnips and onion, cover and cook gently for 5 minutes. Stir in curry powder and cook for another minute. Add water, crumbled stock cube, chutney and seasoning. Bring to the boil and then simmer, covered, for 30 minutes. Remove from heat and blend until smooth. Mix milk powder with 2 tablespoons of water and stir into soup. Reheat gently. Garnish with chopped coriander to serve. Serves 4 at 525 kJ (125 cal) per portion.

| | MASS | KJ | CAL |
|---|---|---|---|
| *pasties* ... 1 | 165g | 1820 | 433 |
| Four' N Twenty/Wedgwood ... cornish pastie ... 1 | 170g | 1855 | 442 |
| Herbert Adams ... 1 | | 1795 | 427 |
| *pastry* ... biscuit crust ... raw | 100g | 2180 | 519 |
| choux ... baked | 100g | 1380 | 329 |
| filo ... baked | 100g | 1560 | 371 |
| raw | 100g | 1180 | 281 |
| flaky ... raw | 100g | 1695 | 404 |
| puff ... baked | 100g | 1875 | 446 |
| raw | 100g | 1515 | 361 |
| shortcrust ... baked | 100g | 2045 | 487 |
| raw | 100g | 1735 | 413 |
| Pampas ... home-style shortcrust pastry sheets ... raw | 100g | 1610 | 383 |
| pizza bases | 100g | 1100 | 262 |
| puff pastry sheets ... raw | 100g | 1470 | 350 |
| sweet shortcrust tart shells ... raw | 100g | 1660 | 395 |
| wholemeal pastry sheets ... raw | 100g | 1425 | 339 |
| *pastry, Danish* see *cakes and pastries* | | | |
| *pastry mix* ... Green's ... made up | 50g | 950 | 226 |
| White Wings ... wholemeal ... not made up | 100g | 365 | 87 |
| *pâté* ... chicken liver ... 1 tbsp | 20g | 105 | 25 |
| *pâté de fois* ... av all brands | 100g | 1240 | 295 |
| *pavlova* see *desserts and puddings* | | | |
| *pawpaw* ... canned | 100g | 275 | 65 |
| fresh ... flesh only ... 1 cup diced | 150g | 185 | 44 |
| glacé ... Winn | 100g | 1420 | 338 |
| *peaches* ... canned in artific. sweet. lliquid ... 1 cup slices | 250g | 260 | 62 |
| drained ... 1 cup slices | 210g | 220 | 52 |
| in pear juice ... 1 cup slices | 260g | 440 | 105 |
| drained ... 1 cup slices | 210g | 355 | 85 |
| in syrup ... 1/2 peach + 25ml syrup | 65g | 140 | 33 |

| | MASS | KJ | CAL |
|---|---|---|---|
| drained ... 1/2 peach | 40g | 85 | 20 |
| dried | 100g | 1130 | 269 |
| stewed ... with sugar | 100g | 630 | 150 |
| raw ... 1 peach | 155g | 185 | 44 |
| stewed ... with sugar | 100g | 395 | 94 |
| without sugar | 100g | 335 | 80 |
| SPC ... jelly fruit ... slices in mango jelly | 100g | 265 | 63 |
| slices in orange jelly | 100g | 255 | 61 |
| SPC Little Big Fruit ... fruit in syrup ... diced | 140g | 405 | 96 |
| Weight Watchers ... artific. sweet. | 100g | 125 | 30 |
| *peanut butter* see *dips and spreads* | | | |
| *peanut oil* | 100g | 3700 | 881 |
| *peanuts* ... choc-coated .. 1/4 cup | 30g | 705 | 168 |
| raw ... 30 | 25g | 590 | 140 |
| roasted ... 30 | 25g | 610 | 145 |
| see also *snack foods* | | | |
| *pear and peach quarters* ... Goulburn Valley ... in fruit juice | 100g | 180 | 43 |
| *pears* ... canned in artific. sweet. liquid ... 1/2 pear + 40 ml liquid | 95g | 105 | 25 |
| drained ... 1/2 pear | 55g | 60 | 14 |
| in pear juice ... drained ... 1/2 pear | 55g | 100 | 24 |
| in syrup ... drained ... 1/2 pear | 55g | 135 | 32 |
| dried | 100g | 1130 | 269 |
| stewed ... with sugar | 100g | 630 | 150 |

| | MASS | KJ | CAL |
|---|---|---|---|
| raw ... stewed ... with sugar | 100g | 385 | 92 |
| without sugar | 100g | 135 | 32 |
| Goulburn Valley ... in fruit juice | 100g | 180 | 43 |
| SPC ... artific. sweet. ... halves | 100g | 135 | 32 |
| fruit in syrup | 100g | 280 | 67 |
| just fruit (fruit in pear juice) ... halves | 100g | 180 | 43 |
| SPC Little Big Fruit (snak pak) ... in jelly | 140g | 405 | 96 |
| in juice ... diced | 140g | 285 | 68 |
| in syrup ... diced | 140g | 390 | 93 |
| Weight Watchers ... artific. sweet. ... halves | 100g | 135 | 32 |
| *pears, brown skin* ... raw ... 1 pear | 145g | 295 | 70 |
| *pears, Packhams Triumph* ... raw ... 1 pear | 235g | 465 | 111 |
| *pears, Williams/Bartlett/Bon Chretien* ... raw ... 1 pear | 155g | 275 | 65 |
| *pears, yellow-green skin* ... raw ... 1 pear | 205g | 390 | 93 |
| *peas, green* ... boiled ... 1 cup | 165g | 335 | 80 |
| canned ... drained ... 1 cup | 175g | 440 | 105 |
| dried ... boiled ... 1 cup | 135g | 260 | 62 |
| frozen ... boiled ... 1 cup | 160g | 335 | 80 |
| raw ... 1 cup | 145g | 360 | 86 |
| split ... boiled | 100g | 480 | 114 |
| dried | 100g | 1455 | 346 |
| Edgell-Birdseye | 100g | 305 | 73 |
| Farmland ... no added salt | 100g | 320 | 76 |
| Golden Circle | 100g | 290 | 69 |
| McCain | 100g | 310 | 74 |
| Watties | 100g | 270 | 64 |
| *pears, snow/sugar* ... boiled ... 10 pods | 30g | 45 | 11 |
| raw ... 10 pods | 33g | 45 | 11 |
| *pecan nuts* ... snack-size sv | 50g | 1440 | 343 |
| *penne* ... dried ... uncooked | 100g | 1540 | 367 |
| *pepino* ... raw ... flesh + seeds ... 1 av | 123g | 115 | 27 |
| *pepper* ... 1/2 tsp | 2g | 25 | 6 |

| | MASS | KJ | CAL |
|---|---|---|---|
| *pepperoni* see *luncheon meat: salami* | | | |
| ***peppers*** ... boiled ... drained ... 1 sv | 50g | 40 | 10 |
| immature, green (hot chilli) ... raw | 100g | 155 | 37 |
| mature, red, inc seeds ... raw | 100g | 390 | 93 |
| ***perch*** ... raw | 100g | 325 | 77 |
| ***perch, northern pearl*** ... baked | 100g | 410 | 98 |
| grilled | 100g | 400 | 95 |
| poached | 100g | 395 | 94 |
| raw | 100g | 320 | 76 |
| smoked | 100g | 335 | 80 |
| steamed | 100g | 350 | 83 |
| ***persimmon*** ... raw ... flesh only ... 1 | 76g | 210 | 50 |
| ***pheasant*** ... roasted ... flesh only | 100g | 890 | 212 |
| inc bone | 100g | 565 | 135 |
| ***pickle*** | 100g | 640 | 152 |
| dill ... 1 large | 100g | 45 | 11 |
| gherkin ... 2 large | 100g | 57 | 14 |
| mustard ... sour | 20g | 25 | 6 |
| sweet | 20g | 95 | 23 |

| | MASS | KJ | CAL |
|---|---|---|---|
| Masterfoods ... sweet mustard | 5g | 15 | 4 |
| tomato | 5g | 20 | 5 |
| *pickle chow* ... sour | 100g | 120 | 29 |
| sweet | 100g | 485 | 115 |
| *pies, savoury* ... beef ... family-size ... 1/4 | 120g | 1130 | 269 |
| individual-size ... 1 | 190g | 1800 | 429 |
| party-size ... 1 | 40g | 465 | 111 |
| fish | 100g | 540 | 129 |
| pork ... 1 | 180g | 2815 | 670 |
| spinach (Lebanese) | 100g | 1215 | 289 |
| steak and kidney ... 1 | 180g | 2430 | 579 |
| Farmland ... meat ... 1 | 90g | 1030 | 245 |
| Four'N Twenty Pies ... meat ... 1 | 170g | 1750 | 417 |
| party pie ... 1 | 50g | 555 | 132 |
| Herbert Adams ... beef and mushroom | 100g | 985 | 235 |
| beefsteak | 175g | 1710 | 407 |
| party pies | 100g | 1050 | 250 |
| chicken ... party pies | 100g | 1010 | 240 |
| meat/steak and kidney | 100g | 1040 | 248 |
| steak and vegetable | 100g | 1785 | 425 |
| *pies, sweet* ... apple ... fresh-baked ... whole | 735g | 7350 | 1750 |
| fruit ... 1 small | 150g | 2330 | 555 |
| fruit mince | 100g | 1140 | 271 |
| fruit pie with pastry top | 100g | 755 | 180 |
| lemon meringue | 100g | 1360 | 324 |
| pecan | 100g | 1755 | 418 |
| pumpkin | 100g | 885 | 211 |
| Edgell-Birdseye ... av fruit pies | 100g | 1000 | 238 |
| snack pies ... | | | |
| little apple/passionfruit | 100g | 875 | 208 |
| little custard and apple | 100g | 900 | 214 |
| little spicy apple | 100g | 880 | 210 |

| | MASS | KJ | CAL |
|---|---|---|---|
| Farmland ... apple ... frozen | 100g | 1005 | 239 |
| Sara Lee ... av fruit pies ... 1/8 pie | 75g | 865 | 206 |
| hi-pies ... apple ... 1/8 pie | 100g | 980 | 233 |
| blackberry/apricot ... 1/8 pie | 100g | 1085 | 258 |
| ***pigeon/squab*** ... roasted | 100g | 960 | 229 |
| ***pike*** ... raw | 100g | 375 | 89 |
| ***pilchards*** ... canned in tomato sauce | 100g | 530 | 126 |
| John West ... in tomato sauce | 100g | 595 | 142 |
| ***pimientos*** ... canned ... solids + liquid ... 3 medium | 100g | 115 | 27 |
| ***pine nuts/kernels*** ... raw ... 1 tbsp | 14g | 350 | 83 |
| ***pineapple*** ... canned in heavy syrup ... 1 cup pieces | 270g | 965 | 230 |
| drained ... 1 cup pieces | 200g | 700 | 167 |
| in pineapple juice ... drained ... 1 slice | 40g | 75 | 18 |
| glacé ... 1 ring | 42g | 555 | 132 |
| raw ... flesh only ... 1 slice | 110g | 175 | 42 |
| Golden Circle ... slices/pieces/crush | 100g | 345 | 82 |
| slices/pieces ... unsweetened | 100g | 85 | 44 |
| Green's ... slices ... in natural juice | 100g | 165 | 39 |
| ***pineapple juice*** see ***fruit juices*** | | | |
| ***pistachio nuts*** ... shelled ... 25 | 15g | 375 | 89 |
| ***pizza*** ... commercial ... ham and pineapple ... 1/2 | 260g | 2535 | 604 |
| supreme ... 1/4 | 205g | 1960 | 467 |
| Edgell-Birdseye ... ham and pineapple | 100g | 1025 | 244 |
| pizza supreme | 100g | 965 | 230 |
| Farmland ... ham and pineapple | 100g | 910 | 217 |
| supreme | 100g | 830 | 198 |
| McCain ... cheese and bacon | 500g | 4900 | 1167 |
| ham and pineapple | 500g | 4580 | 1090 |
| microwave ham and pineapple | 270g | 2225 | 530 |
| microwave supreme | 270g | 2450 | 583 |
| singles ham and pineapple | 450g | 3780 | 900 |
| sub ham and pineapple | 350g | 2775 | 661 |

| | MASS | KJ | CAL |
|---|---|---|---|
| sub supreme | 350g | 2900 | 690 |
| supreme | 500g | 4150 | 988 |
| see also *Pizza Hut* | | | |
| *Pizza Hut* ... cavatini ... 1 sv | 400g | 1470 | 350 |
| Pan Pizza ... cheese ... 2 slices, av | 210g | 2185 | 520 |
| Hawaiin ... 2 slices, av | 250g | 2450 | 583 |
| super supreme ... 2 slices, av | 286g | 2845 | 677 |
| supreme ... 2 slices, av | 272g | 2850 | 678 |
| Thin 'n Crispy ... cheese ... 2 slices, av | 158g | 1815 | 432 |
| Hawaiin ... 2 slices, av | 198g | 2030 | 483 |
| super supreme ... 2 slices, av | 233g | 2425 | 577 |
| supreme ... 2 slices, av | 228g | 2395 | 570 |
| prawn cocktail | 100g | 510 | 121 |
| spaghetti | 100g | 430 | 102 |
| spaghetti and sauce with meat ... 1 entrée sv | 175g | 745 | 177 |
| *plaice* ... crumbed, fried | 100g | 950 | 226 |
| fried in batter | 100g | 1165 | 277 |
| steamed ... with bones + skin | 100g | 210 | 50 |
| without bones | 100g | 390 | 93 |
| *plantain* ... boiled | 100g | 520 | 124 |
| green ... raw | 100g | 475 | 113 |
| ripe ... fried | 100g | 1125 | 268 |

| | MASS | KJ | CAL |
|---|---|---|---|
| *plums* ... fresh ... raw ... 1 av | 110g | 155 | 37 |
| stewed ... with sugar | 100g | 295 | 70 |
| without sugar | 100g | 135 | 52 |
| red-fleshed/damson ... raw ... 1 av | 77g | 120 | 29 |
| stewed ... with sugar | 100g | 295 | 70 |
| wiithout sugar | 100g | 135 | 32 |
| yellow-fleshed ... raw ... 1 av | 70g | 85 | 20 |
| *polenta* ... dry | 100g | 2074 | 494 |
| The Old Grain Mill | 100g | 1485 | 354 |
| *pomegranates* ... fresh ... raw | 100g | 300 | 71 |
| *popcorn* see *snack foods* | | | |
| *pork* | | | |
| *barbecued (Chinese)* | 100g | 995 | 237 |
| *boneless, average cut* ... cooked ... lean ... 1 cup diced | 190g | 1350 | 321 |
| lean+fat ... 1 cup diced | 181g | 2255 | 537 |
| *butterfly steak* ... grilled ... lean ... 1 av | 100g | 675 | 161 |
| lean+fat ... 1 av | 120g | 1310 | 312 |
| *forequarter chops* ... grilled ... lean ... 1 av | 103g | 780 | 186 |
| lean+fat ... 1 av | 144g | 2070 | 493 |
| *leg* ... baked/roast ... lean ... 1 boneless slice | 31g | 225 | 54 |
| lean+fat ... 1 boneless slice | 45g | 635 | 151 |
| *leg steak* ... grilled ... lean ... 1 av | 82g | 535 | 127 |
| lean+fat ... 1 av | 85g | 615 | 146 |
| *medallion steak* ... grilled ... lean ... 1 av | 74g | 580 | 138 |
| lean+fat ... 1 av | 95g | 1230 | 293 |
| *mid-loin* chop ... grilled ... lean ... 1 av | 68g | 495 | 118 |
| lean+fat ... 1 av | 101g | 1535 | 365 |
| *mince* ... cooked | 100g | 1055 | 251 |
| *trotters and tails* ... boiled | 100g | 1160 | 276 |
| *pork buns* | 100g | 1116 | 266 |
| *pork chop suey (Chinese)* | 100g | 510 | 121 |
| *pork in plum sauce (Chinese)* | 100g | 1025 | 244 |

| | MASS | KJ | CAL |
|---|---|---|---|
| *pork pie* see *pies, savoury* | | | |
| *pork rib fingers* ... McCain | 310g | 1790 | 426 |
| *pork spare ribs in black-bean sauce (Chinese)* | 100g | 835 | 199 |
| *porridge* see *breakfast cereals* | | | |
| *port* see *wines, fortified* | | | |
| *potato, baked* ... topped with cheese and bacon | 100g | 630 | 151 |
| topped with sour cream and chives | 100g | 545 | 130 |
| *potato cakes* see *potato scallops* | | | |
| *potato chips* ... commercial ... 1 cup | 95g | 975 | 232 |
| French fries ... 1 cup | | 1135 | 270 |
| home-made ... 10 chips | 45g | 360 | 86 |
| Edgell-Birdseye ... crinkle-cut chips | 100g | 600 | 143 |
| home-style chips/oven fries | 100g | 530 | 126 |
| shoestring chips | 100g | 775 | 185 |
| straight-cut chips ... 10mm | 100g | 590 | 140 |
| McCain ... superfries | 100g | 545 | 130 |
| *potato crisps* see *snack foods* | | | |
| *potato gems* ... Edgell-Birdseye | 100g | 955 | 227 |
| *potato scallops* ... deep-fried ... 1 av | 95g | 1285 | 306 |
| *potatoes* ... dehydrated ... made up | 100g | 390 | 93 |
| not made up | 100g | 1500 | 357 |
| Edgell-Birdseye ... potato whip/with onion ... not made up | 100g | 1505 | 358 |
| Continental ... Deb ... plain/with onion ...1 pkt made up | | 1950 | 465 |
| mashed ... + milk + butter | 100g | 395 | 94 |
| new ... canned ... drained ... 5 av | 175g | 415 | 99 |
| peeled ... boiled ... 1 av | 60g | 160 | 38 |

Plan for proper meals and organise low-kilojoule snacks ahead of time in case you feel tempted.

| | MASS | KJ | CAL |
|---|---|---|---|
| Admiral ... whole new/with mint | 100g | 225 | 54 |
| SPC ... new | 100g | 170 | 40 |
| pale-skinned ... baked ... flesh only (not skin) ... | | | |
| 1 med | 100g | 305 | 73 |
| mashed ... 1 cup | 245g | 685 | 163 |
| peeled ... boiled ... 1 med | 100g | 270 | 64 |
| roasted ... 2 med halves | 85g | 380 | 90 |
| scalloped | 100g | 435 | 104 |
| Edgell-Birdseye ... small whole potatoes | 100g | 265 | 63 |
| tiny taters | 100g | 240 | 57 |
| McCain ... potato patties | 100g | 790 | 188 |
| ***poultry*** see individual types | | | |
| ***prawn chow mein (Chinese)*** | 100g | 605 | 144 |
| ***prawn cocktail*** ... with lettuce + sauce ... 1 sv | 119g | 605 | 144 |
| ***prawn curry*** ... Vesta ... 1 pkt made up ... 2 svs | | 2840 | 679 |
| ***prawn cutlets (Chinese)*** | 100g | 1100 | 262 |
| *prawn satay (Chinese)* | 100g | 590 | 140 |
| ***prawn soup*** see ***soups*** | | | |
| ***prawns*** ... boiled ... with shell | 100g | 170 | 40 |
| without shell | 100g | 450 | 107 |
| canned ... drained solids | 100g | 505 | 120 |
| solids + fluids | 100g | 350 | 83 |
| crumbed, fried | 100g | 1015 | 242 |
| dried | 100g | 1515 | 361 |
| fresh ... raw | 100g | 365 | 87 |
| fried in batter | 100g | 940 | 224 |
| Admiral ... peeled | 100g | 330 | 79 |
| Edgell-Birdseye ... cooked | 100g | 380 | 90 |
| crumbed | 100g | 585 | 139 |
| cutlets | 100g | 565 | 135 |
| Frionor ... crumbed cutlets | 100g | 375 | 89 |
| see also ***garlic prawns*** | | | |

| | MASS | KJ | CAL |
|---|---|---|---|
| *prawns, king* ... cooked ... shelled ... 5 | 80g | 350 | 83 |
| *prawns, school* ... cooked ... shelled ... 1 cup | 135g | 430 | 102 |
| *prawns, sweet-and-sour (Chinese)* | 100g | 1600 | 381 |
| *prickly pear* ... raw ... flesh only ... 1 av | 86g | 145 | 35 |
| *prosciutto* see *ham* | | | |
| *prunes* ... dessert | 100g | 780 | 186 |
| dried... | 100g | 1065 | 254 |
| stewed ... with sugar | 100g | 740 | 176 |
| without sugar | 100g | 500 | 119 |
| *puddings* see *desserts and puddings* | | | |
| *pumello* | 100g | 200 | 48 |
| *pumpernickel* see ***bread:** loaves* | | | |
| *pumpkin* ... average type ... boiled ... 1 cup pieces | 170g | 300 | 71 |
| butternut ... boiled | 100g | 194 | 46 |
| mashed ... 1 cup | 245g | 475 | 113 |
| golden nugget ... boiled ... 1/2 | 130g | 165 | 39 |
| Queensland blue ... boiled ... 1 cup pieces | 170g | 350 | 83 |
| Edgell-Birdseye | 100g | 190 | 45 |
| *pumpkin scones* see *scones* | | | |
| *pumpkin soup* see *soups* | | | |
| *quail* ... roasted ... meat only | 100g | 728 | 173 |
| *quiche* ... lorraine ... 1 sv | 150g | 2435 | 580 |

| | MASS | KJ | CAL |
|---|---|---|---|
| Sara Lee ... light ... ham, tomato, fetta/spinach and ricotta | 100g | 665 | 159 |
| lorraine ... 1/6 | 100g | 1115 | 265 |
| vegetable ... 1/6 | 100g | 980 | 233 |
| *quinces* ... canned | 100g | 350 | 83 |
| raw ... flesh only ... 1 av | 219g | 440 | 105 |
| stewed with sugar | 100g | 350 | 83 |
| *rabbit* ... baked | 100g | 855 | 204 |
| stewed | 100g | 785 | 187 |
| *radish* ... oriental ... raw ... 1 cup sliced | 95g | 70 | 17 |
| red ... raw ... 1 av | 15g | 10 | 2 |
| white ... raw | 60g | 60 | 14 |
| *raisin bread* see *bread* | | | |
| *raisins* ... dried | 30g | 350 | 83 |
| *rambutan* ... 1 av | 14g | 15 | 4 |
| *raspberries* ... canned in juice | 100g | 200 | 48 |
| in syrup | 100g | 425 | 101 |
| fresh | 100g | 240 | 57 |
| stewed ... with sugar | 100g | 290 | 69 |
| without sugar | 100g | 200 | 48 |
| John West ... in syrup | 100g | 370 | 88 |
| *ratatouille* ...SPC | 100g | 105 | 25 |
| *ravioli* | 100g | 565 | 135 |
| Kraft | 100g | 490 | 115 |
| *ravioli Bolognese* ... Griff's | 100g | 1095 | 261 |
| Heinz | 100g | 565 | 135 |
| *ravioli in Bolognese sauce* ... La Deliziosa ... 1 sv | 250g | 1800 | 429 |
| *red emperor* ... baked | 100g | 410 | 98 |
| grilled | 100g | 400 | 95 |
| poached | 100g | 395 | 94 |
| raw | 100g | 320 | 76 |

| | MASS | KJ | CAL |
|---|---|---|---|
| plain/wholemeal | 100g | 1725 | 413 |
| ***rye bread*** see ***bread:*** *loaves* | | | |
| ***rye flour*** see ***flour, rye*** | | | |
| ***rye meal*** | 100g | 1400 | 333 |
| ***saccharin*** see ***sugar substitutes*** | | | |
| ***safflower oil*** | 100g | 3700 | 881 |
| ***sago*** ... dry | 100g | 1500 | 357 |
| ***salad dressing*** ... *blue cheese* ...Bertolli | 100g | 1880 | 448 |
| Hain ... low-energy/no oil | 100g | 305 | 73 |
| *coleslaw* ... Best Foods ... low-energy/no oil | 100g | 140 | 33 |
| ETA | 100g | 1165 | 277 |
| Fountain ... Salad Magic ... no cholesterol | 100ml | 685 | 163 |
| Kraft | 100g | 1700 | 405 |
| light | 100g | 225 | 54 |
| Praise | 100g | 1735 | 413 |
| *French (vinaigrette)* ... av all brands | 100g | 1700 | 405 |
| Best Foods ... low-energy/no oil | 100g | 35 | 8 |
| Fountain ... Salad Magic | 100ml | 145 | 35 |
| Hain ... creamy | 100g | 1660 | 395 |
| oil and vinegar | 100g | 1385 | 330 |
| Kraft | 100g | 925 | 220 |
| light | 100g | 155 | 37 |
| Praise | 100g | 1160 | 276 |
| *herb and garlic* ... Fountain ... Salad Magic ... no oil | 100ml | 165 | 39 |
| Hain ... low-energy/no oil | 100g | 20 | 5 |
| Kraft | 100g | 1105 | 263 |

Try combining half a crushed clove of garlic with 3 tablespoons of apple juice and 1 tablespoon of red wine vinegar for a diet-friendly dressing providing only 20 kJ (5 cal) for four servings. Leave the mixture for 30 minutes before straining and discarding the garlic if desired.

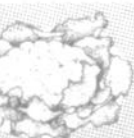

| | MASS | KJ | CAL |
|---|---|---|---|
| Salad Magic ... low-energy/no oil | 100g | 160 | 38 |
| *Italian* ... Best Foods ... low-energy/no oil | 100g | 30 | 7 |
| Fountain ... Salad Magic ... no oil | 100ml | 270 | 64 |
| Hain | 100g | 1970 | 469 |
| Kraft | 100g | 1205 | 287 |
| light | 100g | 35 | 8 |
| Praise | 100g | 1050 | 250 |
| *Miracle Whip* ... Kraft | 100g | 2100 | 500 |
| *Thousand Island* ... Hain | 100g | 1430 | 340 |
| low-energy/no oil | 100g | 220 | 52 |
| Kraft | 100g | 1605 | 382 |
| ***salads*** ... bean ... commercial ... 1 cup | 210g | 1160 | 276 |
| coleslaw ... 1 cup | 200g | 795 | 189 |
| pasta | 100g | 1590 | 379 |
| potato ... canned ... 1 cup | 180g | 900 | 214 |
| commercial ... 1 cup | 180g | 815 | 194 |
| rice | 100g | 2175 | 518 |
| tabouli (Lebanese) | 100g | 610 | 145 |
| waldorf | 100g | 3300 | 786 |
| Green's ... prawn | 100g | 380 | 90 |
| Heinz ... garden bean | 100g | 335 | 80 |
| Hawaiian | 100g | 490 | 117 |
| potato ... varieties | 100g | 390 | 93 |
| traditional veg | 100g | 300 | 71 |
| Masterfoods ... bean 'n' corn | 100g | 410 | 98 |
| mixed beans | 100g | 225 | 54 |
| potato/rice/mixed veg | 100g | 480 | 114 |
| tropical | 100g | 360 | 86 |
| zucchini | 100g | 170 | 40 |
| ***salami*** see ***luncheon meat*** | | | |
| ***salmon*** ... baked | 100g | 760 | 181 |
| canned in brine ... pink ... drained ... 1 cup | 210g | 1290 | 307 |

| | MASS | KJ | CAL |
|---|---|---|---|
| red ... drained ... 1 cup | 210g | 1710 | 407 |
| raw | 100g | 905 | 215 |
| smoked ... 1 slice | 25g | 140 | 33 |
| steamed | 100g | 825 | 196 |
| inc bones + skin | 100g | 665 | 158 |
| Atlantic salmon ... raw | 100g | 755 | 180 |
| Australian salmon ... canned in brine ... drained ... 1 cup | 210g | 1530 | 364 |
| fried | 100g | 845 | 201 |
| raw | 100g | 475 | 113 |
| pink salmon ... Farmland ... no added salt | 100g | 620 | 148 |
| Green's | 100g | 590 | 140 |
| John West | 100g | 650 | 155 |
| red salmon ... Farmland ... no added salt | 100g | 680 | 162 |
| John West | 100g | 705 | 168 |
| medium red | 100g | 670 | 160 |
| ***salt, table*** | 100g | 0 | 0 |
| ***saltimbocca (Italian)*** | 100g | 915 | 218 |
| ***samosas (stuffed with minced lamb)*** | 100g | 2390 | 569 |
| ***sandwiches*** ... (two slices bread, two tsp butter; all salad includes 1 tsp mayonnaise) | | | |

### Salmon and Pasta Salad

*30 g large uncooked macaroni*
*1 45 g egg, hard boiled*
*2 lettuce leaves, torn*
*60 g red salmon, flaked*
*1 Lebanese cucumber or ½ regular cucumber, sliced*
*¼ teaspoon dried thyme*
*1 tablespoon oil-free French dressing*

Cook macaroni in boiling salted water. Drain and set aside. Cool the egg, shell and quarter and add to lettuce with cucumber and salmon. Toss with macaroni to combine. Whisk the thyme with French dressing and pour over salad, tossing gently before serving immediately. Serves 1 at 1290 kJ (310 cal).

| | MASS | KJ | CAL |
|---|---|---|---|
| beef German/Strasbourg ... 1 | | 1295 | 308 |
| cheese ... grated tasty ... 1 | | 1230 | 293 |
| processed slice ... 1 | | 1170 | 279 |
| cheese + salad ... grated tasty ... 1 | | 1430 | 340 |
| processed slice ... 1 | | 1370 | 326 |
| chicken + salad ... 1 | | 1350 | 321 |
| cream cheese + dried apricots + nuts ... 1 | | 1805 | 430 |
| egg + lettuce ... 1 | | 1295 | 308 |
| ham ... (1 slice) ... 1 | | 1110 | 264 |
| ham + salad ... 1 | | 1310 | 312 |
| ham, salad + cheese ... 1 | | 1580 | 376 |
| open salad on rye ... 1 | | 1270 | 302 |
| pocket pita (buttered) + salad ... 1 | | 1520 | 362 |
| roast beef/pork (1 slice) ... 1 | | 1160 | 276 |
| salad roll ... 1 | | 1100 | 262 |
| salad without meat ... 1 | | 1100 | 262 |
| tomato ... 1 | | 940 | 224 |
| tuna + salad ... 1 | | 1240 | 295 |
| vegemite ... 1 | | 900 | 214 |
| *Sanitarium meat analogues* see *meat substitutes* | | | |
| *sardines* ... canned ... in brine | 100g | 820 | 195 |
| in oil | 100g | 1285 | 306 |
| drained ... 5 small | 75g | 715 | 170 |
| in tomato sauce | 100g | 740 | 176 |
| raw | 100g | 563 | 134 |
| Admiral ... in oil | 100g | 1185 | 283 |
| John West ... scottish ... in oil | 100g | 835 | 199 |
| in tomato | 100g | 905 | 215 |
| King Oscar ... oil pack ... drained | 85g | 1090 | 260 |
| tomato pack/mustard pack | 105g | 1005 | 239 |
| *sauces, savoury* | | | |
| *barbecue* | 20ml | 75 | 18 |

| | MASS | KJ | CAL |
|---|---|---|---|
| *bearnaise* ... prepared with milk+butter | 20ml | 230 | 55 |
| *Bolognese* | 20ml | 115 | 27 |
| dried mix | 20g | 325 | 77 |
| *brown onion* ... dried mix | 20g | 310 | 74 |
| *cheese* | 20ml | 150 | 36 |
| *chilli* ... 1 tbsp | 20ml | 20 | 5 |
| *chilli tomato* | 20ml | 85 | 20 |
| *curry* ... dried mix | 20g | 385 | 92 |
| *fish* | 20ml | 50 | 12 |
| *hollandaise* ... dried mix reconst. with water | 20ml | 465 | 111 |
| using milk + butter/butterfat | 20ml | 230 | 55 |
| *meat* | 20ml | 215 | 51 |
| *mushroom* ... dried mix | 20ml | 300 | 71 |
| *oyster* | 20ml | 70 | 17 |
| *parsley* | 20ml | 155 | 37 |
| *soya* | 20ml | 55 | 13 |
| *sweet-and-sour* | 20ml | 110 | 26 |
| *tartare* | 20ml | 420 | 100 |
| *tomato* ... av all brands | 20ml | 75 | 18 |
| no added salt ... White Crow | 20ml | 85 | 20 |
| *white* | 20ml | 135 | 32 |
| dried mix | 20g | 335 | 80 |
| *worcestershire* | 20ml | 65 | 15 |

| | MASS | KJ | CAL |
|---|---|---|---|
| *Cornwell's* ... mint/chick mint/tomato with herb and onion | 20ml | 75 | 18 |
| plum | 20ml | 115 | 27 |
| soy | 20ml | 45 | 11 |
| steak/worcestershire/teriyaki/Lancashire relish | 20ml | 100 | 24 |
| sweet-and-sour | 20ml | 170 | 40 |
| white wine | 20ml | 120 | 29 |
| *Dolmio* ... original | 100g | 165 | 39 |
| with capsicum/garden vegetables/ mushroom | 100g | 195 | 46 |
| with cheese | 100g | 255 | 61 |
| tomato, onion and garlic | 100g | 180 | 43 |
| *ETA* ... barbeque | 20ml | 150 | 36 |
| *Farmland* ... soy | 20ml | 60 | 14 |
| spicy red/mustard | 20ml | 110 | 26 |
| *Fountain* ... fruit chutney | 30ml | 260 | 62 |
| mild chilli | 30ml | 50 | 12 |
| mint | 30ml | 100 | 24 |
| satay | 30ml | 275 | 65 |
| sweet and sour | 30ml | 560 | 133 |
| *Gravox* ... brown onion sauce mix ... made up | 100ml | 135. | 32 |
| roast meat sauce mix/parsley sauce mix ... not made up | 100ml | 285 | 68 |
| white sauce mix ... not made up | 100ml | 285 | 68 |
| *Heinz* ... tomato ketchup | 20ml | 100 | 24 |
| tomato sauce | 20ml | 100 | 24 |
| *Kraft* ... tartare ... 1 tbsp | 20ml | 270 | 64 |
| *Masterfoods* ... chilli | 20ml | 60 | 14 |
| seafood cocktail | 20ml | 170 | 40 |

Eating five small meals a day stimulates the body's metabolism and helps burn up extra kilojoules. Munching between meals is only a problem if you snack on biscuits, sweets, pastries, chocolate and other foods high in fat or sugar.

| | MASS | KJ | CAL |
|---|---|---|---|
| soy | 20ml | 25 | 6 |
| sweet-and-sour | 20ml | 140 | 33 |
| tartare | 20ml | 490 | 117 |
| *Paul Newman's* ... marinara spaghetti/mushroom spaghetti | 100g | 235 | 56 |
| sockarooni spaghetti | 100g | 185 | 44 |
| *Raguletto* ... Basilico pasta | 100g | 120 | 28 |
| Calabrese pasta | 100g | 125 | 29 |
| Capri pasta | 100g | 190 | 45 |
| Sicilian pasta | 100g | 195 | 46 |
| *White Wings* ... bechamel sauce mix | 20ml | 10 | 2 |
| dianne sauce mix | 20ml | 60 | 14 |
| pepper sauce mix | 20ml | 35 | 8 |
| see also ***gravy*** | | | |
| ***sauces, sweet*** ... apple | 20ml | 70 | 17 |
| chocolate topping | 20ml | 163 | 39 |
| cranberry ... canned ... sweetened | 20ml | 125 | 30 |
| fruit flavours, av | 20ml | 150 | 35 |
| low-joule topping ... Cottees | 20ml | 35 | 8 |
| Weight Watchers | 20ml | 25 | 6 |
| maple syrup | 20ml | 50 | 12 |
| topping ... flavoured | 20ml | 115 | 27 |
| white | 20ml | 155 | 37 |
| ***sauerkraut*** ... canned | 100g | 80 | 19 |
| Edgell-Birdseye | 100g | 95 | 23 |
| ***sausage rolls*** ... av commercial brands ... 1 | 130g | 1560 | 371 |
| party size ... 1 | 40g | 505 | 120 |
| Edgell-Birdseye | 100g | 1065 | 254 |
| Four 'N Twenty/Wedgwood ... jumbo | 120g | 1485 | 354 |
| large | 80g | 990 | 236 |
| small | 40g | 495 | 118 |
| Herbert Adams ... party | 100g | 1185 | 282 |
| supa | 100g | 1090 | 260 |

| | MASS | KJ | CAL |
|---|---|---|---|
| *sausages* ... beef ... fried ... 2 | 120g | 1350 | 321 |
| grilled ... 2 | 120g | 1550 | 369 |
| liver | 100g | 1115 | 265 |
| pork ... fried ... 2 | 120g | 1580 | 376 |
| grilled ... 2 | 120g | 1620 | 386 |
| Lebanese | 100g | 1195 | 285 |
| *saveloys* see *frankfurters* | | | |
| *savoury mince* ... canned ... av all brands | 100g | 755 | 180 |
| *savoury noodles* ... Tandaco ... one-pan dinner ... 1/4 pkt | 50g | 675 | 161 |
| *scallops* ... cooked ... 1 cup | 160g | 705 | 168 |
| raw ... 5 | 65g | 145 | 35 |
| Edgell-Birdseye ... crumbed | 100g | 585 | 139 |
| Frionor ... crumbed | 100g | 375 | 89 |
| *scampi* ... fried | 100g | 1015 | 242 |
| *schnitzel* see *chicken schnitzel*; *veal schnitzel* | | | |
| *scone mix* ... White Wings ... plain | 100g | 255 | 61 |
| wholemeal | 100g | 230 | 55 |
| *scones* ... 1 | 36g | 380 | 90 |
| cheese | 100g | 1320 | 314 |
| fruit | 100g | 1335 | 318 |
| plain ... commercial ... 1 | 50g | 565 | 135 |
| home-made ... 1 | 40g | 580 | 138 |
| pumpkin | 100g | 1460 | 348 |

| | MASS | KJ | CAL |
|---|---|---|---|
| sultana | 100g | 1550 | 369 |
| wholemeal | 100g | 1480 | 352 |
| wholemeal | 100g | 1370 | 326 |
| *scotch eggs* | 100g | 1160 | 276 |
| *sea perch* ... fried | 100g | 905 | 215 |
| steamed | 100g | 385 | 92 |
| *seafood* ... Admiral ... seafood mix | 100g | 480 | 114 |
| I & J ... Chinese sea shanties | 100g | 995 | 237 |
| sea cakes | 100g | 535 | 127 |
| sea shanties | 100g | 955 | 227 |
| see also individual types e.g. *crab* | | | |
| *seakale* see *silver beet* | | | |
| *seasoned coating mix* ... Tandaco ... chicken | 100g | 1265 | 301 |
| fish/schnitzel | 100g | 1365 | 325 |
| southern fried chicken | 100g | 1390 | 331 |
| *seasonings* ... Continental ... hotpot base ... curry ... 1 pkt made up | | 1900 | 452 |
| French onion ... 1 pkt made up | | 1250 | 298 |
| mushroom ... 1 pkt made up | | 1420 | 338 |
| savoury ... 1 pkt made up | | 1360 | 324 |
| sweet and sour ... 1 pkt made up | | 2225 | 530 |
| tomato and noodle ... 1 pkt made up | | 1720 | 410 |
| tuna and noodle ... 1 pkt made up | | 2465 | 587 |

Be prepared to accept that you may occasionally break your diet. At these times aim to maintain a constant weight.

| | MASS | KJ | CAL |
|---|---|---|---|
| Kellogg's ... cornflake crumbs/seasoned | 100g | 1580 | 376 |
| *self-raising flour* see ***flour, wheat*** | | | |
| *semolina* see ***breakfast cereals*** | | | |
| ***sesame seeds*** ... 1 tsp | 4g | 95 | 23 |
| ***shallots*** ... boiled ... 2 bulbs | 12g | 10 | 2 |
| raw ... 2 bulbs | 12g | 10 | 2 |
| ***shepherds pie*** ... home-made | 100g | 495 | 118 |
| *sherry* see ***wines, fortified*** | | | |
| ***shish kebab (Lebanese)*** | 100g | 790 | 188 |
| *shortbread* see ***biscuits*** | | | |
| *shortening* see ***butter; lard; margarine*** | | | |
| ***shrimps*** ... boiled ... with shell | 100g | 165 | 39 |
| without shell | 100g | 365 | 87 |
| ***shrimps*** ... canned ... drained solids | 100g | 505 | 120 |
| solids + fluids | 100g | 350 | 83 |
| crumbed, fried | 100g | 1015 | 242 |
| dried | 100g | 1035 | 246 |
| fried in batter | 100g | 940 | 224 |
| frozen ... without shell | 100g | 310 | 74 |
| raw | 100g | 400 | 95 |
| King Oscar ... in brine | 100g | 400 | 95 |
| ***silver beet*** ... boiled ... 1 cup chopped | 115g | 70 | 17 |
| dehydrated | 100g | 1300 | 310 |
| raw ... 1 cup chopped | 45g | 25 | 6 |
| ***silver hake*** ... fillets ... Edgell-Birdseye | 100g | 315 | 75 |
| *silverside* see ***beef*** | | | |
| *sirloin* see ***beef*** | | | |
| ***skate*** ... fried in batter | 100g | 830 | 198 |
| *skordalia (Greek)* see ***dips and spreads*** | | | |
| ***snack foods*** ... beer nuts ... av all brands | 100g | 2330 | 555 |
| Burger Rings | 100g | 2090 | 498 |

| | MASS | KJ | CAL |
|---|---|---|---|
| cashew nuts ... salted ... av all brands | 100g | 2555 | 608 |
| CC's cheese flavour | 50g | 1050 | 250 |
| cheese things | 100g | 2130 | 507 |
| Cheezels | 100g | 2170 | 517 |
| chips/crisps ... flavoured ... 1 small pkt | 35g | 760 | 181 |
| plain ... 1 small pkt | 25g | 735 | 175 |
| chocolate-covered nuts | 30g | 670 | 160 |
| corn chips ... flavoured ... 1 pkt | 25g | 830 | 198 |
| toasted ... 1 pkt | 25g | 790 | 188 |
| nutcrackers | 100g | 1840 | 438 |
| nuts, mixed ... av all brands | 100g | 2440 | 581 |
| peanuts ... salted ... av all brands | 100g | 2340 | 557 |
| popcorn ... regular ... 1 cup | 8g | 155 | 37 |
| sugar-coated | 30g | 2190 | 521 |
| pork rind ... 1 pkt | 25g | 510 | 121 |
| potato straws ... flavoured ... 1 pkt | 25g | 730 | 174 |
| plain ... 1 pkt | 25g | 755 | 100 |
| pretzels ... 20 8-cm sticks | 12g | 185 | 44 |
| Smith's ... Extra Lites Crisps | 100g | 2000 | 476 |
| Less Oil Crisps | 100g | 2075 | 494 |
| Twisties ... cheese | 100g | 2080 | 495 |
| chicken | 100g | 2060 | 490 |
| ETA ... mixed nuts ... salted | 100g | 2545 | 606 |
| peanuts ... granulated/crushed | 100g | 2365 | 563 |
| roasted | 100g | 2475 | 589 |
| salted | 100g | 2440 | 581 |
| Green's ... cashews | 30g | 705 | 168 |
| mixed nuts | 30g | 755 | 180 |
| salted peanuts | 30g | 730 | 174 |
| Farmland ... beer nuts/cashews/roasted peanuts ... no added salt | 100g | 2640 | 629 |
| mixed nuts | 100g | 2500 | 595 |

| | MASS | KJ | CAL |
|---|---|---|---|
| potato chips ... wrinkled ... no added salt | 100g | 2365 | 563 |
| Fullers ... popping corn | 100g | 1605 | 382 |
| Uncle Toby's ... le snak ... cheese spread ... in 1 pack | | 190 | 45 |
| crispbreads (all flavours) ... in 1 pack | | 170 | 40 |
| roll ups ... av all varieties ... 1 roll | | 235 | 56 |
| *snapper* ... battered, deep-fried | 100g | 855 | 204 |
| crumbed, pan-fried | 100g | 835 | 199 |
| steamed | 100g | 510 | 121 |
| *snapper, red* ... fried | 100g | 905 | 215 |
| steamed | 100g | 385 | 92 |
| *snow peas* see *peas, snow/sugar* | | | |
| *soda water* see *drinks, carbonated* | | | |
| *sole* ... baked | 100g | 845 | 201 |
| raw | 100g | 375 | 89 |
| *sole, lemon* ... fried | 100g | 905 | 215 |
| inc bones | 100g | 715 | 170 |
| raw | 100g | 345 | 82 |
| steamed | 100g | 385 | 92 |
| inc bones | 100g | 270 | 64 |
| *soups* | | | |
| *chicken galanga soup (Thai)* | 100g | 470 | 112 |
| *prawn (Thai)* | 100g | 170 | 40 |
| *Alevita* ... carrot/thick vegetable ... made up ... ½ sachet | 250ml | 370 | 88 |
| spring vegetable ... made up ... ½ sachet | 250ml | 110 | 26 |
| tomato ... made up ... ½ sachet | 250ml | 310 | 74 |
| tomato and vegetable ... made up ... ½ sachet | 250ml | 325 | 77 |
| *Campbell's* ... all-natural soups ... diluted with an equal quantity of milk ... | | | |
| creamy asparagus | 250ml | 970 | 231 |

| | MASS | KJ | CAL |
|---|---|---|---|
| creamy broccoli/pumpkin | 250ml | 660 | 157 |
| creamy corn | 250ml | 785 | 187 |
| garden tomato | 250ml | 290 | 69 |
| garden vegetable | 250ml | 170 | 40 |
| chunky soups ... consumed undiluted ... | | | |
| chunky beef | 250ml | 705 | 168 |
| chunky chicken | 250ml | 615 | 146 |
| chunky creamy chicken and corn | 250ml | 755 | 180 |
| chunky minestrone | 250ml | 580 | 138 |
| chunky pea and ham | 250ml | 905 | 215 |
| chunky stockpot | 250ml | 635 | 151 |
| diluted with equal quantity of water ... | | | |
| beef consomme | 250ml | 115 | 27 |
| chicken vegetable | 250ml | 280 | 67 |
| diluted with ½ milk ½ water ... | | | |
| cream of chicken | 250ml | 585 | 139 |
| cream of chicken and corn/chicken and asparagus | 250ml | 490 | 117 |
| cream of oyster/celery | 250ml | 535 | 127 |
| minestrone | 250ml | 385 | 92 |
| old-fashioned stockpot/scotch broth | 250ml | 330 | 79 |
| split pea with ham/cream of asparagus | 250ml | 680 | 162 |
| tomato | 250ml | 430 | 102 |
| vegetable | 250ml | 310 | 74 |
| *Continental* ... packet soups ... made up with water ... | | | |
| cup-a-soup ... 1 sachet made up ... | | | |
| cream of celery | | 325 | 77 |
| cream of chicken | | 175 | 42 |
| French onion | | 175 | 42 |
| pea and ham | | 385 | 92 |
| spring vegetable | | 135 | 32 |
| tomato | | 370 | 88 |

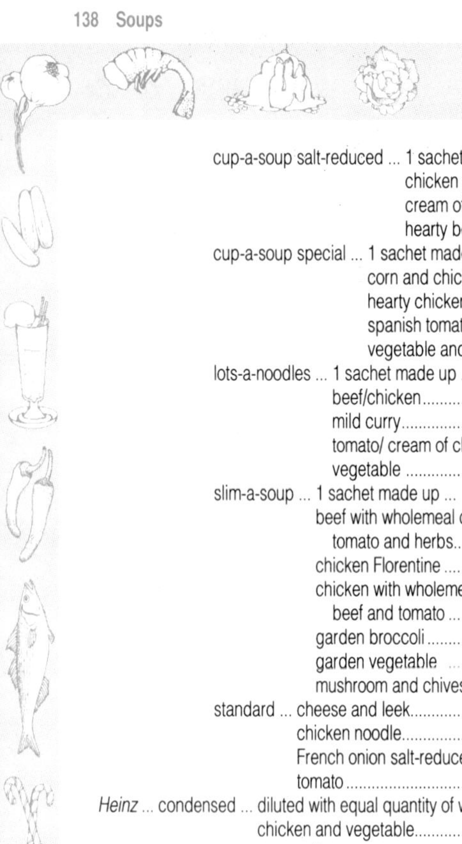

| | MASS | KJ | CAL |
|---|---|---|---|
| cup-a-soup salt-reduced ... 1 sachet made up ... | | | |
| chicken noodle | | 170 | 40 |
| cream of mushroom | | 365 | 87 |
| hearty beef | | 225 | 54 |
| cup-a-soup special ... 1 sachet made up ... | | | |
| corn and chicken | | 470 | 112 |
| hearty chicken | | 490 | 117 |
| spanish tomato | | 445 | 106 |
| vegetable and beef | | 345 | 82 |
| lots-a-noodles ... 1 sachet made up ... | | | |
| beef/chicken | | 500 | 119 |
| mild curry | | 495 | 118 |
| tomato/ cream of chicken | | 545 | 130 |
| vegetable | | 425 | 101 |
| slim-a-soup ... 1 sachet made up ... | | | |
| beef with wholemeal croutons/ tomato and herbs | | 150 | 36 |
| chicken Florentine | | 160 | 38 |
| chicken with wholemeal croutons/ beef and tomato | | 175 | 42 |
| garden broccoli | | 190 | 45 |
| garden vegetable | | 135 | 32 |
| mushroom and chives | | 155 | 37 |
| standard ... cheese and leek | 1 litre | 1075 | 256 |
| chicken noodle | 1 litre | 750 | 179 |
| French onion salt-reduced | 1 litre | 530 | 126 |
| tomato | 1 litre | 990 | 236 |
| *Heinz* ... condensed ... diluted with equal quantity of water ... | | | |
| chicken and vegetable | 100ml | 90 | 21 |
| pea and ham | 100ml | 205 | 49 |
| tomato and bacon/tomato/ vegetable beef | 100ml | 105 | 25 |

| | MASS | KJ | CAL |
|---|---|---|---|
| *sponge cake* see *cake and pudding mixes; cakes and pastries* | | | |
| *sponge pudding* see *cake and pudding mixes; desserts and puddings* | | | |
| *spreads* see *dips and spreads* | | | |
| *spring roll* ... deep-fried ... 1 | 175g | 1670 | 398 |
| *spring roll (Thai)* | 100g | 1130 | 269 |
| *squab* see *pigeon/squab* | | | |
| *squash, button* ... boiled ... 1 av | 35g | 40 | 10 |
| raw ... 1 av | 40g | 40 | 10 |
| *squash, scaloppini* ... boiled ... 1 large | 70g | 60 | 14 |
| raw ... 1 av | 60g | 50 | 12 |
| *squash, summer* see *zucchini* | | | |
| *squash, winter* ... boiled | 100g | 165 | 39 |
| raw | 100g | 190 | 45 |
| *squid* see *calamari* | | | |
| *starch* see *wheat starch* | | | |
| *starfruit* see *carambola* | | | |
| *steak and kidney with vegetables* ... Heinz ... supersnack | 100g | 465 | 111 |
| *steak and onion* ... canned | 100g | 740 | 176 |
| *steak and tomatoes* ... canned | 100g | 630 | 150 |
| *steak dianne* ... McCain | 350g | 1545 | 368 |
| *steak in black-bean sauce (Chinese)* | 100g | 455 | 108 |
| *steak sandwich* | 100g | 940 | 225 |
| *steak* see *beef* | | | |
| *steamed duck and mushrooms (Chinese)* | 100g | 590 | 140 |
| *steamed pudding* see *cake and pudding mixes; desserts and puddings* | | | |
| *stew* ... lean meat + vegetables + flour ... ¾ cup | | 1050 | 250 |
| *stewed steak in gravy* | 100g | 730 | 174 |
| *stifado (Greek)* | 100g | 535 | 127 |
| *stock* ... beef ... Maggi ... recons. with water | 100g | 40 | 10 |
| chicken ... Maggi ... recons. with water | 100g | 35 | 8 |
| *stock cubes* ... 1 cube + 250ml water | 5g | 20 | 5 |
| *stout* ... av all brands | 100g | 165 | 39 |

| | MASS | KJ | CAL |
|---|---|---|---|
| Guinness | 100g | 235 | 56 |
| Tooth Sheaf/Coopers Best Extra | 100g | 195 | 46 |
| *Strasbourg* see *luncheon meat* | | | |
| *strawberries* ... canned ... sweetened | 100g | 245 | 58 |
| unsweetened | 100g | 90 | 21 |
| fresh ... 1 cup whole berries | 145g | 120 | 29 |
| frozen ... whole ... sweetened | 100g | 475 | 113 |
| John West ... in fruit juice | 100g | 345 | 82 |
| *string beans* see *beans, green* | | | |
| *stuffing* ... sage and onion | 100g | 960 | 229 |
| savoury ... bread-based | 100g | 785 | 187 |
| *stuffing mix* ... Tandaco ... seasoned | 100g | 1520 | 362 |
| *suet* | 100g | 3560 | 848 |
| *suet mix* ... Tandaco | 100g | 2395 | 570 |
| *sugar* ... brown/raw/refined | 5g | 80 | 19 |
| *sugar cane* ... juice | 100g | 305 | 73 |
| stem | 100g | 250 | 60 |
| *sugar peas* see *peas, snow/sugar* | | | |
| *sugar substitutes* ... equal ... 1 sachet ... 2 tsp | | 15 | 4 |
| equal/sugarella/hermesetas ... 1 tablet | | 1.5 | 0 |
| saccharin/cyclamate ... 1 tablet/1 drop | | 0 | 0 |
| sugarine ... 4 drops | | 0 | 0 |
| ½ tablet | | 0 | 0 |
| *sultana bran* see *breakfast cereals* | | | |
| *sultanas* ... dried | 100g | 1175 | 280 |
| *summer squash* see *zucchini* | | | |
| *sunflower kernels* ... The Old Grain Mill | 100g | 2345 | 558 |
| *sunflower oil* | 100g | 3700 | 881 |
| *sunflower seeds* | 10g | 235 | 56 |
| *swedes* ... boiled ... 1 cup chopped | 150g | 125 | 30 |
| *sweet-and-sour duck (Chinese)* | 100g | 900 | 214 |
| *sweet-and-sour fish (Chinese)* | 100g | 830 | 198 |

| | MASS | KJ | CAL |
|---|---|---|---|
| *sweet-and-sour pork* | 100g | 1510 | 360 |
| McCain | 300g | 1470 | 350 |
| *sweet-and-sour pork (Chinese)* | 100g | 770 | 183 |
| *sweet-and-sour prawns (Chinese)* | 100g | 490 | 117 |
| *sweet-and-sour sauce* see *sauces, savoury* | | | |
| *sweet curry* ... Harvest ... hot pack | 100g | 260 | 62 |
| *sweet potato* ... orange flesh ... boiled ... 1 cup mashed | 235g | 640 | 152 |
| white flesh ... boiled ... 1 cup mashed | 235g | 755 | 180 |
| *sweetbreads* ... raw | 100g | 860 | 205 |
| *sweetcorn* ... boiled ... kernels only | 100g | 350 | 83 |
| canned ... drained ... baby | 100g | 90 | 21 |
| frozen ... simmered ... on the cob ... 1 cobette | 85g | 470 | 112 |
| raw ... kernels only ... 1 cob | 156g | 605 | 144 |
| Edgell-Birdseye ... kernels/creamed | 100g | 375 | 82 |
| cobs/whole grain | 100g | 390 | 93 |
| Golden Circle ... kernels | 100g | 280 | 67 |
| Green's ... whole kernels in brine | 100g | 385 | 92 |
| McCain ... kernels | 100g | 390 | 93 |
| cobettes ... 1 cobette | 100g | 300 | 71 |
| Farmland ... cream-style | 100g | 435 | 104 |
| cream-style/whole kernels ... no added salt | 100g | 345 | 82 |
| *sweeteners, artificial* see *sugar substitutes* | | | |
| *sweets* see *confectionery* | | | |
| *swiss roll* see *cakes and pastries* | | | |
| *swordfish* | | | |
| *syrup, golden* | 100g | 1225 | 292 |
| | | | |
| *tabouli* see *salads* | | | |
| *taco* | 100g | 905 | 216 |
| *taco salad* | 100g | 590 | 141 |
| with chilli con carne | 100g | 465 | 111 |

| | MASS | KJ | CAL |
|---|---|---|---|
| *tagliatelle* ... dry ... uncooked | 100g | 1540 | 367 |
| *tahini* ... raw/roasted kernels ... 1 tbsp | 20g | 500 | 119 |
| *take-away foods* see *Pizza Hut; McDonalds; Kentucky Fried Chicken; Hungry Jacks* | | | |
| *tamarillo* ... raw ... flesh + seeds ... 1 av | 71g | 80 | 19 |
| *tamarinds* ... raw | 100g | 1000 | 238 |
| *tangelo* ... raw ... flesh only ... 1 av | 115g | 180 | 43 |
| *tangerine* see *mandarins* | | | |
| *tangor* | 100g | 145 | 35 |
| *taramasalata (Greek)* see *dips and spreads* | | | |
| *taro* ... boiled ... 1 cup sliced | 145g | 640 | 152 |
| *tea* ... black | 250ml | 5 | 1 |
| black + 1 sugar | 250ml | 85 | 20 |
| white ... rev | 250ml | 70 | 17 |
| whole milk | 250ml | 90 | 21 |
| white + 1 sugar ... rev | 250ml | 150 | 36 |
| whole milk | 250ml | 170 | 40 |
| *tea, Indian* ... without milk or sugar ... 1 cup | 250ml | 5 | 1 |
| *tempeh* | 100g | 835 | 199 |
| *tofu* ... canned ... fried | 100g | 1265 | 301 |
| fresh | 100g | 380 | 90 |
| steamed | 100g | 290 | 69 |
| stirfried | 100g | 625 | 149 |
| *tomato juice* see *fruit juices* | | | |
| *tomato paste* ... Heinz/Raguletto | 20g | 75 | 18 |
| IXL | 20g | 90 | 21 |
| *tomato puree* ... av all brands | 100g | 145 | 35 |
| *tomato sauce* see *sauces, savoury* | | | |
| *tomato supreme* ... Edgell-Birdseye | 100g | 210 | 50 |
| *tomatoes* ... fried | 100g | 290 | 69 |
| raw ... 1 av | 129g | 70 | 17 |
| Edgell-Birdseye ... peeled | 100g | 140 | 33 |

| | MASS | KJ | CAL |
|---|---|---|---|
| Heinz ... crushed | 100g | 110 | 26 |
| whole ... peeled | 100g | 100 | 24 |
| IXL ... whole ... peeled ... in juice | 100g | 85 | 20 |
| SPC ... whole ... peeled | 100g | 100 | 24 |
| *tomatoes, cherry* ... raw ... 5 | 74g | 40 | 10 |
| *tomatoes, egg* ... raw ... 1 av | 75g | 45 | 11 |
| *tomatoes, stuffed (Greek)* | 100g | 460 | 110 |
| *tommy ruff* see *ruff, tommy/orange* | | | |
| *tongue* see *beef; lamb* | | | |
| *toppings* see *sauces, sweet* | | | |
| *tortellini Bolognese* ... Heinz | 100g | 395 | 94 |
| *treacle* ... 1 tbsp | 22g | 242 | 58 |
| *trevally* ... fried | 100g | 845 | 201 |
| raw | 100g | 475 | 113 |
| *tripe* ... cooked ... with parsley sauce | 100g | 420 | 100 |
| raw | 100g | 250 | 60 |
| stewed | 100g | 420 | 100 |
| *trout* ... brook ... raw | 100g | 425 | 101 |
| brown ... steamed | 100g | 565 | 135 |
| inc bones | 100g | 375 | 89 |
| lake | 100g | 1010 | 240 |
| rainbow ... raw | 100g | 815 | 194 |
| *tuna* ... canned ... in brine ... drained ... 1 cup | 190g | 985 | 235 |

| | MASS | KJ | CAL |
|---|---|---|---|
| in oil ... drained ... 1 cup | 205g | 1890 | 450 |
| sandwich type ... in oil ... 2 tbsp | 40g | 420 | 100 |
| raw | 100g | 1010 | 240 |
| John West ... in brine/in spring water | 100g | 480 | 114 |
| in oil | 100g | 865 | 206 |
| *tuna lasagne* ... Findus Lean Cuisine ... 1 sv | 275g | 1090 | 260 |
| *turkey* ... roasted | 100g | 1145 | 273 |
| Tegel ... flavour-basted ... breast/buffe | 100g | 625 | 149 |
| thigh | 100g | 500 | 119 |
| hindquarter ... uncooked | 100g | 500 | 119 |
| smoked buffe | 100g | 615 | 146 |
| *turkey breast with tagliatelle* ... Findus Lean Cuisine ... 1 sv | 240g | 1110 | 264 |
| *turkey dijon* ... Findus Lean Cuisine ... 1 sv | 270g | 1180 | 281 |
| *turkish delight* see *confectionery* | | | |
| *turnip, white* ... boiled ... 1 cup diced | 240g | 215 | 51 |
| *turtle* ... raw ... flesh only | 100g | 470 | 112 |
| *two fruits* ... SPC ... artific. sweet. | 100g | 130 | 31 |
| in syrup | 100g | 250 | 60 |
| iust fruit (in pear juice) | 100g | 210 | 50 |
| SPC Little Big Fruit (snak pak) ... in juice | 140g | 295 | 70 |
| in syrup | 140g | 310 | 74 |
| Weight Watchers ... artific. sweet. | 100g | 130 | 31 |

## Smoked Trout Paté

*75 g dill pickles*
*200 g smoked trout, skin and bones removed*
*275 g tofu, crumbled*
*2 tablespoons cider vinegar*
*1 level teaspoon French mustard*

Drain dill pickles on paper towel and chop. Roughly flake the trout flesh and mix in a blender with tofu, vinegar and mustard until smooth. Stir in the chopped dill pickles. Divide between eight small containers. Label and freeze. Thaw at room temperature for 3 hours when required.

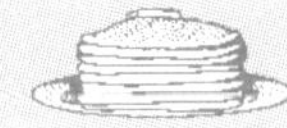

| | MASS | KJ | CAL |
|---|---|---|---|
| *tyropita (Greek)* | 100g | 1550 | 369 |
| *tzatziki (Greek)* see *dips and spreads* | | | |
| *veal* | | | |
| *boneless, average cut* ... cooked ... lean ... 1 cup diced | 190g | 1185 | 282 |
| lean+fat ... 1 cup diced | 173g | 1155 | 275 |
| *brains* ... boiled | 100g | 450 | 107 |
| crumbed, fried | 100g | 1220 | 290 |
| *cutlets* ... crumbed, fried | 140g | 1265 | 301 |
| *forequarter* ... simmered ... lean ... 1 cup diced | 148g | 1075 | 256 |
| lean+fat ... 1 cup diced | 158g | 1235 | 294 |
| *leg* ... baked ... lean ... 1 slice | 44g | 255 | 61 |
| lean+fat ... 1 slice | 45g | 270 | 64 |
| *leg steak* ... fried ... lean ... 1 av | 65g | 420 | 100 |
| lean+fat ... 1 av | 67g | 450 | 107 |
| *liver* ... grilled ... 1 slice | 85g | 670 | 160 |
| *loin chop* ... grilled ... lean ... 1 av | 51g | 310 | 74 |
| lean+fat ... 1 av | 54g | 365 | 87 |
| *shank* ... simmered ... lean ... 3 slices | 80g | 490 | 117 |
| lean+fat ... 3 slices | 90g | 670 | 160 |
| *shoulder steak* ... grilled ... lean ... 1 av | 51g | 310 | 74 |
| lean+fat ... 1 av | 53g | 345 | 82 |
| ***veal casserole*** ... with vegetables | 100g | 500 | 119 |
| without vegetables | 100g | 590 | 140 |
| ***veal schnitzel*** ... frozen ... fried ... av all brands | 100g | 1425 | 339 |
| Baron's Table ... 1 sv | 150g | 1565 | 373 |
| Edgell-Birdseye | 100g | 1050 | 250 |
| ***vegekabana*** ... tempeh ... 1 slice | 16g | 155 | 37 |
| ***vegemite*** see ***dips and spreads*** | | | |
| ***vegetable and sausage*** ... Harvest ... hot pack | 100g | 265 | 63 |
| ***vegetable and steak*** ... Harvest... hot pack | 100g | 240 | 57 |
| ***vegetable beef casserole*** | 100g | 465 | 111 |
| ***vegetable curry*** | 100g | 755 | 180 |

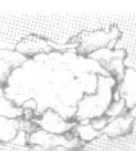
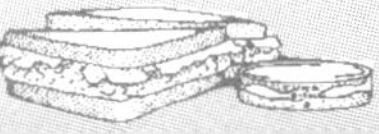

| | MASS | KJ | CAL |
|---|---|---|---|
| *vegetable juice* ... canned | 100ml | 75 | 18 |
| Campbell's ... V8 | 100ml | 85 | 20 |
| *vegetable* see individual vegetables | | | |
| *vegetables and noodles* ... Dewcrisp ... easy serve | 100g | 320 | 76 |
| *vegetables and sausages* ... Farmland | 100g | 425 | 101 |
| Kraft | 100g | 385 | 92 |
| *vegetables and steak* ... Farmland | 150g | 470 | 112 |
| no added salt | 100g | 295 | 70 |
| *vegetables, mixed* ... Edgell-Birdseye | 100g | 185 | 44 |
| 7-vegetable mix | 100g | 240 | 57 |
| McCain | 50g | 50 | 12 |
| Florentine | 100g | 240 | 57 |
| Mediterranean mix | 100g | 170 | 40 |
| Normandie | 100g | 205 | 49 |
| *venison* ... roasted | 100g | 830 | 198 |
| *vermicelli* ... dry ... uncooked | 100g | 1540 | 367 |
| *vine leaves* | 100g | 65 | 15 |
| stuffed | 100g | 455 | 108 |
| vegetarian | 100g | 715 | 170 |
| *vinegar* ... brown/red/white | 100g | 50 | 12 |
| cider | 100g | 60 | 14 |

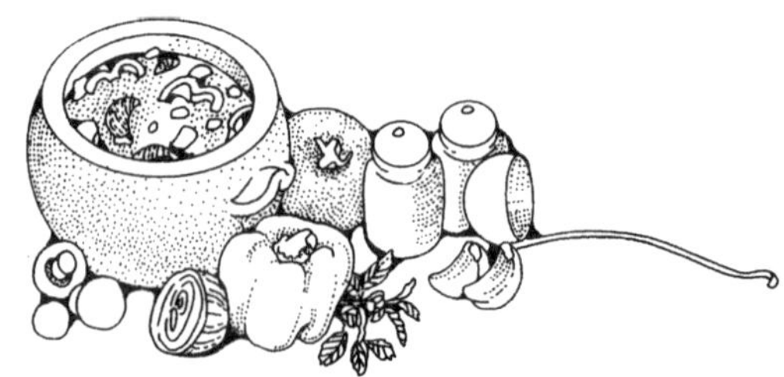

| | MASS | KJ | CAL |
|---|---|---|---|
| Cornwell's ... white/salt/cider/wine/spiced | 100g | 60 | 14 |
| *vita brits* see *breakfast cereals: Uncle Toby's* | | | |
| *vodka* see *spirits* | | | |
| *vol-au-vent* ... case without filling | 100g | 2400 | 571 |
| | | | |
| *waffles* ... 1 | | 600 | 143 |
| Edgell-Birdseye | 100g | 575 | 137 |
| *walnuts* ... shelled ... chopped ... 1 tbsp | 12g | 320 | 76 |
| snack size | 50g | 1340 | 319 |
| *water buffalo* ... feral | 100g | 645 | 154 |
| *water chestnuts* ... canned ... drained solids | 100g | 205 | 49 |
| Admiral | 100g | 230 | 55 |
| *watercress* ... raw ... ¼ cup chopped | 8g | 5 | 1 |
| *watermelon* see *melon* | | | |
| *wax gourd* see *gourd, wax* | | | |
| *wax jambu* ... raw ... 1 av | 45g | 40 | 10 |
| *weet-bix* see *breakfast cereals* | | | |
| *weeties* see *breakfast cereals* | | | |
| *Welsh rarebit* | 100g | 1525 | 363 |
| *wheat starch* | 100g | 1455 | 346 |
| *wheatgerm* see *breakfast cereals* | | | |
| *whisky* see *spirits* | | | |
| *whitebait* ... fried | 100g | 2175 | 518 |
| *whiting, King George* ... battered, deep-fried | 100g | 1315 | 313 |
| floured, pan-fried | 100g | 635 | 151 |
| steamed | 100g | 435 | 104 |
| Edgell-Birdseye | 100g | 440 | 105 |
| *wines* ... chablis/champagne ... 1 sv | 100ml | 350 | 83 |
| dry red/dry white/rosé ... 1 sv | 100ml | 295 | 70 |
| red ... 1 sv | 100ml | 360 | 86 |
| sauterne ... 1 sv | 100ml | 375 | 89 |
| sweet ... red ... 1 sv | 100ml | 505 | 120 |

| | MASS | KJ | CAL |
|---|---|---|---|
| sparkling ... 1 sv | 100ml | 315 | 75 |
| white ... 1 sv | 100ml | 420 | 100 |
| white chardonnay/semillon/riesling ... 1 sv | 100ml | 355 | 85 |
| *wines, fortified* ... port | 100ml | 655 | 156 |
| sherry ... dry | 100ml | 465 | 111 |
| sweet | 100ml | 610 | 145 |
| *witloof* see *chicory* | | | |
| *yeast* ... dried ... bakers | 100g | 1270 | 302 |
| brewers | 100g | 1210 | 288 |
| fresh compressed ... bakers | 100g | 360 | 86 |
| Tandaco ... dried | 100g | 715 | 170 |
| Winn ... lite yeast mix | 100g | 1600 | 381 |
| wholemeal yeast mix | 100g | 1630 | 388 |
| *yoghurt* | | | |
| *fruit* | 100g | 370 | 88 |
| low-fat | 100g | 315 | 75 |
| *natural* | 100g | 360 | 85 |
| low-fat | 100g | 250 | 60 |
| *Bulla* ... plain | 100g | 315 | 75 |
| reduced-fat fruit | 100g | 400 | 95 |
| reduced-fat fruit drinking yoghurt | 100g | 335 | 80 |
| *Calorie Counters* ... skim milk | 100g | 230 | 55 |
| *Dairy Farmers* ... traditional low-fat natural | 100g | 210 | 50 |
| traditional natural | 100g | 320 | 76 |
| *Danino* ... reduced-fat fruit ... strawberry/tropical fruits/apricot | 100g | 375 | 89 |
| vanilla | 100g | 400 | 95 |
| *Danone* ... diet-lite low-fat ... av all flavours | 100g | 195 | 46 |

Although salads usually contain little fat, the addition of oily dressings or mayonnaise can increase their fat content considerably. A low-fat, yoghurt-based dressing can help keep the kilojoule count down.

| | MASS | KJ | CAL |
|---|---|---|---|
| fruit ... av all flavours | 100g | 395 | 94 |
| lite and fruity low-fat | 100g | 310 | 74 |
| *Jalna* ... honey | 100g | 300 | 71 |
| leben/natural | 100g | 280 | 67 |
| premium blend creamy | 100g | 435 | 104 |
| skim-milk | 100g | 215 | 51 |
| vanilla | 100g | 250 | 60 |
| *Oak* ... frozen | 100g | 630 | 150 |
| fruit | 100g | 425 | 101 |
| plain | 100g | 390 | 93 |
| *Pauls* ... extra low-fat fruit ... av all flavours | 100g | 308 | 73 |
| plain | 100g | 220 | 52 |
| vanilla | 100g | 400 | 95 |
| fruit ... av all flavours | 100g | 395 | 93 |
| low-fat ... plain | 100g | 220 | 52 |
| natural set yoghurt ... plain | 100g | 350 | 83 |
| *Peters Farm* ... apple and vanilla | 100g | 475 | 113 |
| black cherry/blueberry/double berry/apricot | 100g | 410 | 96 |
| natural | 100g | 305 | 73 |
| peach and mango/tropical fruit/raspberry | 100g | 395 | 93 |
| peach melba | 100g | 465 | 111 |
| vanilla/strawberry | 100g | 435 | 104 |
| *Peters Farm low-fat* ... apricot/strawberry | 100g | 340 | 82 |
| peach melba/vanilla | 100g | 385 | 92 |
| *Ski* ... av all flavours | 100g | 405 | 96 |
| apricot | 100g | 400 | 95 |
| *Ski life* ... av all flavours | 100g | 325 | 78 |
| berries and cherries | 100g | 355 | 85 |
| *Weight Watchers* ... natural | 100g | 205 | 49 |
| *Yomix* ... av all flavours | 100g | 325 | 77 |
| fruit base ... av all flavours | 100g | 320 | 76 |
| natural | 100g | 215 | 51 |

| | MASS | KJ | CAL |
|---|---|---|---|
| *Yoplait* ... apricot/strawb/fruit tango/redberry cocktail ... pack | 200g | 765 | 181 |
| banana and passionpeach/orchard fruit/ tropical fruit/fruit of the forest/fruit salad ... pack | 200g | 795 | 188 |
| kiwifruit and mango/peach and guava ... pack | 200g | 785 | 187 |
| pineapple and mandarin ... pack | 200g | 740 | 176 |
| *Yoplait low-fat* ... blueberry/strawb and guava ... pack | 200g | 705 | 168 |
| fruit salad/peach and cherry/strawb and peach/tropical fruit ... pack | 200g | 720 | 171 |
| natural ... pack | 200g | 420 | 100 |
| strawb/strawb and banana/apricot ... pack | 200g | 685 | 162 |
| ***Yogo*** ... Peters Farm ... banana/creamy rice/strawb/caramel | 100g | 435 | 104 |
| chocolate | 100g | 450 | 107 |
| raspberry/vanilla/tropical banana | 100g | 410 | 98 |
| ***Yorkshire pudding*** | 100g | 900 | 214 |
| ***youngberries*** ... fresh ... raw | 100g | 245 | 58 |
| ***zucchini*** ... average type ... boiled ... 1 cup sliced | 155g | 100 | 24 |
| raw ... 1 cup sliced | 130g | 75 | 18 |
| golden ... boiled ... 1 cup sliced | 155g | 120 | 29 |
| raw ... slices | 60g | 40 | 10 |
| green-skinned ... boiled ... 1 cup sliced | 155g | 95 | 23 |
| raw ... 1 av | 84g | 50 | 12 |
| ***zucchini lasagne*** ... Findus Lean Cuisine ... 1 sv | 310g | 1090 | 260 |
| ***zucchini, stuffed (Lebanese)*** | 100g | 535 | 127 |

# INTRODUCTION TO THE TABLE

Five food components – fat, cholesterol, sodium, calcium and fibre – have important implications for our health, either because we may be eating too much of them (in the case of fat, cholesterol and sodium) or because we may not be eating enough (in the case of calcium and fibre).

This section of *The Australian Calorie Counter* explains how each component affects health and suggests practical ways of keeping your intake at a desirable level. To find specific information about the amounts of the five components in a wide range of foods, consult the table given on pages 174–203.

## FAT

For most people, the type of fat eaten is characteristic of their culture, for example butter in Northern Europe, olive oil in Mediterranean countries and soya bean and sesame seed oils in Asia. The fat obtained from animals and dairy products is also characteristic of different cultures.

### The purpose of fat

Whatever the source, dietary fats generally serve the same purpose: they add flavour and texture to food and supply energy and essential nutrients, including fat-soluble vitamins A, D, E and K, and the fatty acids needed by the body.

## The three main types

The fats in our diet have different compositions depending on the types of fatty acids they contain. There are three main types of fatty acids: **saturated**, **mono-unsaturated** and **poly-unsaturated**. All fats contain a mixture of these but the predominance of one type gives the fat its main characteristics.

In general, most saturated fats, for example butter, meat fat, copha and solid cooking fats, are solid at room temperature. Mono-unsaturated fats, for example olive oil and canola oil, are usually liquid at room temperature. Polyunsaturated fats, for example the vegetable, seed and nut oils (sunflower, peanut and safflower), are also normally liquid at room temperature.

Polyunsaturated margarines are made from vegetable oils that have been processed to give them a spreading consistency. The lower-fat dairy spreads and margarines are processed to incorporate a higher water content.

The oils present in fish contain a special class of polyunsaturated fatty acids, which some researchers suggest may protect against coronary heart disease.

## Fat and health

The amount and type of fat in our diet receives a great deal of attention. Research shows that a high-fat diet, particularly a diet high in saturated fats, can increase blood cholesterol and increase the risk of heart disease, stroke and some cancers.

For these reasons health authorities recommend that we reduce the total fat in our diet to 30–33 per cent of the daily energy intake (measured in kilojoules or calories). At present the average Australian diet contains about 40 per cent energy from fat. In effect this means that we should eat not more than 9 grams of fat for every 1000 kilojoules (220 calories) of energy.

*Note*: This fat restriction does not apply to children under five years of age.

A further recommendation is that not more than one-third of the fat eaten should come from saturated fats: accordingly, you should replace saturated fats with mono-unsaturated and poly-unsaturated fats wherever possible.

Remember that the most important step is to cut down the total amount of fat and foods that contain fat. This is an efficient way of reducing calorie intake because fat is the most concentrated source of energy in our diet, supplying 37 kilojoules (9 calories) per gram.

## How to reduce your fat intake

Eat more of the following non-fat or low-fat foods:

- fruit, vegetables and legumes (dried peas, beans, lentils and chick peas)
- pasta and cereals, including cereals such as rice, cracked wheat, barley and corn, and wholegrain breakfast cereals
- wholemeal bread, flat bread and crispbread
- low-fat milk and yoghurt, reduced-fat tasty and processed cheese, cottage and ricotta cheese
- fish, fat-trimmed meat and skinless chicken.

Limit the following:

- butter and margarine (to 20 grams per day), cream, sour cream, full-fat cheeses and standard ice-cream

- croissants, cream buns, doughnuts, pastries, chocolate and cream cakes, and biscuits
- chocolate, chocolate bars, carob bars, caramels and fudge
- avocados, olives and nuts
- fat-basted foods and fried, crumbed and battered foods – including oven-baked crumbed and battered convenience foods
- soups and sauces made with roux, cream, butter, eggs or cheese
- high-fat snack foods, including potato crisps
- the hidden-fat foods – traditional mayonnaises and dressings, certain 'dry' biscuits, frozen and packaged convenience meals, packet cake and pudding mixes, take-away foods, and toasted muesli.

Practise some cunning dodges:

- buy lean cuts of meat
- trim fat from meat, skin from poultry
- skim all fat from casseroles, cooked mince, soup stock and gravy juices
- use a non-stick frying pan, and a rack for roasting meat and vegetables
- steam or microwave vegetables rather than frying them
- use purees of fruit or vegetables as sauces
- spread butter or margarine thinly, and omit it when you are using moist sandwich fillings
- choose low-fat alternatives in the supermarket – light salad dressings, reduced-fat spreads
- look for low-fat take-away and convenience foods.

# CHOLESTEROL

Cholesterol is a fatty substance not present in plant foods but found in all animal tissue (including human tissue), where it is essential to life and present in all body cells. It carries out many important functions and is produced by the liver as it is needed, regardless of whether cholesterol is consumed in the diet.

## Blood cholesterol

Blood carries cholesterol to any part of the body that requires it, but if the level of blood cholesterol is too high it is likely that deposits of cholesterol will form on the lining of arteries, causing them to narrow and harden. This condition is known as atherosclerosis. If atherosclerosis becomes severe the arteries can become blocked by small blood clots. A heart attack can occur if the blockage is in a blood vessel of the heart.

There are different types of cholesterol in the blood and, although there are special methods to measure them separately it is usual to measure total blood cholesterol. The National Heart Foundation recommends that the total blood-cholesterol level for Australians should be not more than 5.5 mmol/L (millimoles per litre). Your doctor can arrange for you to have your level checked. Many Australians have high levels (6.5 mmol/L or more), increasing their risk of coronary heart disease.

## What determines blood-cholesterol level?

The amount of cholesterol in the blood depends on several factors, including hereditary influences, overweight, exercise, smoking and diet. Of these factors we have some control over all but the first. If high blood cholesterol is a characteristic of your family it is important to have regular checks and to keep to the recommended lifestyle and dietary guidelines.

The most important dietary factors implicated in raised blood-cholesterol levels are:

- high-fat diets
- diets high in saturated fats
- diets in which the proportion of saturated fat is high in comparison to mono-unsaturated and polyunsaturated fats.

Other dietary factors related to high blood-cholesterol levels are:

- a high intake of cholesterol from food
- a low intake of dietary fibre.

Control your blood cholesterol with the following measures:

- aim for the healthy weight range (see 'Health and eating habits', p. 4)
- reduce total intake of fat and oil, and of saturated fats (see 'Fat', p. 155)
- include some mono-unsaturated and polyunsaturated fat in your daily fat intake
- limit cholesterol intake from food sources (not more than 300 milligrams of cholesterol per day)
- increase foods high in dietary fibre (see 'Fibre', p. 169)
- keep to a regular exercise and activity programme
- avoid smoking
- avoid excess alcohol.

# SODIUM

The sodium we eat comes mainly from the chemical compound we call **salt** (sodium chloride), although it is also found in other chemical compounds in our food (for example bicarbonate of soda and monosodium glutamate [msg]) and also occurs naturally in some fresh foods (for example meat and vegetables). In the table (see pages 174–203) figures are given for the sodium content of food; in most cases, but not all, that sodium is part of the salt that has been added to food in cooking and processing.

## Why cut down on salt?

The Australian Dietary Guidelines advise using less salt as a practical way of keeping sodium intake down to a healthy level.

Our 'Western' diet has conditioned us to like salt added to our food; but research indicates that for some people a high intake of sodium can lead to high blood pressure, and it has been shown that where the overall salt intake is high a larger proportion of the population has higher-than-normal blood pressure. On the other hand, among communities eating only naturally occurring sodium (for example Australian Aborigines eating traditional food) there is no increase in blood pressure with advancing age as there commonly is in communities eating a 'Western' diet.

## How much salt?

For most people there is enough naturally occurring sodium in a varied diet. The average person's requirement is 230 milligrams per day – the amount of sodium in about one-tenth of a teaspoon of salt (one teaspoon [6 grams] of salt contains 2.3 grams of sodium).

At present the average Australian consumes one-and-a-half to two teaspoons of salt per day (9–12 grams of salt or 3.5–4.6 grams of sodium). Government health recommendations, which work towards ideal targets from the starting point of what people are actually eating, advise that we reduce our daily intake to half to one teaspoon (3–6 grams) of salt (1.2–2.3 grams of sodium).

## Salt regulation in the body

Most sodium in the human body occurs as sodium chloride, or salt. The body, particularly by means of the kidneys, has a marvellous capacity to regulate its water and salt levels. Even during hot weather, when people perspire more, there is no need for most to take extra salt because the body conserves salt if it is needed. It is much more important to replace the water lost through perspiration.

## Salt in our food

Our dietary habits provide us with four main ways of taking in sodium:

- through sodium naturally present in fresh foods
- through salt added to many processed foods
- in salt added during the cooking
- in salt added at the table.

About half our daily intake of sodium comes from the salt in processed foods, some of them basic items of the daily diet, for example bread, butter, margarine, cheese and processed breakfast cereals.

Your excess sodium may come from the salt used in preserving processes, as in the case of corned beef, ham, bacon, salami, smoked cod, smoked salmon, caviar, anchovies, olives and vegemite; from salty sauces and seasonings, for example soy sauce, fish sauce, and stock cubes; or from salt added more directly for flavour, as in the case of many take-away foods, including hamburgers, chips and crisps, salted nuts, and other snack foods.

Then there are the hidden-sodium foods – sweet biscuits, breakfast cereals, cakes and pastries. In addition, there is sodium in soda water, fizzy drinks taken for indigestion, and some common painkillers. Consult your doctor if you are concerned about the sodium levels in any drugs you take regularly.

## A brief guide to sodium levels in foods

The following information refers to standard foods rather than to low-salt versions.

Highest in sodium (more than 2.5 g/100g) are:

- all types of salt including table salt, cooking salt, rock salt, sea salt, and vegetable salts such as celery salt and garlic salt
- stock cubes, gravy powders, soy sauce, fish sauce, msg, seasoning powders, yeast and vegetable extracts (vegemite and marmite), anchovies, and anchovy paste.

Foods high in sodium (1.0–2.5g/100g) include:

- commercial and home-made bottled sauces and pickles, gherkins and olives, French dressing, prepared mustard
- ham, bacon, corned beef, salami, luncheon meats, frankfurts, sausages and pâté
- salted snack foods – pretzels, twisties, crisps, cracker biscuits

- parmesan, processed cheddar, fetta, haloumy and pepato cheeses
- take-away foods – meat pies, sausage rolls, pizza, hamburgers and Chinese food
- standard butter and margarine
- packet soups
- canned sardines, salmon and tuna, and smoked salmon, caviar, and fish paste.

Foods moderately high in sodium (0.3–1.0 g/100g) include:

- potato chips and salted nuts
- sweet biscuits, cakes and pastries
- canned vegetables and vegetable juice
- some breakfast cereals, including toasted muesli
- canned soups
- toffees.

Foods low in sodium (less than 0.3 g/100 g) include:

- fresh and frozen fruits and vegetables
- fresh meat, poultry, fish and eggs
- most beverages, including fruit juice, milk, beer, wine and many soft drinks
- cereals and pasta cooked without salt, plain white and wholemeal flour, dried beans and lentils, unsalted seeds and nuts
- untoasted muesli, puffed wheat and rice, unprocessed bran
- quark, cottage and ricotta cheese
- sugar, jam, honey, plain boiled sweets, jelly beans and peppermints
- herbs, spices and oils.

## Reducing your intake

To meet the Dietary Guidelines and the demand created by an increasingly health-conscious public, some companies produce low-salt or salt-reduced versions of standard products, for example low-salt butter, margarine, cheese, or canned soup. Choose low-salt versions for preference; however, remember that a low-salt food may not be appropriate in other ways, perhaps by having a high fat or high sugar content: so use your judgement.

It can take up to three months to adjust to a lower salt taste. It is best if babies and young children don't acquire the taste for salty foods in the first place. Adding salt to food is a habit for many people. Good advice is to:

- taste food before adding salt
- use a salt shaker with smaller holes, or better still put it away
- gradually reduce the amount of salt used in cooking
- try different herbs and spices in cooking to give extra flavour and variety
- don't add salt to dessert, cake, pastry and biscuit recipes
- refrigerate fetta cheese in water
- bring corned beef or smoked cod to the boil in water, and discard the water before proceeding with the usual cooking process
- limit the quantity of salty foods eaten
- read the labels, and choose reduced-salt or salt-free varieties of processed foods as often as possible.

# CALCIUM

Calcium has many important functions in the body, the most easily recognised being its role in bone formation; in fact more than 99 per cent of the calcium in the body is present in the bones. It is well known that babies and children need the calcium supplied by milk and milk products to develop strong, healthy bones and teeth.

Calcium is essential in several other body processes, including blood clotting, nerve transmission, muscle contraction and some enzyme actions.

## Your calcium intake

Your intake of calcium should come from foods – calcium supplements should be taken only on medical advice. The following table gives the recommended intakes for children and adults.

**Recommended dietary intakes of calcium**
*(mg/day)*

| Subject | Age | Recommended intake |
|---|---|---|
| Infants | 0–6 months (breast milk) | 300 |
| | 0–6 months (cow's milk) | 500 |
| Children | 1–3 years | 600 |
| (both sexes) | 4–7 years | 700 |
| Girls | 8–11 years | 900 |
| | 12–15 years | 1000 |
| | 16–18 years | 800 |

| | | |
|---|---|---|
| Boys | 8–11 years | 800 |
| | 12–15 years | 1200 |
| | 16–18 years | 1000 |
| Women | 19–50* years | 800 |
| | After menopause | 1000 |
| | Pregnant | +300** |
| | Lactating | +500 |
| Men | 19–64 years | 800 |
| | 65+ years | 800 |

* Menopause
** Third trimester

Taken from: Nordin, B.E.C. Ch. 17, 'Calcium', in *Recommended Nutrient Intakes: Australian Papers*. A.S. Truswell (ed.), Australian Professional Publications, 1990, p.213.

## Osteoporosis

Like other body tissues, bone is continually being broken down and rebuilt, so throughout life a daily intake of calcium in food is needed for the rebuilding process. With increasing age this rebuilding process slows down: in the elderly more calcium may be lost from bone than is re-absorbed, causing the bones to become weaker and more porous, a condition known as osteoporosis. Bone-thinning is a normal condition of ageing occurring in both men and women; however, it occurs more rapidly in women following menopause when levels of the hormone oestrogen are reduced.

There are three main factors associated with the development of osteoporosis.

1 Genetic characteristics influence bone strength – small-boned, white Caucasian women are the most susceptible to osteoporosis.

2 Exercise is a major factor. Lack of exercise increases bone loss, for example in the bedridden; conversely, women can suffer bone loss if they exercise so much that their hormone levels drop to the point where menstruation is delayed or ceases (a situation similar to menopause). This can occur in ballet dancers and athletes.
3 Heavy drinkers and smokers increase their risk of calcium loss.

*Note*: Bone calcium loss can also occur in people suffering from the 'dieting disease' anorexia nervosa, particularly in women if the condition results in the cessation of menstruation.

## Guarding against osteoporosis

In particular, girls and young women should build up their bone stores of calcium so that they can withstand the natural depletion in middle and old age. The following are general recommendations.

- Keep up the recommended calcium intake.
- Develop the habit of moderate, regular, weight-bearing exercise. Walking, jogging, tennis, golf and dancing are all suitable. While swimming has many benefits it doesn't qualify as a weight-bearing exercise.
- Limit alcohol consumption.
- Avoid smoking.
- Limit caffeine consumption.
- Use less salt.

## Useful dietary sources of calcium

The best dietary sources of calcium are milk, cheese and yoghurt. For adults, low-fat milk and milk products are recommended as these do not provide excess calories, fat or cholesterol.

Other useful dietary sources are certain green vegetables, including broccoli and haricot beans; certain nuts, for example almonds; dried fruits, for example figs; and fish with edible bones, for example sardines and salmon. Soy drinks used as milk substitutes provide some calcium; certain brands add extra calcium to make the drink more like milk in the nutrients it supplies, so check the labels.

## FIBRE

In the days of our grandparents dietary fibre was described as roughage, the indigestible part of food – a waste product of no nutritional value. It is now recognised as a most important constituent of our diet, essential for good health.

There are two main types: insoluble fibre and soluble fibre. Each serves a different function in the body and is found in different plant foods. Animal foods, meat and dairy products do not contain dietary fibre.

### Insoluble fibre

Cereal foods, particularly in the bran portion of wheat and rice, are the main sources of insoluble fibre. It is present in wholegrain breakfast cereals made from wheat; wheat bran; wholemeal and mixed-grain breads; cakes, biscuits and muffins made from wholemeal flour; wholemeal pasta products; and brown rice and rice bran.

These cereal fibres help in the prevention and relief of constipation. Fibre absorbs water in the bowel and in the process softer, bulkier stools are formed. In the longer term this can help prevent bowel diseases such as diverticulitis and haemorrhoids.

## Soluble fibre

This type of fibre is found particularly in rolled oats and oat bran; barley; and brown rice and rice bran (which contain both insoluble and soluble fibres); legumes such as beans, lentils and chick peas; and fruit and vegetables.

Soluble fibre has little laxative effect but is valuable in helping to reduce blood-cholesterol levels.

## Fibre in the diet

Foods high in dietary fibre – fruit, vegetables, legumes and wholegrain breads and cereals – are generally low in fat. (The main exception is nuts.) Most of these foods are bulky, giving a feeling of fullness and satisfying the appetite without supplying excess calories, so making them useful in weight control. Because they are digested more slowly than refined foods they are also recommended in diabetics' diets.

Health authorities recommend an intake of 25–30 grams of fibre per day from a wide variety of sources to ensure the benefits of the different types. Large amounts of one type of fibre (for example wheat bran or a fibre supplement) is not recommended.

To make the most of fibre foods consumed it is important to drink plenty of fluid. If your fibre intake has been low it is advisable to increase it gradually to avoid possible bowel discomfort.

## How to increase your dietary fibre

Eat more of the following:

- fruit and vegetables – fresh, dried, frozen and canned. Use raw and unpeeled fruit and vegetables whenever possible.

- legumes – baked beans, bean-mix salads, homous and casseroles (for example chilli con carne), and lentils, kidney beans and chick peas added to soups (for example minestrone and split-pea)
- wholemeal breads, wholegrain and bran breakfast cereals, wholemeal pasta and brown rice.

Add nuts and seeds to increase variety – in sandwiches, salads and snacks.

The following on page 172 shows you how to make changes to your menu to include more dietary fibre and less fat.

| Choose this ... | ... instead of this. |
| --- | --- |
| fresh or stewed fruit | fruit juice, flavoured milk |
| wholegrain cereal, natural muesli | rice bubbles, fruit loops |
| wholemeal toast | white toast |
| marmalade | butter, honey |
| dried fruit, wholemeal muffin | potato crisps, doughnut |
| wholemeal salad roll (with tuna, lean roast beef or skinless chicken pieces) | meat pie, pastie |
| crispbread with low-fat cheese | crackers with cheddar cheese |
| new potatoes in jackets | peeled or mashed potatoes |
| steamed or microwaved vegetables, brown rice | fried chips |
| stir-fried vegetables (minimum oil) | vegetables with a knob of butter |
| wholemeal dinner roll | garlic bread |
| fruit salad with low-fat yoghurt | cheesecake, apple pie, steamed pudding with custard |

# THE TABLE

| ⁺Values are given for 100g unless specified otherwise. | FAT g/ 100g⁺ | CHOL mg/ 100g⁺ | SOD mg/ 100g⁺ | CALC mg/ 100g⁺ | FIBRE* g/ 100g⁺ |
|---|---|---|---|---|---|
| ***Biscuits*** | | | | | |
| *anzac* | 24 | 18 | 230 | 61 | 3.6 |
| *carob* | 30 | 7 | 160 | 140 | 1.4 |
| *choc-coated/chip* ... av type | 24 | 14 | 300 | 60 | 1.4 |
| *crackers* ... cheese | 22 | 14 | 960 | 120 | 3.4 |
| jatz/salada | 24 | 10 | 670 | 60 | 3.4 |
| rye crispbreads | 2.5 | tr** | 480 | 38 | 14 |
| salada/premium | 14 | 16 | 930 | 20 | 3.6 |
| sao/thin captain | 14 | 7 | 720 | 63 | 2.9 |
| savoury shapes | 24 | 8 | 1100 | 64 | 3.4 |
| vitawheat | 10 | 0 | 410 | 29 | 12.5 |
| water | 9.3 | 3 | 600 | 47 | 2.8 |
| wholemeal + sesame | 15.7 | 6 | 730 | 53 | 7 |
| *cream-filled* | 24 | 23 | 450 | 60 | 1.4 |
| *shortbread* | 25 | 29 | 480 | 35 | 1.9 |
| *sweet* ... fruit-filled | 10 | 13 | 150 | 40 | 2.8 |
| iced | 12.8 | 16 | 250 | 24 | 1.5 |
| jam-filled | 17.7 | 18 | 130 | 34 | 1.8 |
| nut | 27 | 31 | 440 | 90 | 1.9 |
| plain | 16 | 15 | 300 | 36 | 2 |
| *wafers* ... cream-filled | 28 | 19 | 110 | 52 | |
| ***Breads*** | | | | | |
| *bread* ... brown | 2.5 | 0 | 500 | 60 | 5 |
| white | 2.5 | 0 | 450 | 60 | 2.7 |
| 1 slice av type ... 28g | 0.7 | 0 | 130 | 14 | 0.8 |
| *breadcrumbs* ... dried | 3.6 | 0 | 670 | 64 | 4.1 |

**Dietary fibre values are derived from figures based on the AOAC (Association of Official Analytical Chemists) method.*

*** The figure 0 indicates an absence of this nutrient in the food. A trace of the nutrient is indicated by the abbreviation 'tr'. No entry indicates that no figures are yet available.*

| ⁺Values are given for 100g unless specified otherwise. | FAT g/ 100g⁺ | CHOL mg/ 100g⁺ | SOD mg/ 100g⁺ | CALC mg/ 100g⁺ | FIBRE g/ 100g⁺ |
|---|---|---|---|---|---|
| *bread roll* ... white | 2.6 | tr | 700 | 60 | 3.1 |
| wholemeal | 2.4 | tr | 720 | 48 | 5.7 |
| *croissant* ... 1 ... av type ... 65g | 15.3 | 18 | 240 | 50 | 2.9 |
| *crumpet* ... 2 ... av type ... 100g | 0.7 | tr | 950 | 83 | 2.3 |
| *garlic bread* | 17.4 | 12 | 380 | 72 | 2.6 |
| *Lebanese/pita/flat* ... white | 2.3 | 0 | 520 | 20 | 2.8 |
| wholemeal | 2 | 0 | 450 | 20 | 6.3 |
| *muffin* ... English | 1.4 | tr | 420 | 120 | 2.4 |
| fruit | 1.7 | 0 | 470 | 110 | 2.5 |
| *raisin/fruit loaf* | 3.9 | 0 | 190 | 45 | 3 |
| *rye* ... dark | 1.8 | 0 | 510 | 73 | 7.1 |
| light | 2 | 0 | 510 | 39 | 4.5 |
| *white* ... high fibre | 2.7 | 0 | 440 | 60 | 4.3 |
| *wholemeal* | 2.9 | 0 | 470 | 54 | 6.5 |
| high fibre | 3.2 | 0 | 450 | 48 | 7.8 |
| *Buttercup* ... salt-reduced wholemeal | 2.5 | 0 | 245 | 60 | 5 |
| *Vogel* ... wholemeal + sesame | 6 | 0 | 550 | | 1.8 |

| +Values are given for 100g unless specified otherwise. | FAT g/ 100g+ | CHOL mg/ 100g+ | SOD mg/ 100g+ | CALC mg/ 100g+ | FIBRE g/ 100g+ |
|---|---|---|---|---|---|
| ***Breakfast Cereals*** | | | | | |
| *bran* ... oat, raw | 7 | 0 | 4 | 58 | 15.9 |
| rice | 20.4 | 0 | 8 | 58 | 25.5 |
| wheat | 4.5 | 0 | 18 | 87 | 44.7 |
| *branflakes* ... Kelloggs | 2.4 | 0 | 1000 | 66 | 16 |
| *cornflakes* | 1 | 0 | 1190 | 5 | 3.3 |
| *muesli* ... non-toasted ... av | 9.2 | 0 | 55 | 110 | 12.5 |
| toasted ... av sample | 16.6 | 0 | 170 | 65 | 8.7 |
| *oatmeal/rolled oats* ... boiled ... no salt | 1.1 | 0 | 1 | 8 | 1.3 |
| *rice bubbles* | 0.8 | 0 | 970 | 23 | 1 |
| *vita brits/weet-bix* ... av sample | 2.3 | 0 | 390 | 30 | 10.5 |
| *weeties* | 2.1 | 0 | 510 | 29 | 11 |
| *wheat, puffed* | 2.1 | 0 | 1 | 29 | 12.1 |
| *wheatgerm* | 7.8 | 0 | 240 | 41 | 41.7 |
| *Farmland* ... no-added-salt toasted muesli | 19 | | 25 | | 4 |
| *Kellogg's* ... all-bran | 3.3 | 0 | 1020 | 66 | 31 |
| plus fruit | 3.3 | 0 | 580 | | 19.5 |
| coco pops | 2.5 | | 720 | 30 | 1.7 |
| cornflakes | 1.3 | 0 | 933 | | 3.3 |
| just right | 2.3 | 0 | 250 | | 10.6 |
| komplete | 20.8 | | 109 | | 7.6 |
| nutrigrain | 2.7 | 0 | 666 | | 1.7 |
| rice bubbles | 1.3 | 0 | 1093 | | 3.3 |
| sustain, low-salt | 4.3 | 0 | 110 | | 7 |
| ***Butter, Margarines, Fats and Oils*** | | | | | |
| *butter* ... salt-reduced ... av type | 81.3 | 260 | 350 | 17 | 0 |
| standard ... salted | 81.3 | 260 | 843 | 17 | 0 |

Watch out for any hidden fats and cholesterol in the food you buy. Many vegetable oils contain saturated fats.

| +Values are given for 100g unless specified otherwise. | FAT g/ 100g+ | CHOL mg/ 100g+ | SOD mg/ 100g+ | CALC mg/ 100g+ | FIBRE g/ 100g+ |
|---|---|---|---|---|---|
| 10g ... 2 tsp | 8.1 | 26 | 84 | 1.7 | 0 |
| unsalted ... av type | 81.3 | 260 | 8 | 17 | 0 |
| *ghee* | 99 | 300 | 5 | 10 | 0 |
| *margarine* ... cooking | 81 | 105 | 840 | 18 | 105 |
| polyunsaturated ... av type | 81 | 0 | 833 | 20 | 0 |
| reduced-fat ... av type | 40 | 0 | 300 | 5 | 0 |
| table ... av type | 81 | 31 | 840 | 20 | 0 |
| Meadowlea ... low-salt | 81 | | 390 | 20 | 0 |
| *vegetable oils* | 99.7 | 0 | tr | tr | 0 |

*Cakes, Pastries and Puddings*

| | FAT | CHOL | SOD | CALC | FIBRE |
|---|---|---|---|---|---|
| *apple crumble* | 7.8 | | 450 | 65 | |
| *apple pie* | 11.6 | 14 | 288 | 6 | 1.5 |
| McDonald's | 20.1 | 19 | 232 | 22 | 1.6 |
| *apple strudel* | 9.7 | 11 | 340 | 28 | 1.5 |
| *baklava* | 19.8 | 17 | 260 | 42 | 2 |
| *black forest cake* | 19.3 | 57 | 280 | 57 | 0.7 |
| *bun, fruit* | 8 | 4 | 200 | 100 | 3.3 |
| *carrot cake* | 17.7 | 54 | 330 | 50 | 2.5 |
| *cheesecake* | 22.2 | 46 | 270 | 110 | 1 |
| *chocolate cake* | 17.9 | 105 | 500 | 77 | 1.5 |
| *chocolate eclair* | 25.9 | 97 | 160 | 48 | 0.5 |
| *chocolate pudding, self-saucing* | 6.8 | 50 | 200 | 33 | 1 |
| *Christmas pudding* | 6.7 | 40 | 317 | 99 | 3 |
| *cupcake, plain, iced* | 14.9 | 54 | 370 | 4 | 1.1 |
| *custard* | 3 | 11 | 85 | 100 | 0 |
| *custard powder* ... dry | 0.7 | | 320 | 15 | 0 |
| *custard tart* | 13.1 | 54 | 270 | 74 | 1 |
| *Danish pastry* | 15.5 | 35 | 40 | 45 | 2.3 |
| *date and nut loaf* | 11.5 | 30 | 375 | 64 | 3 |
| *doughnut* | 20.6 | 34 | 380 | 41 | 2.2 |

| ⁺Values are given for 100g unless specified otherwise. | FAT g/ 100g⁺ | CHOL mg/ 100g⁺ | SOD mg/ 100g⁺ | CALC mg/ 100g⁺ | FIBRE g/ 100g⁺ |
|---|---|---|---|---|---|
| *fruit cake* ... boiled | 9.7 | 37 | 392 | 40 | 2.9 |
| light | 13.9 | 52 | 360 | 43 | 3.3 |
| dark | 11.6 | 24 | 312 | 56 | 3.4 |
| *fruit mince slice* | 9.4 | 20 | 220 | 35 | 2.1 |
| *jam tart* | 14.9 | 16 | 200 | 13 | 0.9 |
| *jelly crystals* | 0 | 0 | 500 | 4 | 0 |
| *lamington* | 12 | 31 | 140 | 6 | 2.3 |
| *madeira cake* ... home-made | 17 | 91 | 550 | 70 | 1.6 |
| *meringue* | 1.4 | 0 | 40 | 3 | 0 |
| *muesli slice* | 23 | 29 | 300 | 45 | 3 |
| *pancakes, plain* | 15 | 45 | 90 | 100 | 1 |
| *pastry* ... biscuit crust | 23.4 | 7 | 405 | 80 | 1.9 |
| filo ... raw | 2.2 | tr | 800 | 18 | 1.4 |
| puff ... baked | 26.5 | 30 | 545 | 10 | 1.6 |
| shortcrust ... baked | 30 | 36 | 460 | 12 | 2 |
| wholemeal ... baked | 26.3 | 28 | 465 | 23 | 10.4 |
| *plum pudding* ... canned | 7 | 22 | 350 | 51 | 2.6 |
| *quiche* | 22 | 130 | 530 | 14 | 0.7 |
| *scones* ... plain | 8.2 | 10 | 620 | 138 | 1.7 |
| sultana | 9 | 11 | 310 | 100 | 3 |
| *sponge* ... plain | 6 | 68 | 170 | 55 | 0.9 |
| filled | 14 | 130 | 240 | 46 | 0.9 |
| *Swiss roll* | 7 | 36 | 250 | 26 | 1.5 |
| *vanilla slice* | 8.9 | 8 | 170 | 70 | 0.4 |
| ***Cereals*** | | | | | |
| *barley, pearl* ... boiled | 0.8 | 0 | 8 | 10 | 3.5 |
| *bulgur* ... soaked | 0.9 | 0 | 2 | 12 | 8 |
| *flour* ... plain, white | 1.2 | 0 | 2 | 20 | 3.8 |
| self-raising, white | 1.2 | 0 | 700 | 107 | 3.8 |
| wholemeal | 2.1 | 0 | 3 | 30 | 11.2 |

| *Values are given for 100g unless specified otherwise. | FAT g/ 100g* | CHOL mg/ 100g* | SOD mg/ 100g* | CALC mg/ 100g* | FIBRE g/ 100g* |
|---|---|---|---|---|---|
| *pasta* ... white ... cooked ... no added salt | 0.5 | 0 | 3 | 8 | 1.7 |
| wholemeal | 0.8 | 0 | 5 | 28 | 5.7 |
| see also *Fish and Fish Foods; Meats; Take-away and Convenience Meals* | | | | | |
| *rice* ... white ... boiled ... with salt ... | | | | | |
| av salting | 0.6 | 0 | 300 | 7 | 0.2 |
| without salt | 0.6 | 0 | 5 | 17 | 0.2 |
| brown ... boiled | 0.6 | 0 | 9 | 11 | 0.5 |
| fried see *Take-away and Convenience Meals* | | | | | |
| *rye flour* | 2.3 | 0 | 4 | 44 | 1.5 |
| *soya flour* | 20 | 0 | 2 | 210 | 21 |
| ***Cheese and Cheese Foods*** | | | | | |
| *cheese* ... blue vein | 32.5 | 120 | 1000 | 540 | 0 |
| brie | 29.1 | 96 | 604 | 468 | 0 |
| camembert | 26.3 | 93 | 652 | 478 | 0 |
| cheddar | 33.8 | 102 | 647 | 779 | 0 |
| processed | 27.5 | 83 | 1350 | 625 | 0 |
| reduced salt and fat | 25 | 75 | 300 | 800 | 0 |
| cottage | 9.3 | 36 | 200 | 67 | 0 |
| cream | 33 | 97 | 420 | 104 | 0 |
| edam | 27.9 | 88 | 676 | 848 | 0 |
| fetta | 23.3 | 75 | 1060 | 353 | 0 |
| mozzarella | 23.1 | 71 | 367 | 817 | 0 |
| parmesan | 31.5 | 101 | 1371 | 1091 | 0 |

### Nutty Blue Cheese Spread

*25 g walnuts, chopped*
*75 g Danish blue cheese, crumbled*
*275 g low-fat cottage cheese*
*3 tablespoons skim milk*

Blend blue cheese, cottage cheese and skim milk until smooth. Stir in walnuts. Divide between 6 small containers. Label and freeze. Thaw at room temperature for 3 hours, as needed. Makes 6 servings at 480 kJ (115 cal) per portion.

| +Values are given for 100g unless specified otherwise. | FAT g/ 100g+ | CHOL mg/ 100g+ | SOD mg/ 100g+ | CALC mg/ 100g+ | FIBRE g/ 100g+ |
|---|---|---|---|---|---|
| quark | 9.6 | 32 | 100 | 85 | 0 |
| quark/cottage ... low-fat ... av type | 1.2 | 11 | 130 | 77 | 0 |
| ricotta | 11.3 | 48 | 200 | 223 | 0 |
| *cheese souffle* | 16.9 | 450 | 590 | 236 | tr |
| *cheese spreads* | 27 | 75 | 1400 | 400 | 0 |
| *Kraft light* | 25 | | 1300 | | 0 |
| ***Confectionery*** | | | | | |
| *caramels* ... plain | 11.1 | 14 | 226 | 138 | tr |
| with nuts | 16.3 | 13 | 203 | 140 | 5 |
| *carob drink powder* | 8.4 | | | | 19 |
| *chocolate* ... dark | 30 | tr | 55 | 50 | 1 |
| milk | 28 | 18 | 90 | 250 | 0.8 |
| *muesli bars, Gold Crest* ... | | | | | |
| apricot choc chip ... 35g | 7 | | 29 | | 0.8 |
| apricot muesli lite ... 25g | 2.1 | | 22 | | 0.6 |
| bites, cherry and choc ... 20g | 3.1 | | 15 | | 0.7 |
| choc chip ... 35g | 5.5 | | 22 | | 1.4 |
| peanut choc ... 35g | 6.9 | | 23 | | 1.4 |
| *toffee fudge* ... av type | 15 | 20 | 300 | 80 | 1.5 |
| ***Eggs*** | | | | | |
| *egg* ... av sample | 10.1 | 450 | 122 | 54 | 0 |
| fried in oil ... 55g | 21.3 | 201 | 51 | 25 | 0 |
| poached ... 55g | 5.3 | 180 | 41 | 24 | 0 |
| raw ... 55g | 4.8 | 180 | 64 | 19 | 0 |
| scrambled | 15 | 500 | 145 | 90 | 0 |
| *egg omelette* | 13.1 | 410 | 145 | 52 | 0 |
| *egg white* ... 31g | 0 | 0 | 54 | 2 | 0 |
| *egg yolk* ... 17g | 4.8 | 180 | 10 | 17 | 0 |

| †Values are given for 100g unless specified otherwise. | FAT g/ 100g† | CHOL mg/ 100g† | SOD mg/ 100g† | CALC mg/ 100g† | FIBRE g/ 100g† |
|---|---|---|---|---|---|
| ***Fish and Fish Foods*** | | | | | |
| *anchovies, fillets* ... canned | 9 | 77 | 5500 | 170 | 0 |
| *anchovy paste* | 11.2 | 80 | 9604 | 14 | 0 |
| *bream* ... steamed | 5.4 | 85 | 80 | 25 | 0 |
| *calamari* ... fried | 10 | 200 | 320 | 14 | 0 |
| *caviar* ... black | 5.4 | 286 | 2120 | 10 | 0 |
| red | 8.2 | 350 | 1850 | 30 | 0 |
| *cod* ... smoked ... simmered | 1.5 | 60 | 550 | 31 | 0 |
| *crab* ... canned | 0.6 | 84 | 700 | 170 | 0 |
| in black-bean sauce | 10.1 | 56 | 720 | 120 | |
| *eel* ... smoked | 28 | | 100 | 20 | 0 |
| *fish* ... in batter ... frozen ... oven-fried | 19.3 | 27 | 320 | 17 | 0.4 |
| deep-fried in batter ... av sample | 12 | 70 | 200 | 24 | 0.4 |
| floured, pan-fried in oil | 10 | 75 | 130 | 40 | tr |
| steamed ... av sample | 3 | 85 | 100 | 45 | 0 |
| in white sauce | 5 | 100 | 200 | 60 | tr |
| *fish cakes* ... deep-fried | 14.6 | 20 | 980 | 160 | 0.7 |
| *fish cocktail* ... deep-fried | 16.9 | 26 | 460 | 24 | 0.9 |
| *fish fingers* ... frozen ... fried | 16 | 26 | 300 | 33 | 0.9 |
| grilled ... no added salt | 11.3 | 31 | 80 | 35 | 0.4 |
| *fish paste* ... canned | 4.2 | 80 | 1400 | 280 | 0 |
| *flake* ... in batter ... deep-fried | 5.6 | 43 | 250 | 13 | 0.4 |
| *gemfish/mullet* ... crumbed ... fried | 18.5 | 70 | 120 | 16 | 0.4 |

| ⁺Values are given for 100g unless specified otherwise. | FAT g/ 100g⁺ | CHOL mg/ 100g⁺ | SOD mg/ 100g⁺ | CALC mg/ 100g⁺ | FIBRE g/ 100g⁺ |
|---|---|---|---|---|---|
| *herring fillets in tomato sauce* | 4.9 | | 1580 | 100 | tr |
| *lobster* | 0.9 | 116 | 400 | 50 | 0 |
| *mussels* ... smoked ... canned in oil | 10.4 | 92 | 460 | 70 | 0 |
| *oysters* ... fresh ... raw | 2.4 | 80 | 300 | 134 | 0 |
| smoked ... canned in oil | 12 | 76 | 400 | 40 | 0 |
| *prawn chow mien* | 10.9 | 26 | 330 | 34 | 2 |
| *prawn cocktail* | 7.4 | 86 | 830 | 25 | 0.1 |
| *prawn cutlets* | 14.8 | 164 | 650 | 50 | 0 |
| *prawn omelette* | 15.6 | 173 | 480 | 45 | tr |
| *prawns* ... cooked | 0.9 | 188 | 480 | 135 | 0 |
| garlic | 7.4 | 190 | 490 | 100 | 0 |
| *rollmops* | 11.3 | 70 | 1270 | 100 | 0 |
| *salmon, pink/red* ... canned ... | | | | | |
| no added salt | 6.5 | 65 | 120 | 200 | 0 |
| in brine | 10 | 65 | 530 | 200 | 0 |
| smoked | 4.6 | 50 | 1710 | 15 | 0 |
| *sardines* ... canned in brine | 12 | 110 | 760 | 303 | 0 |
| in oil | 15.7 | 114 | 600 | 360 | 0 |
| *scallops* ... simmered | 1.4 | 61 | 150 | 27 | 0 |
| *shrimps* ... fried in batter | 10.8 | 190 | 186 | 72 | 0.4 |
| *spaghetti marinara* | 4.6 | 41 | 250 | 36 | 0.9 |
| *taramasalata* | 19.4 | 32 | 630 | 20 | tr |
| *tuna* ... canned in brine | 2.6 | 53 | 440 | 10 | 0 |
| in oil | 13.7 | 40 | 440 | 7 | 0 |
| raw/canned ... no added salt | 2 | 50 | 90 | 10 | 0 |
| *whiting* ... in batter ... deep-fried | 19.6 | 114 | 460 | 40 | 0.6 |
| floured ... pan-fried | 6.2 | 98 | 70 | 30 | tr |
| steamed | 1.1 | 104 | 70 | 30 | 0 |
| *Findus Lean Cuisine* ... | | | | | |
| fish in lemon sauce ... 1 serve ... 225g | 13 | 100 | 1482 | | |

| +Values are given for 100g unless specified otherwise. | FAT g/ 100g+ | CHOL mg/ 100g+ | SOD mg/ 100g+ | CALC mg/ 100g+ | FIBRE g/ 100g+ |
|---|---|---|---|---|---|
| **_Fruit and Fruit Foods_** | | | | | |
| *apple* ... raw ... av type | tr | 0 | 1 | 5 | 1.6 |
| *apricot* ... raw/canned ... av type | tr | 0 | 2 | 16 | 1.9 |
| *banana* | tr | 0 | 1 | 5 | 1.4 |
| *boysenberry* ... John West ... canned | tr | 0 | 3 | 5 | 3.3 |
| *cherry/grape* | tr | 0 | 5 | 10 | 0.7 |
| *date* | tr | 0 | 15 | 50 | 5.2 |
| *melon* ... cantaloupe/honeydew | tr | 0 | 25 | 25 | 0.6 |
| *nectarine* | tr | 0 | 1 | 10 | 1.5 |
| *orange* | tr | 0 | 2 | 30 | 1.4 |
| *passionfruit* | tr | 0 | 20 | 10 | 3.9 |
| *pawpaw* | tr | 0 | 7 | 30 | 1.1 |
| *peach* ... canned | tr | 0 | 5 | 5 | 1.9 |
| peeled | tr | 0 | 2 | 5 | 1.5 |
| unpeeled | tr | 0 | 2 | 5 | 2.1 |

*Fruit (fresh, canned, cooked, frozen or dried), without added ingredients, contains only a trace of fat, no cholesterol and very low levels of sodium and calcium. The fruits listed here are included for their significant contribution of dietary fibre to the diet.*

| +Values are given for 100g unless specified otherwise. | FAT g/ 100g+ | CHOL mg/ 100g+ | SOD mg/ 100g+ | CAL mg/ 100g+ | FIBRE g/ 100g+ |
|---|---|---|---|---|---|
| *pear* ... canned | tr | 0 | 3 | 5 | 2.8 |
| peeled | tr | 0 | 2 | 5 | 3.2 |
| unpeeled | tr | 0 | 2 | 5 | 5 |
| *pineapple* ... raw/canned ... av type | tr | 0 | 3 | 10 | 1.2 |
| *plum* | tr | 0 | 2 | 10 | 1.2 |
| *prune* | tr | 0 | 10 | 50 | 4 |
| *strawberry* | tr | 0 | 5 | 15 | 0.9 |
| *watermelon* | tr | 0 | 2 | 10 | 0.3 |
| *jams* ... av all varieties | 0 | 0 | 15 | 15 | 1.3 |
| *orange juice* | 0 | 0 | 2 | 10 | 0.2 |
| *prune juice* | 0 | 0 | 3 | 142 | 0.8 |
| *raisins* | tr | 0 | 50 | 68 | 5 |
| *sultanas* | tr | 0 | 35 | 53 | 4 |

### *Meats*

*Animal foods (meat, fish, poultry, eggs, milk and dairy foods) by themselves contain no dietary fibre. Some sausages, hamburgers, luncheon meats and convenience meats are manufactured with added cereals and/or vegetable protein, which may contribute small amounts of dietary fibre.*

| | FAT | CHOL | SOD | CAL | FIBRE |
|---|---|---|---|---|---|
| *bacon* ... fried | 30 | 74 | 1540 | 10 | 0 |
| grilled | 22 | 88 | 2000 | 10 | 0 |
| *beef* ... | | | | | |
| cooked ... av trim | 13.5 | 78 | 60 | 10 | 0 |
| lean | 6.3 | 75 | 60 | 9 | 0 |
| chuck steak ... cooked ... av trim | 13.7 | 86 | 45 | 7 | 0 |
| lean | 6 | 82 | 50 | 7 | 0 |
| corned brisket ... boiled | 24 | 70 | 820 | 6 | 0 |
| corned silverside ... boiled ... av trim | 12.9 | 70 | 1280 | 5 | 0 |
| lean | 3.5 | 70 | 1420 | 5 | 0 |
| fillet steak ... grilled ... av trim | 13.2 | 85 | 60 | 6 | 0 |
| lean | 8.3 | 82 | 60 | 6 | 0 |

| *Values are given for 100g unless specified otherwise. | FAT g/ 100g+ | CHOL mg/ 100g+ | SOD mg/ 100g+ | CALC mg/ 100g+ | FIBRE g/ 100g+ |
|---|---|---|---|---|---|
| hamburger mince ... cooked | 12.1 | 93 | 62 | 15 | 0 |
| kidney ... cooked | 2.7 | 549 | 110 | 17 | 0 |
| liver ... cooked | 11.7 | 409 | 70 | 9 | 0 |
| mince ... regular ... cooked | 9.8 | 69 | 60 | 9 | 0 |
| oxtail | 29.3 | 59 | 50 | 15 | 0 |
| rump steak ... grilled ... av trim | 16.8 | 86 | 50 | 5 | 0 |
| lean | 7 | 82 | 50 | 5 | 0 |
| tongue ... simmered | 25 | 60 | 80 | 6 | 0 |
| topside roast ... baked ... av trim | 10 | 68 | 50 | 5 | 0 |
| lean | 5 | 66 | 50 | 5 | 0 |
| tripe ... stewed | 4.5 | 160 | 73 | 150 | 0 |
| *beef in black-bean sauce* | 7.2 | 21 | 560 | 214 | 0.5 |
| *beef casserole with vegetables* | 11 | 30 | 330 | 14 | 2.4 |
| *beef chow mein* | 8.7 | 8 | 420 | 15 | 2.4 |
| *beef in oyster sauce* | 9.6 | 20 | 550 | 11 | 0.5 |

| +Values are given for 100g unless specified otherwise. | FAT g/ 100g+ | CHOL mg/ 100g+ | SOD mg/ 100g+ | CALC mg/ 100g+ | FIBRE g/ 100g+ |
|---|---|---|---|---|---|
| *beef satay* | 12.9 | 23 | 450 | 18 | 2 |
| *beef sausage* ... grilled | 18 | 65 | 900 | 14 | 2.2 |
| *canelloni* | 8.4 | 24 | 260 | 67 | 3 |
| frozen | 6.7 | 18 | 310 | 57 | 3 |
| *chicken* ... | | | | | |
| breast ... with skin ... baked | 12.7 | 99 | 60 | 10 | 0 |
| without skin ... baked | 4.8 | 92 | 65 | 10 | 0 |
| breast quarter roast ... with skin | 12.3 | 75 | 180 | 10 | 0 |
| cooked ... av trim ... with skin | 16.3 | 128 | 75 | 14 | 0 |
| without skin | 8.1 | 128 | 80 | 16 | 0 |
| croquette ... deep-fried ... 2 | 17.6 | 29 | 610 | 20 | tr |
| drumstick ... with skin | 15 | 151 | 91 | 20 | 0 |
| without skin | 10.6 | 154 | 96 | 20 | 0 |
| leg quarter roast ... with skin | 18.6 | 92 | 190 | 10 | 0 |
| *Kentucky/McDonalds* see *Take-away and Convenience Meals.* | | | | | |
| *chicken a la king* | 14 | 80 | 310 | 52 | 1 |
| *chicken and almonds* | 9.8 | 46 | 430 | 28 | 1 |
| *chicken cacciatore* | 7.5 | 61 | 240 | 26 | 1 |

| +Values are given for 100g unless specified otherwise. | FAT g/ 100g+ | CHOL mg/ 100g+ | SOD mg/ 100g+ | CALC mg/ 100g+ | FIBRE g/ 100g+ |
|---|---|---|---|---|---|
| *chicken chop suey* | 6.5 | 20 | 230 | 16 | 2.4 |
| *chicken, lemon* ... crispy skin ... av sample | 14 | 85 | 465 | 20 | tr |
| *chicken omelette* | 18 | 101 | 420 | 25 | tr |
| *corned beef* see *beef* | | | | | |
| *dim sim* | 8.6 | 7 | 1070 | 67 | 1.3 |
| *duck, Chinese* see *Take-away and Convenience Meals* | | | | | |
| *duck, roast* | 29 | 150 | 200 | 20 | 0 |
| *frankfurters* ... boiled | 20 | 60 | 770 | 30 | 1.8 |
| cocktail | 24 | 60 | 360 | 6 | 1.5 |
| *ham* ... canned ... leg | 4.5 | 42 | 1250 | 14 | 0 |
| shoulder | 6.3 | 42 | 1430 | 16 | 0 |
| cooked ... leg | 7.6 | 53 | 1515 | 8 | 0 |
| shoulder | 6 | 52 | 1270 | 9 | 0 |
| *hamburger* ... plain | 10.2 | 26 | 660 | 21 | 1.8 |
| see also *Take-away and Convenience Meals* | | | | | |
| *lamb* ... brains ... simmered | 9.4 | 1886 | 110 | 10 | 0 |
| crumbed, fried | 21.1 | 1900 | 380 | 43 | 0.4 |
| chump chops ... grilled ... av trim | 18.4 | 109 | 70 | 20 | 0 |
| lean | 7.8 | 109 | 75 | 17 | 0 |
| cutlets ... crumbed, fried | 38.2 | 109 | 500 | 9 | 0.4 |
| kidney ... simmered | 4.3 | 550 | 200 | 20 | 0 |
| leg ... baked ... av trim | 11.9 | 109 | 70 | 5 | 0 |
| lean | 5.6 | 109 | 70 | 4 | 0 |
| liver ... fried | 13.7 | 585 | 100 | 7 | 0 |
| midloin chops ... grilled ... av trim | 31.4 | 110 | 90 | 8 | 0 |
| 75% trim | 15.2 | 109 | 90 | 7 | 0 |
| lean | 7.2 | 109 | 100 | 7 | 0 |
| shank | 10.5 | 109 | 80 | 20 | 0 |
| tongue ... simmered | 20.4 | 146 | 90 | 9 | 0 |
| *lamb casserole with vegetables* | 7.9 | 100 | 350 | 12 | 2.4 |
| *lamb's fry and bacon* ... fried | 38.2 | 500 | 550 | 7 | 0 |
| *lasagne* | 6 | 18 | 240 | 39 | 2 |

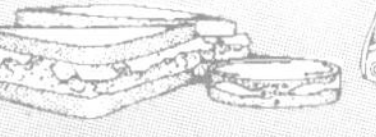

| +Values are given for 100g unless specified otherwise. | FAT g/ 100g+ | CHOL mg/ 100g+ | SOD mg/ 100g+ | CALC mg/ 100g+ | FIBRE g/ 100g+ |
|---|---|---|---|---|---|
| *Lebanese sausages* | 18.1 | 71 | 650 | 28 | |
| *luncheon meats ...* | | | | | |
| beef, German | 17.4 | 48 | 800 | 37 | 1 |
| Berliner fleischwurst | 18.2 | 60 | 750 | 26 | 1 |
| black pudding | 18.6 | 72 | 970 | 48 | 1 |
| cabanossi | 31.6 | 71 | 810 | 31 | 1 |
| chicken Devon | 17.8 | 64 | 920 | 38 | 1 |
| chicken roll | 7.6 | 47 | 670 | 32 | 1.3 |
| Devon | 18 | 45 | 770 | 38 | 1 |
| fritz | 19 | 51 | 830 | 32 | 1 |
| garlic roll | 18.9 | 51 | 840 | 34 | 2.4 |
| ham and chicken roll | 18 | 50 | 800 | 30 | 1.7 |
| ham sausage | 23.8 | 67 | 630 | 21 | 1 |
| liverwurst ... calf | 26.2 | 140 | 700 | 23 | 1 |
| chicken | 26.4 | 130 | 670 | 21 | 1 |
| mortadella | 29.3 | 64 | 770 | 45 | 1.4 |
| salami ... Danish | 40.2 | 115 | 1370 | 23 | 0 |

| +Values are given for 100g unless specified otherwise. | FAT g/ 100g+ | CHOL mg/ 100g+ | SOD mg/ 100g+ | CALC mg/ 100g+ | FIBRE g/ 100g+ |
|---|---|---|---|---|---|
| Hungarian | 37.4 | 92 | 1860 | 27 | 0 |
| mettwurst | 37.5 | 81 | 1470 | 18 | 0 |
| Milano | 36.9 | 104 | 1390 | 39 | 0 |
| pepperoni | 36.1 | 129 | 1200 | 25 | 0 |
| Polish | 17.8 | 50 | 880 | 19 | 0 |
| **strasbourg** | 19.2 | 51 | 870 | 31 | 1.8 |
| *meat paste* | 13 | 90 | 800 | 200 | 1 |
| *meat pie* ... see *Take-away and Convenience Meals* | | | | | |
| *moussaka* | 9.6 | 40 | 310 | 70 | 0.9 |
| *osso bucco* | 9.6 | 77 | 310 | 37 | 0.5 |
| pastie see *Take-away and Convenience Meals* | | | | | |
| *pâté* | 24.7 | 159 | 970 | 24 | 1.3 |
| *pork* ... butterfly steak ... grilled ... av trim | 17.6 | 86 | 45 | 8 | 0 |
| 75% trim | 8.4 | 84 | 50 | 8 | 0 |
| lean | 4.7 | 83 | 50 | 8 | 0 |
| Chinese, barbecued | 15.2 | 63 | 1070 | 18 | tr |
| chop ... grilled | 28 | 92 | 75 | 32 | 0 |
| 75% trim | 14.4 | 92 | 80 | 30 | 0 |
| chop suey | 8.8 | 15 | 550 | 26 | 2.4 |
| cooked ... av trim | 22 | 89 | 60 | 14 | 0 |
| leg ... baked ... av trim | 26.7 | 15 | 50 | 6 | 0 |
| 75% trim | 11.4 | 92 | 50 | 7 | 0 |
| sausage ... grilled | 22 | 60 | 1000 | 15 | 1.5 |
| spare ribs ... in black-bean sauce | 14.6 | 38 | 800 | 36 | 0.5 |
| in plum sauce | 17.4 | 43 | 500 | 20 | 0.5 |
| sweet-and-sour | 9.4 | 60 | 390 | 14 | 1.5 |
| steak ... grilled ... av trim | 5.9 | 93 | 60 | 6 | 0 |
| lean | 5.2 | 84 | 60 | 13 | 0 |
| *ravioli* | 5.4 | 20 | 310 | 77 | 1.5 |
| frozen | 4.6 | 14 | 280 | 65 | 1.5 |
| *saltimbocca* | 14.1 | 59 | 500 | 77 | 0.4 |
| *sausage roll* | 17.6 | 20 | 650 | 20 | 1.3 |

| +Values are given for 100g unless specified otherwise. | FAT g/ 100g+ | CHOL mg/ 100g+ | SOD mg/ 100g+ | CALC mg/ 100g+ | FIBRE g/ 100g+ |
|---|---|---|---|---|---|
| *sausages* ... with meat ... deep-fried | 25.2 | 48 | 800 | 13 | 0.4 |
| grilled | 17.3 | 60 | 810 | 14 | 2.8 |
| *saveloy* ... in batter, deep-fried | 20.8 | 23 | 1020 | 35 | 0.1 |
| *shish kebab* | 10 | 135 | 170 | 10 | 0 |
| *souvlakia* | 11.3 | 94 | 320 | 10 | 0 |
| *spaghetti Bolognese* | 4 | 10 | 240 | 29 | 1 |
| *veal* ... boneless ... cooked ... av trim | 3.9 | 111 | 80 | 7 | 0 |
| lean | 2.5 | 111 | 80 | 7 | 0 |
| chops ... grilled ... av trim | 4.8 | 111 | 100 | 8 | 0 |
| trimmed | 2.3 | 82 | 90 | 8 | 0 |
| cutlets ... crumbed, fried | 28.5 | 110 | 211 | 4 | 0.4 |
| kidney ... grilled | 6.7 | 434 | 230 | 15 | 0 |
| liver ... cooked | 8.1 | 244 | 100 | 7 | 0 |
| shank ... simmered | 2.4 | 82 | 100 | 23 | 0 |
| *veal marsala* | 10.6 | 82 | 210 | 7 | tr |
| *Findus Lean Cuisine* ... | | | | | |
| beef oriental ... 245g | 3 | 95 | 1270 | | |
| chicken and coconut ... 260g | 8 | 40 | 760 | | |
| spaghetti beef and mushroom ... 325g | 7 | 20 | 1400 | | |
| ***Milk, Ice-cream, Yoghurt and Non-dairy Substitutes*** | | | | | |
| *coconut cream* | 20 | 0 | 20 | 4 | 1.7 |

You don't have to buy full-cream milk to be sure that you get the valuable calcium it contains. Modified fat and skim milks are just as high in calcium as whole milk. They may have lost some of the A and D vitamins through having the fat skimmed off, but many producers are putting these lost vitamins back into their low-fat products. Even hardened whole-milk drinkers can make the transition to skim milk by changing to fat-modified milk first. If you use skim milk for cooking you will probably be unable to taste the difference.

| *Values are given for 100g unless specified otherwise. | FAT g/ 100g* | CHOL mg/ 100g* | SOD mg/ 100g* | CALC mg/ 100g* | FIBRE g/ 100g* |
|---|---|---|---|---|---|
| *coconut milk* ... from fresh nut | tr | 0 | 20 | 15 | tr |
| *cream/sour cream/thickened cream* | 35 | 100 | 36 | 60 | 0 |
| *cream* ... reduced-fat | 25 | 85 | 40 | 97 | 0 |
| *ice-cream* ... vanilla ... tub variety | 11 | 32 | 80 | 140 | 0 |
| Streets ... paddle pop ... 1 | 3.4 | | 91 | 100 | 0 |
| gaytime/ cornetto ... 1 | 12.3 | | 95 | 100 | 1.3 |
| cal control ... 1 | 1.2 | | 38 | 62 | 0 |
| *milk* ... cow's, whole | 3.8 | 14 | 51 | 120 | 0 |
| flavoured ... av all varieties | 3.5 | 14 | 55 | 110 | 0 |
| goat's, UHT | 2.6 | 9 | 66 | 110 | 0 |
| human | 3.9 | 16 | 14 | 31 | 0 |
| reduced-fat ... Rev | 1.5 | 5 | 60 | 145 | 0 |
| PhysiCAL | 1.4 | 5 | 37 | 205 | 0 |
| skim | 0.1 | 4 | 54 | 120 | 0 |
| Farmhouse | 4.8 | 20 | 50 | 118 | 0 |
| *milk, condensed* ... sweet. ... full-cream | 9.2 | 27 | 104 | 250 | 0 |
| skim | 0.3 | 6 | 120 | 320 | 0 |
| *milk, evaporated* ... unsweet. ... full-cream | 8.1 | 20 | 100 | 250 | 0 |
| skim | 0.3 | 5 | 100 | 250 | 0 |
| *milk powder* ... full-cream | 26.2 | 6 | 300 | 780 | 0 |
| skim | 1 | 13 | 425 | 1310 | 0 |
| *sour cream* ... reduced-fat | 19.7 | 47 | 56 | 135 | 0 |
| *sour-cream dip* | 17.4 | 36 | 600 | 130 | 0 |
| *soya curd/tofu* ... fried | 25 | 0 | 10 | 507 | 0.4 |
| steamed | 4 | 0 | 10 | 507 | 0.4 |
| *soya milk* | 2 | 0 | 70 | 12 | 0.1 |
| *Vitari fruit ice* | tr | 0 | 38 | 0 | – |
| *yoghurt* ... fruit ... av all flavours | 2.1 | 8 | 65 | 130 | 0.2 |
| low-fat | 0.2 | 2 | 68 | 173 | 0.2 |
| plain | 4.4 | 14 | 77 | 195 | 0 |
| low-fat | 0.2 | 2 | 97 | 260 | 0 |

| +Values are given for 100g unless specified otherwise. | FAT g/ 100g+ | CHOL mg/ 100g+ | SOD mg/ 100g+ | CALC mg/ 100g+ | FIBRE g/ 100g+ |
|---|---|---|---|---|---|
| ***Nuts and Seeds*** | | | | | |
| *almonds* ... roasted, salted | 56.7 | 0 | 198 | 245 | 9 |
| sugar-coated | 18.6 | 0 | 20 | 100 | 8 |
| *brazil* | 68 | 0 | 2 | 180 | 9 |
| *cashew* | 45 | 0 | 11 | 50 | 5 |
| *coconut* ... desiccated | 62 | 0 | 13 | 23 | 15 |
| fresh | 36 | 0 | 20 | 13 | 7 |
| *peanut butter* | 50 | 0 | 300 | 45 | 10 |
| Farmland ... no added salt | 49 | 0 | 25 | 65 | 10 |
| *peanuts* ... raw | 47.9 | 0 | 4 | 57 | 9 |
| roasted, salted | 48.6 | 0 | 440 | 72 | 8 |
| Farmland ... no added salt | 51 | 0 | 10 | 65 | 1.9 |
| *sesame seeds* | 55 | 0 | 24 | 60 | 10 |
| *sunflower seeds* | 51 | 0 | tr | 100 | 10 |
| *tahini paste* | 60 | 0 | 80 | 330 | 13 |
| see also *Snack Foods* | | | | | |
| ***Salad Dressings*** | | | | | |
| *French dressing* ... av brand | 35.2 | 0 | 1200 | 7 | 0.5 |
| *Italian dressing* ... Bertolii/Kraft | 26.7 | 0 | 865 | 12 | 1.2 |
| *mayonnaise* ... home-made ... av sample | 78.9 | 90 | 360 | 20 | 0.5 |
| low-energy, low-oil ... av all brands | 0.9 | 0 | 890 | 36 | 1 |
| Eta | 16.1 | 29 | 720 | 16 | 1.4 |
| Fountain Salad Magic, cholesterol-free | 10.7 | 0 | 710 | | 0.6 |
| Hain | 81.7 | 14 | 360 | 20 | 0.6 |
| Kraft Free | 12 | 0 | 1110 | | 0.5 |
| Miracle Whip | 51.1 | 81 | 190 | | 0.7 |
| Natural | 27.5 | 32 | 800 | | 0.5 |
| McCormick/Praise | 74 | 25 | 630 | | 0.6 |

| *Values are given for 100g unless specified otherwise. | FAT g/ 100g* | CHOL mg/ 100g* | SOD mg/ 100g* | CALC mg/ 100g* | FIBRE g/ 100g* |
|---|---|---|---|---|---|
| Praise Light | 29 | 55 | 550 | | 0.4 |
| Lo-Salt | 73 | 20 | 270 | | 0.4 |
| *salad dressing ...* | | | | | |
| condensed-milk, home-made | 5 | 14 | 840 | 90 | 0 |
| thousand island ... av sample | 36 | 28 | 840 | 10 | 1.4 |

## *Salt, Sauces, Gravies and Seasonings*

*Most of the foods and condiments in this section are included for the comparison of their sodium values. Unless indicated otherwise, they contain no significant levels of the other nutrients listed in these tables.*

| | FAT | CHOL | SOD | CALC | FIBRE |
|---|---|---|---|---|---|
| *baking powder* | 0 | 0 | 11600 | 11300 | 0 |
| 1 tsp | 0 | 0 | 580 | 565 | 0 |
| *beef extract* | 0.2 | tr | 6400 | 100 | 0 |
| *bicarbonate of soda* | 0 | 0 | 26000 | | 0 |
| 1 tsp | 0 | 0 | 1300 | | 0 |
| *chutney* ... av sample | 0.5 | 0 | 650 | 25 | 2 |
| 1 tsp | tr | 0 | 40 | 1 | tr |

| ⁺Values are given for 100g unless specified otherwise. | FAT g/ 100g⁺ | CHOL mg/ 100g⁺ | SOD mg/ 100g⁺ | CALC mg/ 100g⁺ | FIBRE g/ 100g⁺ |
|---|---|---|---|---|---|
| *curry powder* | tr | 0 | 450 | 640 | |
| 1 tsp | tr | 0 | 22 | 32 | |
| *gravy* ... made from roast-meat drippings | 8.5 | 23 | 470 | 3 | |
| *gravy powder* ... made up ... 1/4 cup | 0.1 | 0 | 630 | 3 | |
| 1 tsp ... dry ... av sample | 0.4 | 0 | 250 | tr | 0 |
| *marmite* | 1.6 | 0 | 3050 | 25 | 0 |
| 1 tsp | tr | 0 | 152 | 5 | 0 |
| *meat/chicken seasoning* | tr | 0 | 17600 | 70 | 0 |
| *meat tenderiser* | tr | 0 | 28000 | | 0 |
| 1 tsp | tr | 0 | 1400 | | 0 |
| *monosodium glutamate (msg)* | 0 | 0 | 12500 | | 0 |
| 1 tsp | 0 | 0 | 700 | | 0 |
| *mustard* ... hot ... English | 3 | 0 | 4400 | 80 | 4 |
| prepared ... av sample | 3 | 0 | 1500 | 80 | 4 |
| *mustard powder* ... 1 tsp ... dry ... av sample | 2 | 0 | 240 | 20 | tr |
| *pepper/herbs/spices* ... in normal use | | | tr | | |
| *salt* ... cooking | 0 | 0 | 39000 | 30 | 0 |
| rock | 0 | 0 | 39000 | 230 | 0 |
| sea | 0 | 0 | 39000 | 30 | 0 |
| table | 0 | 0 | 39000 | 30 | 0 |
| vegetable/celery/garlic | 0 | 0 | 28000 | 20 | 0 |
| 1 tsp | 0 | 0 | 2000 | tr | 0 |
| *salt-free substitutes* | 0 | 0 | tr | | 0 |
| *salt substitute* ... lite salt | 0 | 0 | 20000 | | 0 |
| 1 tsp | 0 | 0 | 1000 | | 0 |
| *sauces** ... barbecue | tr | 0 | 815 | 15 | 1 |
| cheese | 13 | 30 | 546 | 280 | 0.5 |
| chilli | 0.6 | 0 | 1338 | 9 | 1 |
| curry, home-made | 2.1 | 5 | 376 | 11 | 1 |
| parsley, home-made | 8 | 21 | 300 | 160 | 0.5 |
| satay | 10.6 | 0 | 500 | 40 | 2.5 |

**For 1 tbsp of these sauces calculate one-fifth of values given – a useful approximate measurement.*

| +Values are given for 100g unless specified otherwise. | FAT g/ 100g+ | CHOL mg/ 100g+ | SOD mg/ 100g+ | CALC mg/ 100g+ | FIBRE g/ 100g+ |
|---|---|---|---|---|---|
| *soya* | 1.3 | 0 | 7500 | 20 | 0 |
| low-salt | 1 | 0 | 3400 | 20 | 0 |
| tartare | 53.8 | 90 | 707 | 19 | 1 |
| tomato | 0.4 | 0 | 1042 | 20 | 1.9 |
| white | 8.9 | 21 | 300 | 160 | tr |
| worcestershire ... Holbrooks | tr | 0 | 690 | 160 | 0 |
| Farmland ... tomato ... no added salt | 0.4 | 0 | 35 | 20 | 1.5 |
| *sauces, dehydrated* ... Bolognese | 11.4 | | 11300 | 45 | tr |
| brown onion | 10.7 | | 13500 | 140 | 3 |
| curry | 13.2 | | 10600 | 200 | 1 |
| mushroom | 11.2 | | 12500 | 140 | 4 |
| white | 13 | | 10800 | 600 | tr |
| *stock cubes and powders* ... av | 9 | tr | 10000 | 70 | 0 |
| *stuffing, savoury* ... for chicken | 8.4 | 13 | 520 | 30 | 2 |
| *tomato paste* | tr | 0 | 400 | 30 | 3 |
| *vegemite* | tr | 0 | 3200 | 50 | 0 |
| 1 tsp | tr | 0 | 150 | 2 | 0 |
| *vinegar* | 0 | 0 | tr | tr | 0 |
| ***Snack Foods*** | | | | | |
| *beer nuts* | | | | | |
| salted | 50 | 0 | 330 | | 2 |
| Farmland ... no added salt | 51 | 0 | 10 | 50 | 2.1 |
| Nobby's salted peanuts | 40.6 | 0 | 350 | 40 | 15.4 |
| *corn chips* ... flavoured | 29 | 2 | 640 | 120 | 5 |
| toasted | 26.7 | 0 | 600 | 110 | 4.9 |
| *extruded snack foods* ... cheese | 27.9 | 8 | 1002 | 120 | 2.7 |
| *French fries* | 31.3 | 0 | 660 | 25 | 4.5 |
| *popcorn* ... plain | 24.4 | 6 | 980 | 9 | 8.5 |
| *pork rind snack* | 28.5 | 75 | 4260 | 17 | 0 |
| *potato crisps* ... cheese and onion | 35 | 3 | 470 | 60 | 3.5 |

| +Values are given for 100g unless specified otherwise. | FAT g/ 100g+ | CHOL mg/ 100g+ | SOD mg/ 100g+ | CALC mg/ 100g+ | FIBRE g/ 100g+ |
|---|---|---|---|---|---|
| flavoured | 33.4 | 1 | 460 | 37 | 3.5 |
| plain | 32.1 | 0 | 638 | 25 | 3.6 |
| Farmland no added salt | 37 | 0 | 20 | 30 | 0.2 |
| Lites | 31.8 | 0 | 530 | 30 | 6.5 |
| chicken | 28.9 | 1 | 310 | 30 | 3.5 |
| *potato straws* ... plain | 31.3 | 0 | 660 | 31 | 3 |
| *pretzels* ... av sample | 7.2 | 0 | 1980 | 25 | 3 |
| *Bigs* | 32 | 2 | 860 | 115 | 5.8 |
| *C C's tangy bbq corn chips* | 29 | 3 | 640 | 115 | 6.1 |
| ***Soups*** | | | | | |
| *canned, condensed* ... av all varieties | 3 | tr | 810 | 20 | tr |
| *chicken noodle* ... made up | tr | 2 | 1136 | 5 | tr |
| *cream of chicken* ... canned, condensed | 2.7 | tr | 710 | 20 | tr |
| diluted with water | 1.3 | tr | 350 | 10 | tr |
| *dried, packet mix* ... av all varieties | 3 | 9 | 6120 | 40 | tr |
| *tomato* ... canned, condensed | tr | 0 | 810 | 10 | 2 |
| diluted with water | tr | 0 | 410 | 5 | 1 |
| *Continental* ... chicken noodle ... salt-reduced ... made up | tr | 2 | 160 | 5 | tr |
| ***Take-away and Convenience Meals*** | | | | | |
| *bean salad* | 4.8 | 0 | 450 | 20 | 3.7 |
| *cannelloni* | 6.7 | 21 | 285 | 60 | 3.3 |
| *chiko roll* | 10.4 | 7 | 690 | 30 | 1.3 |
| *Chinese duck* | 7.4 | 40 | 400 | 25 | tr |
| *Chinese fried rice* | 6.3 | 30 | 500 | 10 | 2 |
| *coleslaw* ... see *Kentucky (below)* | | | | | |
| *combination chow mien* | 9.5 | 40 | 410 | 12 | 2 |
| *croissant with egg, cheese and bacon* | 22 | 167 | 689 | 117 | 1.5 |
| *dim sim* ... fried | 8.6 | 7 | 1070 | 60 | 1.3 |

| *Values are given for 100g unless specified otherwise. | FAT g/ 100g* | CHOL mg/ 100g* | SOD mg/ 100g* | CALC mg/ 100g* | FIBRE g/ 100g* |
|---|---|---|---|---|---|
| *fish in batter* ... see *Fish and Fish Foods* | | | | | |
| *fish cake* ... see *Fish and Fish Foods* | | | | | |
| *hamburger* ... bacon | 13.1 | 29 | 780 | 20 | 1.7 |
| cheese | 13.3 | 34 | 760 | 83 | 1.7 |
| egg | 11.8 | 110 | 600 | 26 | 1.6 |
| plain | 10.2 | 26 | 660 | 21 | 1.8 |
| see also *Meats*; *McDonalds (below)* | | | | | |
| *hot dog* ... 1 av | 24 | | 900 | 30 | 1.2 |
| *lasagne* see *Meats* | | | | | |
| *meat pie* | 13.8 | 20 | 600 | 11 | 1.1 |
| 1 ... 170g | 23 | 34 | 1000 | 18 | 1.8 |

| ⁺Values are given for 100g unless specified otherwise. | FAT g/ 100g⁺ | CHOL mg/ 100g⁺ | SOD mg/ 100g⁺ | CALC mg/ 100g⁺ | FIBRE g/ 100g⁺ |
|---|---|---|---|---|---|
| *Mexican* ... enchirito + cheese, beef and beans | 8.3 | 26 | 648 | 113 | 1 |
| frijoles with cheese | 4.7 | 22 | 528 | 113 | 2.3 |
| nachos with cheese | 16.8 | 16 | 722 | 241 | 1.7 |
| taco | 12 | 33 | 469 | 129 | 1.2 |
| with salad | 7.5 | 22 | 385 | 97 | 1.3 |
| with chilli con carne | 5 | 2 | 339 | 94 | 2 |
| *pastie* | 6.8 | 17 | 640 | 18 | 1.3 |
| 1 ... 165g | 11 | 28 | 1000 | 30 | 2 |
| *pizza* ... ham and pineapple ... frozen ... av sample | 11.1 | 14 | 700 | 140 | 2.6 |
| *pizza supreme* ... frozen ... av sample | 11.5 | 20 | 720 | 160 | 2.6 |
| *potato, baked* ... + sour cream and chives | 7.4 | 8 | 60 | 35 | 0.5 |
| + cheese and bacon | 8.7 | 10 | 325 | 103 | 0.5 |
| *potato chips* | 14 | 12 | 250 | 10 | 3.7 |
| *potato salad* see *Kentucky (below)* | | | | | |
| *potato scallop* ... deep-fried | 21.6 | 21 | 260 | 17 | 3 |
| *ravioli* see *Meats* | | | | | |
| *sausage roll* | 17.6 | 20 | 650 | 20 | 1.3 |
| *spaghetti in meat sauce* ... canned | 2.3 | 4 | 510 | 8 | 0.9 |
| *spaghetti in tomato/cheese sauce* ... canned | 0.4 | 1 | 400 | 9 | 0.9 |
| *spanakopita (spinach and cheese pie)* | 20.6 | 32 | 750 | 90 | 1.3 |
| *spring roll* ... fried | 9.8 | 11 | 780 | 26 | 1.3 |

It has been a popular misconception that bread and potatoes are the most fattening foods. To gain 1 kg of body fat would mean eating more than 120 smallish (100 g) potatoes. What's more, you would not put on that 1 kg if you ate 1 potato per day for 120 days, because the body prefers to burn carbohydrate kilojoules for physical activity. The potato only becomes the dieter's enemy if accompanied by butter, margarine, sour cream, oil or some other type of fat.

| *Values are given for 100g unless specified otherwise. | FAT g/ 100g* | CHOL mg/ 100g* | SOD mg/ 100g* | CALC mg/ 100g* | FIBRE g/ 100g* |
|---|---|---|---|---|---|
| *steak sandwich* | 6.9 | 36 | 391 | 30 | 1.3 |
| *tofu burger* | 8 | | 130 | | |
| *Farmland* ... Irish stew ... no added salt | 2.4 | 30 | 110 | 12 | 1.5 |
| *Kentucky* ... bacon and cheese chicken fillet burger | 13.4 | | | | 0.6 |
| bean salad | 4.8 | 0 | 450 | 19 | |
| chicken fillet burger | 13.3 | | | | 0.6 |
| chicken original recipe | 22 | 98 | 588 | 15 | |
| coleslaw | 4 | 12 | 270 | 35 | |
| Colonel Burger | 12.9 | | | | 0.5 |
| French fries | 16.3 | 5 | 60 | | |
| small sv ... 1 | 19.7 | 6 | 73 | | |
| Kentucky Nuggets | 16.4 | | | | |
| mashed potato and gravy ... 1 | 4.6 | 12 | 386 | 7 | |
| potato salad | 5.7 | 9 | 380 | 10 | |
| medium sv ... 1 | 22.5 | 35 | 1500 | 38 | |
| *McDonalds* ... apple pie ... 1 | 17.1 | 16 | 197 | 19 | |
| big breakfast ... 1 | 33.9 | 433 | 840 | 140 | 1.1 |
| big mac ... 1 | 31 | 85 | 1092 | 153 | 1.1 |
| cheeseburger ... 1 | 16 | 35 | 815 | 104 | 1.3 |
| chicken mcnuggets ... 6 pieces with sauce | 21.8 | 117 | 630 | 31 | |
| cookies ... 1 box | 13.1 | 12 | 132 | 22 | 1.5 |
| egg mcmuffin ... 1 | 21.3 | 382 | 610 | 100 | 1.1 |
| English muffin ... 1 | 6.4 | 12 | 200 | 61 | 2.4 |
| filet-o-fish ... 1 | 21.5 | 44 | 962 | 80 | 1.4 |
| French fries | 15.5 | 21 | 152 | 9 | 3 |
| regular ... 81g | 12.6 | 17 | 123 | 7 | 2.4 |
| hash browns ... 1 | 12.2 | 21 | 290 | | |
| hot cakes with syrup ... 1 | 11.8 | 30 | 1130 | 120 | |
| junior burger | 11.1 | 21 | 193 | 12 | 0.1 |
| mcfeast | 29.1 | 32 | 896 | 65 | 0.8 |

| +Values are given for 100g unless specified otherwise. | FAT g/ 100g+ | CHOL mg/ 100g+ | SOD mg/ 100g+ | CALC mg/ 100g+ | FIBRE g/ 100g+ |
|---|---|---|---|---|---|
| quarter pounder + cheese | 34.8 | 37 | 1380 | 12 | 0.8 |
| sausage mcmuffin ... 1 | 19.8 | 56 | 540 | 170 | |
| sundae ... 1 | 7 | 11 | 120 | 160 | 0 |
| thick shake ... 1 | 10 | 10 | 210 | 210 | 0 |
| *Pizza Hut* ... cavatini | 3.2 | 4 | 360 | 50 | 0.9 |
| garlic bread | 17.4 | 12 | 380 | 72 | 2.6 |
| pizza ... av sample | 11 | 36 | 600 | 135 | 2 |
| prawn cocktail | 7.4 | 86 | 830 | 25 | tr |
| spaghetti and meat sauce | 2.7 | 5 | 310 | 8 | 1 |
| ***Vegetables and Vegetable Foods*** | | | | | |
| *artichoke, Jerusalem* ... boiled | tr | 0 | 5 | 20 | 3.2 |
| *asparagus* ... boiled | tr | 0 | 2 | 20 | 2.1 |
| canned | tr | 0 | 295 | 10 | 1 |
| Farmland ... no added salt | tr | 0 | 5 | 10 | 0.8 |
| *aubergine (eggplant)* ... baked | tr | 0 | 5 | 20 | 3.5 |

## Ratatouille

*225 g eggplant, sliced*
*1 tablespoon oil*
*1 medium-sized onion*
*300 g zucchini, sliced*
*1 green capsicum, seeded and sliced*
*225 g tomatoes, sliced*
*2 level tablespoons dried thyme*
*salt and pepper to taste*
*1 level teaspoon crushed garlic*
*1 level teaspoon finely chopped parsley*

Cook eggplant in boiling water for 10 minutes and then drain. Heat oil in a non-stick pan and fry sliced onion until soft. Add eggplant and fry for another 2 minutes. Add zucchini, capsicum and tomato to onion and eggplant mixture, together with thyme. Season to taste. Cover and simmer for 20 minutes. Stir in parsley and cook for a further 5 minutes. Makes 2 servings at 695 kJ (165 cal) per portion.

| +Values are given for 100g unless specified otherwise. | FAT g/ 100g+ | CHOL mg/ 100g+ | SOD mg/ 100g+ | CALC mg/ 100g+ | FIBRE g/ 100g+ |
|---|---|---|---|---|---|
| *avocado* | 22.6 | 0 | 2 | 20 | 1.5 |
| *baked beans* ... Heinz ... canned | 0.7 | 0 | 480 | 37 | 4.8 |
| salt-reduced | 0.7 | 0 | 270 | 37 | 4.8 |
| *beans* ... 4-bean mix ... canned | tr | 0 | 150 | 20 | 4 |
| green ... canned | tr | 0 | 330 | 30 | 2 |
| raw/boiled/frozen | tr | 0 | 2 | 30 | 2.2 |
| red kidney ... boiled | tr | 0 | 8 | 34 | 7 |
| canned | tr | 0 | 320 | 36 | 6.5 |
| *beetroot* ... canned | tr | 0 | 236 | 8 | 2.8 |
| *broccoli* ... boiled | tr | 0 | 20 | 31 | 3.7 |
| *brussels sprouts* ... boiled | tr | 0 | 30 | 14 | 2.9 |
| *cabbage* ... boiled | tr | 0 | 20 | 24 | 1.6 |
| *capsicum, green* ... raw | tr | 0 | 2 | 8 | 1.3 |
| *carrot* ... raw ... av type | tr | 0 | 40 | 30 | 3 |
| *carrots* ... canned | tr | 0 | 148 | 30 | 2.5 |
| no added salt | tr | 0 | 50 | 30 | 2.5 |
| *cauliflower* ... av | tr | 0 | 14 | 13 | 2.1 |
| *celery* ... raw | tr | 0 | 90 | 36 | 1.3 |
| *corn* see *sweetcorn* | | | | | |
| *cucumber* ... peeled | | 0 | 20 | 13 | 0.4 |
| pickled | tr | 0 | 1353 | 20 | 2.2 |
| unpeeled | tr | 0 | 20 | 13 | 1.1 |
| *felafel* | 14.9 | 0 | 610 | 68 | 3.5 |
| *gherkin* ... pickled | tr | 0 | 1000 | 20 | 2.2 |
| *homous* | 17.1 | 0 | 310 | 45 | 3 |
| *leek* ... boiled | tr | 0 | 20 | 30 | 2.9 |
| *lentils* ... boiled | tr | 0 | 10 | 20 | 3.7 |
| *lettuce* | tr | 0 | 23 | 16 | 1.7 |
| *mushrooms* ... raw | tr | 0 | 7 | 2 | 2.5 |
| *olives* ... black ... pickled | 21.2 | 0 | 900 | 100 | 1 |
| green ... pickled | 12.9 | 0 | 2480 | 76 | 8 |

| *Values are given for 100g unless specified otherwise. | FAT g/ 100g* | CHOL mg/ 100g* | SOD mg/ 100g* | CALC mg/ 100g* | FIBRE g/ 100g* |
|---|---|---|---|---|---|
| *onion* ... fried | 20 | | 15 | 24 | 1.5 |
| raw | tr | 0 | 13 | 18 | 1.5 |
| spring | tr | 0 | 13 | 22 | 2.2 |
| *parsley* | tr | 0 | 50 | 200 | 4.7 |
| *parsnip* ... boiled | tr | 0 | 20 | 36 | 2.5 |
| *peas* ... canned | tr | 0 | 230 | 27 | 7.4 |
| Farmland ... no added salt | tr | 0 | 5 | 27 | 7 |
| fresh ... boiled | tr | 0 | 1 | 18 | 6.5 |
| frozen ... boiled ... av type | tr | 0 | 3 | 27 | 5.8 |
| *potato* ... chips ... fried | 14.2 | 12 | 160 | 10 | 1.2 |
| frozen, fried | 12.2 | 10 | 300 | 10 | 1.2 |
| dehydrated ... made up | 2.3 | 1 | 240 | 40 | 3.6 |
| mashed with full-cream milk | 0.4 | 3 | 300 | 10 | 1.2 |
| salad | 9.2 | 7 | 380 | 10 | 1.2 |
| scallop ... deep-fried | 21.6 | 21 | 260 | 17 | 3 |
| *pumpkin* ... boiled ... av type | tr | 0 | 1 | 20 | 2.1 |
| *silver beet* ... boiled ... no added salt | tr | 0 | 185 | 68 | 2.5 |
| *spinach* ... boiled | tr | 0 | 20 | 50 | 1.9 |
| *swede* ... boiled | tr | 0 | 12 | 20 | 3.4 |
| *sweetcorn* ... boiled on the cob | 1.9 | 0 | 5 | 3 | 1.7 |
| canned | 0.6 | 0 | 260 | 4 | 2.7 |
| Farmland ... no added salt | 1 | 0 | 5 | 3 | 2.7 |
| frozen ... cooked | 1 | 0 | 5 | 3 | 2.6 |
| kernels ... cooked | 1.2 | 0 | 5 | 3 | 4.8 |
| *sweet potato* | tr | 0 | 10 | 26 | 1.8 |

Raw onions are 30 kJ (7 cal) per 30 g; sliced and fried they soar to 190 kJ (45 cal). If a recipe requires that chopped onions be pre-fried, poach them instead in a little liquid until softened.

| +Values are given for 100g unless specified otherwise. | FAT g/ 100g+ | CHOL mg/ 100g+ | SOD mg/ 100g+ | CALC mg/ 100g+ | FIBRE g/ 100g+ |
|---|---|---|---|---|---|
| *tomato* ... canned | tr | 0 | 230 | 9 | 0.8 |
| no added salt | tr | 0 | 5–20 | 9 | 0.8 |
| raw | tr | 0 | 6 | 8 | 1.3 |
| *tomato juice* ... canned | tr | 0 | 230 | 7 | 1 |
| low-salt | tr | 0 | 1–20 | 7 | 1 |
| *tomato paste* | 1 | 0 | 160 | 15 | 3 |
| Farmland ... no added salt | 1 | 0 | 60 | 15 | 3.3 |
| *tomato puree* | tr | 0 | 350 | 12 | 2 |
| *turnip* ... boiled | tr | 0 | 20 | 20 | 2.5 |
| *vine leaves* | 2.9 | 0 | 600 | 60 | 2.5 |

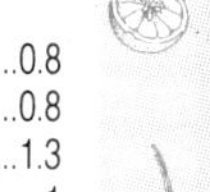

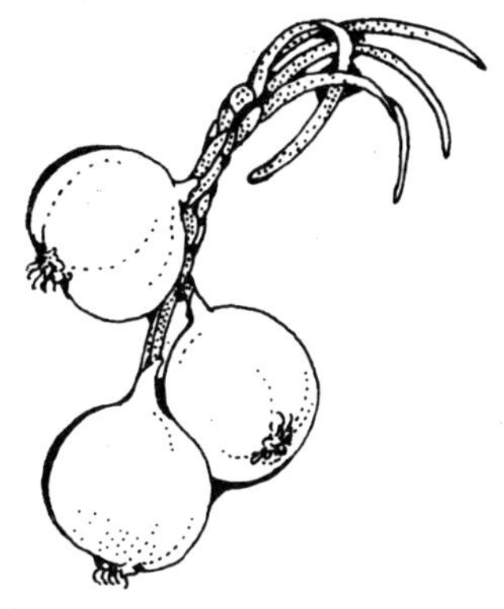

***Other books in the Penguin Pocket Series***

THE AUSTRALIAN EASY SPELLER
CHOOSING AUSTRALIAN WINES
FAMILY FIRST AID
HOW TO MAKE OVER 200 COCKTAILS
MICROWAVE TIPS AND TECHNIQUES
WEDDING ETIQUETTE
YOUR NEW BABY